Inside Insurgency

Inside Insurgency

*Violence, Civilians,
and Revolutionary
Group Behavior*

Claire Metelits

NEW YORK UNIVERSITY PRESS

New York and London

NEW YORK UNIVERSITY PRESS
New York and London
www.nyupress.org

Library of Congress Cataloging-in-Publication Data

Metelits, Claire.
Inside insurgency : violence, civilians, and revolutionary group
behavior / Claire Metelits.
p. cm.
Includes bibliographical references and index.
ISBN-13: 978-0-8147-9577-4 (cl : alk. paper)
ISBN-10: 0-8147-9577-3 (cl : alk. paper)
ISBN-13: 978-0-8147-9578-1 (pb : alk. paper)
ISBN-10: 0-8147-9578-1 (pb : alk. paper)
1. Violence. 2. Political violence. 3. Insurgency. I. Title.
HM886.M48   2009
303.6'4—dc22   2009029209

New York University Press books are printed on acid-free paper,
and their binding materials are chosen for strength and durability.
We strive to use environmentally responsible suppliers and materials
to the greatest extent possible in publishing our books.

Manufactured in the United States of America

c   10 9 8 7 6 5 4 3 2 1
p   10 9 8 7 6 5 4 3 2 1

To my parents

Contents

Preface

When folks find out what, or more specifically whom, I study, I get either one of two questions: "Why do you study insurgents?" or "How do you study insurgents?" The questions are usually more along the lines of, "Why the #*!* do you study them?" or "How the #*!* do you get into those places?" These are often accompanied by comments on my sanity or (on the odd occasion) suspicions about my patriotism. The "how" is a matter for another time—or if you are a student of mine, you've already heard my stories on more than a few occasions. The "why," however, is somewhat more convoluted, but—I hope—no less interesting.

My first experience traveling outside the United States was in apartheid-era South Africa. I was nineteen years old. An uncle of mine—a Foreign Service officer who at the time had no children of his own—had years before promised me and my two younger siblings that when we were old enough he would take us each on a trip outside the United States. (I imagine he wanted our cultural horizons to expand beyond our hometown of Phoenix, Arizona.) Upon finishing my first rather tumultuous year of college as a journalism student, I wrote to my uncle and told him I was ready for my trip. "To where are we going?" he inquired. "South Africa," I wrote.

Still very far from discovering political science, I nevertheless was fascinated by the politics of South Africa in 1993. One could say my interests were more along the lines of social activism. Making good on his promise, my uncle (on a much-needed break from war-torn Angola) met me in Johannesburg for what would be a month-long traipse around the country. He had devised a detailed and elaborate itinerary filled with what to most people would be wonderful tourist destinations. However, as we whisked through animal parks, the wine country, and diamond-mining communities, I could not pull my eyes or my curiosity from other, more obvious elements of the place: the people and the conditions. Instead of photo albums filled with pictures of Krueger National Park and gorgeous areas such as Stellenbosch, I came home with snapshots of shantytowns and people living in destitution on the streets. What interested me about South Africa was the way the politics of the place had trickled down in such a devastating way to those who had so little say in the matter.

Fast-forward several years. Still unimpressed with the idea of being a scholar of political science, I nevertheless remained fascinated by countries wracked with instability—particularly conflict. I managed to get myself a very informal internship in southern Africa the summer before I began my master's degree. One of the places I told the administrators I wanted to visit was Angola. I wanted to see how the war there had affected the civilian population. Who was the greater enemy, really, the government of Angola or the insurgent group called the National Union for the Total Independence of Angola (UNITA)? I was sent to Luanda, Angola's capital, to research the peace movement that was gaining momentum there. However, once I reached the country, I found myself more interested in the actual war, and how this war had turned the country into a humanitarian disaster.

Luanda and the surrounding countryside shocked me. It was in Angola that I saw despair in the eyes of civilians, acts of criminality because there was no other mode of survival, and starvation. It was also in Angola that I was enormously humbled when a local family invited me to share a meal with them and insisted I take the only soda available. It was in Angola that I was first mugged, not once but twice over the course of a week, and where I learned to stop being angry about such acts; it is where I started to understand these acts, instead. It is where I learned that survival is a human instinct and can drive people to do things others may perceive as unthinkable.

These travels led to other trips in Africa and later to ones in other continents. I also discovered that I wanted to keep researching conflict, the actors involved, and the civilians affected. It was during a summer internship in Oslo, Norway, when I met with a scholar who had recently returned from southern Sudan and the conflict that was raging there. He mentioned that the insurgent group fighting the government, the SPLA, was requiring that foreigners who travel through the areas under its control be issued a rebel visa.

"You mean like a state would issue?" I asked him, shocked at how organized and bureaucratic this insurgent group sounded.

"Like a state," he told me. Fascinating! I thought. "And," he continued, "the SPLA is allowing southerners to vote in local elections."

Even more fascinating! An insurgent group that walked like a state, talked like a state, but wasn't really a state. How, I wondered, did this affect southern Sudanese? What did they think of the insurgents? Did they find the SPLA's bureaucracy to be beneficial to them and to their survival? A few months later I found myself on a tiny airplane heading out of southern Sudan, where I had spent several weeks conducting interviews. Reading from my field notes today, I see that I wrote, "I believe there is something useful to be taken from the experiences of the SPL[A]. Don't know what—yet. But I want to study it further." This book is the result of my studies.

I would not have been able to accomplish nearly a fraction of the fieldwork and other research that went into this book without the support of numerous organizations and people. I would like to thank several individuals who provided me with guidance and support during and after my research. In particular I thank William Reno, Timothy Earle, and Frank Safford at Northwestern University, for their mentorship. Thanks also to Reuel Rogers at Northwestern, who advised me on the initial book-proposal stages. Ato Kwamena Onoma helped formulate my original questions and thoughts for this project, as did J. Andrew Grant. A special thanks goes to Jeremy Weinstein, who, in a phone conversation with me, helped inspire this study. Many thanks to Kendra Koivu, a fantastic political scientist and an even greater friend and fellow fieldwork junkie. Øystein Rolandsen at the International Peace Research Institute, Oslo (PRIO) took the time to read early drafts of my SPLA chapter, and for that I am grateful. Thanks to Nils Petter Gleditsch at PRIO and his staff for facilitating the initial stages of my research in their library in Oslo. Joakim Kruetz at the University of Uppsala provided me with the initial one-sided violence data. Jorge Restrepo also helped me gather data on the FARC.

This work would have been impossible, of course, without the financial support of several institutions. I am deeply indebted to the Dispute Resolution and Research Center at Northwestern University's Kellogg School of Management for funding a political scientist. I am grateful to the Roberta Buffet Center for International and Comparative Studies at Northwestern University, which facilitated several of my trips to the field. In particular I thank Andrew Wachtel, former director of the institute. I also thank the Northwestern University Alumnae Association for providing me with financial support. Thanks go as well to my current colleagues at the Department of Political Science at Washington State University for supporting me in this book endeavor.

In the countries to which I traveled in order to conduct fieldwork, I met people who went out of their way to assist me. Many of these people became close friends. While researching the SPLA, David Mozersky of the International Crisis Group in Nairobi provided me with much-needed information. John Ashworth gave me direction and shared his thoughts with me on the SPLA while I was in Nairobi. I am grateful to Chris in Rumbek and Ashwil in Nairobi for their assistance, but most of all for their friendship. Thanks go to the administrative staff at the New Sudan Council of Churches in Nairobi for getting me on several planes into Sudan and for being so welcoming. Extra special thanks goes to Gillian Cull, who nursed me through a bout of dysentery.

My research on the PKK took me to Turkey and Iraq and also would not have been possible without the support of several key individuals. Ibrahim Sirkeci provided assistance and friendship while I was researching the PKK in Ankara. I am grateful for the eager assistance of my expert translator and friend, Mahmut, and for the hospitality of Angel and Nishtiman while I was in Diyarbakir. I also thank Kani in Washington, D.C., and Daniel in Baghdad for making my trip into Iraq and southeastern Turkey possible.

While researching the FARC in Colombia, I had help from several individuals. I thank Amanda Martin and Kath Nygard for their amazing guidance while I was in the northern regions of Colombia. Thanks go to Stephen Dudley in Bogotá for his advice and his time, and a special thanks goes to the anonymous couple who gave me a ride to the U.S. embassy after a rather distressing (and educational) experience in a Bogotá cell-phone shop.

The civilians and insurgents with whom I spoke, traveled, and at times developed friendships were many. I have changed many of their names in this book, using pseudonyms in some cases and leaving them anonymous in others. This is for their protection. Many of these individuals risked their own safety to talk with me. The impressions they made on me has been indelible. I thank them for that.

Special thanks to the staff at New York University Press. In particular, I thank Ilene Kalish, for her enthusiasm for this book and her editorial expertise. Thank you also to Aiden Amos, for her guidance in the whole process.

I also thank my friends and family for continuing to weather my travel schedules. Thanks go to Amy, Ed, Sisouvanh, Lisa, and M'Linda at Washington State University: your friendship and support means so much to me. Thank you especially to Michael (my uncle), who—though he may not be overjoyed at the places to which I find myself traveling—none-theless understands why I do so, and to Joy and Steph for being a great cheering section. A special thank you goes to my sister, Molly, and to her husband, Scott. Finally, thanks go to my parents, Maryann and Robert, to whom this work is dedicated.

1

Insurgents and Civilian-Targeted Violence

Wars teach us not to love our enemies, but to hate our allies.
—W. L. George

I sit across a desk from Daniel. It is past sundown in Yei, a small village in southern Sudan ringed by a mixture of jungle and grassland. A three-hour-long downpour has subsided and left behind intense humidity but also a light breeze that blows through the doorway of the crumbling building in which we sit. We are both exhausted. I have accompanied him on a thirteen-hour drive from Kampala, Uganda, across the border into the "liberated" zones of the Sudan People's Liberation Army/Movement (SPLA/M)—the insurgent group he has belonged to since joining in 1984.¹ Much of our day was spent lurching along deeply rutted mud roads, with the occasional delay to extricate our vehicle or our fellow travelers' vehicle in front of us from the sticky mud. The standing joke along our journey has been the story of the foreign-aid donor who comes to visit the region and naively asks, "Why do they put the roads in the rivers?" Everyone has laughed at this joke along the way, though the irony is not lost on anyone, for when the rainy seasons arrive the dirt roads do actually turn into rivers.

As we are jostled along in our vehicles, the drivers are careful not to veer too far from the dirt road, because the area has been heavily mined. These land mines are one of the many remnants of the civil war between the government of Sudan in the north and the insurgents of the south. It is November 2001, and much of Yei lies in a state of destruction or reconstruction. After being bombed several times by government forces between 1998 and 2000, the people of this town, along with the SPLA, have attempted to fix or make do with what has been left standing.

However, the SPLA did not always help its own people, the southern Sudanese. Following its formation in 1983, the SPLA became notorious for committing massive human-rights abuses against communities on whose behalf it claimed to fight. This group's coercive behavior included looting villages, kidnapping children, carrying out summary executions, and creating famine conditions in southern Sudan.[2] I ask Daniel to recall these earlier years, when war atrocities by both the government of Sudan and the SPLA abounded. I look up at him expectantly. The room is lit only by a flashlight, yet I can see him stare at me for several seconds before answering. "The movement ran from the opposition," he says, "but we replicated the system we ran away from." Daniel shakes his head. "Human-rights violations, little tolerance of different ideas," he recalls.[3]

In 1994, the SPLA's treatment of civilians changed. The level of civilian-targeted violence decreased as the group separated its military arm from its civil administration and established structures of governance that involved local communities. Daniel comments on this change. "We ran away from dictatorship," he explains. "We cannot be dictators [then]." The mission of the SPLA is to liberate the south of Sudan from the north. Then, he continues, it is up to the people of the south to create their own system. "We are the luckiest Africans," he says with a small smile. I ask him to explain this remark. He tells me that the southern Sudanese have seen what mistakes were made in Sudan and in other countries on the African continent. They can learn from these mistakes.[4] It is reasonable that the SPLA would strive for unity and greater legitimacy. It is not clear, however, why the change in the group's behavior and treatment of southern civilians occurred when it did and against the personal interests of faction leaders who continued to have resources at their disposal.

This book is about the change in insurgent behavior toward civilians. Unlike much of the recent research on insurgencies, which analyzes these groups from afar, this book takes a different approach. I draw from information I gathered by interviewing over one hundred insurgent soldiers and commanders, government officials, scholars, and civilians in Sudan, Kenya, Colombia, Turkey, and Iraq, as well as from historical analyses and data on civilian deaths. Much of this book is based on information I collected while traveling with detachments of insurgent groups. I also collected information while traveling through insurgent areas of operation and major cities where these groups have constituencies. Whereas some recent studies base their work on conflicts that have come to an end, thus making information less timely, research for this book was conducted *during* the period of the conflicts, on armed actors in their own environments.

Defining Cases, Refining Concepts

This book examines three insurgent groups to explore their shifting treatment of civilians whom they claim to represent. First, I examine the SPLA (chapter 3), the group described in this chapter's opening. In its formative years during the 1980s as a Marxist group supported by Ethiopian backers, the SPLA committed human-rights abuses against southern Sudanese populations. The group, however, transformed into a nascent state that garnered the support of both southern Sudanese and the international aid community.

I also analyze the Fuerzas Armadas Revolucionarias de Colombia, or Revolutionary Armed Forces of Colombia (FARC) (chapter 4). The FARC, like the SPLA, underwent a massive shift in its treatment of Colombian peasants. However, it evolved in the opposite direction from what the Sudanese insurgents did. The FARC found its roots in peasant self-defense organizations in the mid-1970s, supported in part by the Colombian Communist Party. It supported better working conditions for peasant farmers. In expanding its military strategy, the FARC began acquiring resources from the coca-growing and drug-trafficking industries. Eventually, the group became infamous for the killing of local civilians, kidnapping, and extortion.

The third group I examine in this book is the Partiya Karkerên Kurdistan, or Kurdistan Workers' Party (PKK) (chapter 5). Like the SPLA and the FARC, the PKK also began with Marxist roots. As a student-led movement in Turkey during the 1970s, the PKK soon adopted a military strategy that quickly alienated Kurdish civilians. Characterized by human-rights abuses and other coercive behavior perpetrated against civilians, the PKK, despite retaining support in parts of Turkey, was noted for its brutal treatment of its own people. However, the PKK's behavior, like that of the SPLA and the FARC, shifted over time. This case in particular demonstrates how national factors such as government policies influence insurgent groups' strategy.

The groups I analyze in this book are referred to as "insurgents," which I define as nonstate armed actors that use violence to reformulate or destroy the foundation of politics in an existing country.[5] Insurgents have been referred to as "guerrillas," "separatists," "liberators," and "terrorists," depending on the period in which they have fought. During the late 1960s, the government of Nigeria referred to the leaders of the breakaway Eastern Region as "ethnic separatists" or "rebels," whereas in the 1970s, Portuguese colonizers faced "communist insurgents" in their African colonies, and locals considered the combatants "freedom fighters" dedicated to ending colonial rule. Insurgent groups are, at their core, political, though many engage in criminal activities.[6] Most insurgent groups fight to take control of a state, in part because of the very fact that the current international political order takes the form of a system of states instead of empires or networks of small, autonomous polities. As this book demonstrates, this system shapes warfare and the violence we see in today's wars.

Several insurgent groups around the world have changed the way they treat civilians—the noncombatant host communities that the insurgents claim to represent. The treatment of civilians by insurgent groups ranges along a spectrum from *coercive* (which I also refer to as *violent*) to *contractual* behavior. Coercive behavior is characterized by the forcible extraction of resources from civilians without establishing a reciprocal relationship—without providing services in return. Coercion can include kidnapping children for use as soldiers or slaves, burning villages, raping women, and looting to invoke fear in civilians, as well as the intentional withholding of humanitarian aid from populations in need. During the 1991–2002 war in Sierra Leone, the Revolutionary United Front (RUF) inflicted highly coercive behavior on civilians when, for example, it kidnapped children to use as soldiers. Likewise, the ongoing abuses committed against noncombatants since the late 1980s in northern Uganda by the Lord's Resistance Army (LRA) is clearly coercive behavior. In contrast, contractual behavior describes the relationship between a controlling power (state or insurgent group) and local residents when the controlling power provides services in return for resources.

Other insurgent groups often protect a specific ethnic group or another community of solidarity. These groups' state-building urges bear some resemblance to historical events in Europe. Like their predatory competitors, they mobilize commercial networks and exploit resources. However, at the same time, they produce different outcomes that reflect the comparative advantages and leverage of actors in commercial networks, local community organizations, and others with whom leaders of armed groups bargain, in some ways similar to what the scholar Charles Tilly describes in his book *Coercion, Capital, and European States*.[7] In the FARC's nascent years, for example, the group maximized its legitimacy among its targeted membership by providing basic services for peasants, such as protection against the harsh policies of large landowners and education, in exchange for resources such as food and money.[8]

In this book, I use a broad definition of *resources*. Resources include, but are not limited to, any material item that helps an insurgent group achieve its goal, including food, guns, and money. Resources also include nonmaterial goods that can produce material items. For example, popular support from civilian populations is a resource because it can produce food and shelter as well as recruits. I understand that this definition is quite all-encompassing, and some people may argue that it is overinclusive. However, the research I have done on insurgent groups in their areas of operation indicates that resources are, in fact, very broad.[9] That is understandable, as many of the regions where insurgent groups operate lack infrastructure and resources. Thus, these armed actors make use of many types of elements to support their causes.

Understanding insurgent behavior is a challenging task that bears relevancy beyond the specific events this book treats. Parties that fight a governing regime often use both violent (coercive) and nonviolent (contractual) means to achieve their objectives. Insurgent violence is primarily a tool that nonstate groups use to maintain political order.[10] Yet the relationship between violence and order can just as easily be a component of state building.[11] Some contemporary insurgent groups reject violence as part of their state-creating strategy; this kind of strategy is often crucial in building strong connections with civilians. Other groups are exceptionally brutal toward civilians. Furthermore, some groups change their behavior over the course of their existence, beginning as violent organizations as the SPLA did and evolving into groups that provide public goods and services such as food and security. The behavior these groups display while interacting with civilians reveals a great deal about their military strength and their ability to control resources that are important to the civilian population. This dynamic, I argue, helps explain why some insurgent groups treat communities they claim to represent either coercively or contractually. The aim of this book is to uncover why transformations such as those of the SPLA and other insurgent groups occur.

Is Insurgent Violence Rational?

The central question that frames this book is, why did the insurgent groups in this study change the way they treated constituent communities? In many ways, this question requires us to look at several other issues: Why do some insurgent groups mistreat host populations? Why do other groups develop strong ties with host communities, creating desirable alternatives to the existing government and forming what these groups and their supporters call "liberated" zones?[12] What types of resources are most important to insurgent groups? Do certain kinds of resources result in specific behaviors? To answer these questions, I uncover what causes certain types of insurgent violence in the first place. What goal drives the violence? Is it a need to exercise raw power? Is it a matter of physical or political survival?

These questions in turn require an understanding of local forces that influence insurgent treatment of civilians. Some political studies emphasize the actions and responses of states at the cost of including what is happening on the front lines.[13] Too frequently nonstate armed actors such as insurgents are misunderstood as being acted *upon*. In this structural view, power flows inward from larger entities such as the state or the international community of states and affects local actors. A state-centered analysis narrows the understanding of insurgent groups by failing to consider the amount of agency these groups possess. Although state policies and international events do influence insurgent groups, local politics are just as important—if not more so—in shaping these groups' decisions about the use of violence against civilians. Thus, insurgents become actors with choices, not merely groups that respond to the whim of outside forces. Insurgent groups operate rationally within a defined space and therefore have choices (albeit narrow ones at times) about the strategies they adopt. Thus, as some recent studies of insurgents demonstrate, violence is a byproduct of unintended consequences of both outside forces and local forces *including insurgent choices*.

A second major focus of this book is evaluating current explanations of insurgent violence against civilians. Theories that claim to account for insurgent violence (or nonviolence) are not in short supply. Some researchers emphasize "new wars" as a driving force for contemporary violence against civilians.[14] Other scholars argue that greed is a motivating factor, emphasizing the recruitment of opportunistic individuals and the lack of discipline. The list of conceivable explanations is plentiful, but the problems with them are threefold: they lack timely data collected directly from these conflicts rather than after the wars have ended, and they thus mix with hindsight to shape perceptions; they fail to address the changes witnessed in insurgent behavior toward civilians; and they portray resources as static in nature. This book utilizes on-the-ground evidence from the field to evaluate the factors that drive the transformation of insurgent violence against host communities.

This book also develops an explanation of insurgent behavior that gets at the micropolitics of violence and accounts for the shift from violence to nonviolence (or vice versa) at the local level. Some of the state-building literature is useful in this context because, though insurgents do use violence to transform politics, these armed actors can also create a distinct political order. For example, when doing research on the SPLA, I had to acquire an insurgent-issued "visa" in order to travel into areas of Sudan under the group's control. Once inside these "liberated" zones, my visa (which consisted of a thick piece of paper with my passport photo stapled to it and my occupation and the purpose of my visit typed out) was checked by the local SPLA administrator. All of this was done with a good degree of ostentation, as though the group wanted to prove that it too could behave like a state. In this same context, for insurgents, violence against other armed forces serves a purpose: it is one of the primary political tools they use to reshape the foundation of politics in a state. When insurgents resort to violence in order to acquire the resources needed for survival, their behavior is comparable to state building. There have been cases in which states grew out of the social contract developed between armed groups and civilians. Groups that ensured local communities could continue to produce wealth by permitting basic social transactions and providing security enjoyed more success in the long run.[15] Some insurgencies, such as the SPLA, established quasi-states or states-within-states in areas under their control.[16]

Although the focus of this book is the SPLA, the FARC, and the PKK, the ideas that frame this study are more general than parochial. These three groups are critical cases, or cases with strategic importance, for scholars, policymakers, military personnel, and students whose work addresses political violence and war. I strategically selected these three insurgent groups to see whether groups with different backgrounds, geographies, and directions of transformation can have similar causes of changing behavior. Likewise, several explanations of insurgent violence toward civilians derive from case studies of insurgencies. Hence, the purpose of the book is not only to evaluate and develop an explanation of insurgent violence in Sudan, Turkey, and Colombia but also to treat these groups as test cases for general theories of violence and order. Macrolevel as well as microlevel theories of such violence will find application in the SPLA, for example. By the same token, my arguments about these three insurgent groups offer insight into the dynamics guiding other instances of insurgent violence and conflict.

Researching Insurgents in Zones of Conflict

Recent studies of insurgent violence emphasize the systematic collection of data in postconflict areas.[17] Some of these studies employ surveys of civilians and perpetrators of violence. Survey data, however, is not always an optimal tool for tracing the process of civil war and change in insurgent behavior. Surveys carry with them a deep concern about issues of truthfulness. Survey respondents may possess incentives to present facts in ways that justify their roles or points of view. Furthermore, respondents' willingness to answer questions about war and violence is largely a factor of the relationship between the researcher and the interviewees. My work involved returning to field sites more than once over the course of several years, which allowed me to establish relationships with individuals and collect increasingly sensitive levels of information. I also kept in constant contact with several key sources involved in the three cases I studied.

To explore the shifts in insurgent treatment of civilians, I asked direct participants in insurgencies and civilians they claimed to represent why the group changed its behavior. Such grassroots research is rare; scholarly analysis of civil wars too often relies on official or elite sources to the exclusion of truly "raw" data.[18] In particular, the study of peasant insurgency often relies on the memoirs of leaders who belong to a different class than the peasants themselves.[19] Local actors, however, are important in the study of insurgent violence because they provide the primary perspectives from which to draw conclusions.[20] Although recent work on conflict and insurgents in particular does a good job of beginning to correct the use of older and less-varied data on insurgent groups, the fact remains that the work is still plagued with historical speculation and single-case vagaries. This book attempts to correct this imbalance.

I gathered information for this book in several ways. First, I conducted interviews in each of the places where the three insurgent groups operated. I traveled in these places and interviewed individuals *during* the separate conflicts and after the change in the groups' behavior occurred. I asked insurgent leaders and their cadres, civilians, leaders of local nongovernmental organizations (NGOs), government officials, and local scholars and journalists questions concerning the behavior of the insurgent group as it developed, including its violence against civilians and the emergence of local systems of governance in "liberated" zones. That this analysis relies largely on open-ended or unrestricted interviews raises issues of reliability. How do I know the information I collected from individuals is accurate? Is the data merely a reflection of what individuals wanted me to hear? How do I know whether the people I interviewed told me the truth? Such questions should constantly plague the researcher, and I am in no way immune from these worries. I did my best to confirm the data I collected during interviews by checking information with at least two additional sources.

My work on the SPLA began in the fall of 2001 when I traveled to Nairobi, Kenya, where the SPLA carried out much of its administrative affairs. Nairobi was also the city where much of the international aid community that worked in southern Sudan was based. I returned to the region to continue fieldwork on the Sudanese insurgents in 2003 and 2005. I also traveled to Lokichokio in northern Kenya to Kakuma Refugee Camp, which was created to deal with the thousands of refugees fleeing the war. At the time of my stay there, the camp held over eighty thousand refugees. I spoke with the leaders of several different ethnic Sudanese communities, including the head of the Nuer as well as several elder Dinka. Eventually I moved my study of the SPLA to Sudan itself. I visited the southern towns of Rumbek, Yei, and Nimule, where I continued to interview SPLA cadres, commanders, NGO representatives, church officials, and southern Sudanese civilians.

My study of the FARC took me to several different settings in Colombia on two separate occasions during 2006. I traveled to large urban areas such as Bogotá and Cartagena, where I spoke with Colombian scholars and journalists who study this group. I also spoke with local grassroots organizations working on behalf of the displaced individuals who have streamed into the cities to escape the war. I also traveled to rural towns such as Chinulito, where I spoke with victims of the conflict, local police, church officials, and the members and leaders of local NGOs.

As part of my study of the PKK, I collected data and conducted interviews in Turkey and Iraq. In 2003 I began work in Istanbul and Ankara, speaking with scholars who study the Kurds. I then traveled to Diyarbakir, the center of Turkey's Kurdish community. I returned to Turkey and the Kurdish region again in the latter part of 2003 and early 2004. I spoke with Kurdish students, human-rights activists, politicians, members of local NGOs, and civilians. This work led me to travel to PKK bases in northern Iraq. There I stayed with a contingent of the PKK and spent time conducting interviews with PKK soldiers and Kurdish civilians.

The second stage of my research was a microcomparative study of insurgents' coercion or violence toward civilians in their regions of operation. Violence was intense in all cases at various points in time. Insurgents and civilians at times established a noncoercive, contractual relationship with one another in these regions as well. I discovered that the violent treatment of civilians on various continents occurred under similar circumstances. After 1994, the SPLA extended voting rights to local residents in the midst of reduced faction fighting. The FARC provided a similar environment for *campesinos* (peasant farmers) in Tolima prior to the advent of state- and cartel-sponsored militia. The Kurdish insurgents received criticism for their treatment of local Kurds in southeastern Turkey while dealing with rival ethnic factions, though after state repression of Kurds increased and several of these groups disbanded or found themselves in jail, the PKK addressed issues linked to how they treated civilians.

Scholars who study violence and the creation (or collapse) of order often draw from past studies of stability. I have done the same. This approach has allowed me to draw on a rich political-economy literature on state behavior to further the understanding of nonstate actors who created order, with or without the use of violence. Some scholars may have difficulty viewing insurgent groups as analogous to states, but indeed, states themselves can be excessively violent toward civilians during times of war. States have used highly coercive tactics, ranging from massacre and chemical warfare to aerial bombardment against civilians. As will become clear in the following chapter, the logic put forth in this book can be applied to explaining the behavior of states in similar circumstances. I use the state-building literature to develop what I see as an "ideal type" of infrastructural order and power. This ideal type practices restraint and discipline. It orders local structures of governance and engages civilians in the process of effecting political change. It builds specific administrative units tasked only with the extraction of resources, while other units focus on public goods such as protection and education. No nation-state (or insurgent group, for that matter) measures up to this ideal type completely, but in generating theory, it is at times necessary to develop such standards in order to measure reality. In this book, the ideal type is, at one end of the spectrum, the purveyor of nonviolent order. At the opposite end, order is maintained through extreme coercion—violence.

Rivalry and Insurgent Violence: A Theory

Insurgents shape their strategies toward local communities according to whether they face competition, or what I call *active rivalry*. The presence of rivals that feed from the same pool of resources leads to competition. If insurgent groups can achieve or maintain the role of the sole extractors of resources with relatively little threat from other armed organizations, they will be likely to seek mutually beneficial ties with local populations. However, once insurgents perceive a threat to extraction—most often in the form of rival groups or state reform—they are more likely to protect their perceived interests through means that can harm locals. They do this to acquire more-immediate access to resources and to prevent rival groups from establishing political authority over these communities.

Why is rivalry the key to insurgent behavior? When an insurgent group does not face competition over resources, the level of violence against civilians is more likely to be low. In contrast, when an insurgent group faces competition—a threat to control of resources—the level of violence against civilians is likely to rise. If an insurgent group gets much of its resource base from taxing drug traffickers who move through its territory, the group would want to monopolize taxing these traffickers. Similarly, if an insurgent group obtains food for its soldiers from local farmers, it wants to be the only group doing so.

The objective for insurgent groups is opportunity. Survival is rarely a long-term guarantee for these organizations. The supply of resources can be tenuous; resources often are limited in part because of a group's illegitimate position in the international environment[21] but also as a result of the conditions of the countries in which these groups operate. Hence, insurgents want to have as much opportunity as possible to collect resources. The best way to do that is to control the extraction of these resources within the country and outside their areas of operation. In most cases insurgents microgather resources by looking to local communities, where they can best avoid competition from other groups. Insurgents will prefer the most efficient way in which to extract resources, and in the short run it is more effective for insurgent groups to extract resources from local communities because these resources are readily available. Rather than taking the time to raise their own crops, for example, rebels can simply take agricultural goods from local farmers. It turns out, then, that security-driven motivations can be predatory. Insurgent concerns over security are often intertwined with predatory goals, which explains why security seekers are likely to take any opportunity to exploit others in order to build up strategic resources. An insurgent group that faces rivals is more likely to use coercive behavior toward noncombatants because increasing its security while rivals are present means reducing the security of others.[22]

Broadly speaking, insurgent groups extract resources from local communities in two ways: coercively or contractually. The latter is comparable to the Maoist approach of honoring peasants and thereby winning their active support. By permitting basic social transactions such as engagement in independent economic activity, armed groups create a more secure environment for civilians. The more physically secure civilians there are in their locality, the more productive they are likely to be. The result is an increase in the amount of resources the armed groups can collect from local communities (without endangering the survival of the local populace), despite the lower rate of imposition, or lesser degree of violence.[23] When an insurgent group does not confront competition for resources, it can more efficiently mobilize popular support, collecting resources and recruiting cadres to gain autonomy from the state and potential rivals.

Rivals are any armed entity that threatens or has the potential to threaten an insurgent group's control over strategic resources. Some studies of civil-war violence use a narrow conception of entities that fight insurgents. One recent study emphasizes the state-insurgent relationship, leaving aside effects of local militia and other armed actors in the area.[24] Another recent study leaves the state out of the analysis completely and focuses only on nonstate armed groups.[25] For purposes of this study, rivals are *any* state or nonstate entity that challenges an insurgent group's control over strategic resources.

Implications of the Insurgent Rationale

The arguments put forward in this book have several important implications for uncovering why insurgent groups treat civilians violently or nonviolently and for addressing the matter of changing insurgent behavior. First, I provide a unique interpretation and a detailed account of the local-level dynamics of the conflicts in Sudan, Colombia, and Turkey.

Although each of these conflicts is contextually unique, together they paint a vivid and at times personal account of the nature of contemporary civil wars. Along these same lines, this book sheds some understanding on why so many armed actors today appear to be excessively violent and at times seem to be irrational. I offer considerable evidence and theory for why insurgent behavior is in fact quite rational. Although I mean in no way to forgive insurgent behavior, my research will hopefully help people understand insurgent violence.

In a more general sense, my research has theoretical implications that extend beyond the behavior of the SPLA, the PKK, and the FARC. This book also offers a further examination of the relationship between political order and violence. I draw from Weber's concept of "legitimate domination," the expectation of obedience based on a belief that those who execute orders also share a community of interests.[26] Herein lies the reciprocal relationship between communities and "stable bandits" that defines the contractual end of the scale of insurgent behavior in relation to civilians.[27] Coercive and contractual behavior are ideals in their extreme and this book finds that insurgent groups exhibit degrees of these elements of behavior. My findings support the idea that some insurgents reject violence as a tool for enforcing order. For example, the FARC could have used violence from the beginning but chose instead to act as part of a structure of social welfare. The group adjudicated disputes and social conflicts and worked with peasant communities to create cooperatives and provide political education.[28]

This book looks at how connections between insurgent groups and local communities are institutionalized. I explain why under certain circumstances insurgents, rather than treating civilians in a coercive manner, will act more like a state engaged in the social contract of providing goods and services to its citizens in exchange for support and taxes. I detail how several groups establish order with and without the use of violence.

Additionally, my findings point to the importance of security for contemporary insurgents, with self-preservation being a mechanism that can lead to increased levels of violence against civilians. In the three cases I examine, the leadership as well as the soldiers became perpetrators of violence against noncombatants because they feared for their survival in the face of advancing rivals. The nature of the environments in which these groups operated and the levels of repression by the state mattered for the calculations the groups made. However, the broader implication is that insurgent groups will choose to commit violence to maintain their survival. In the face of possible extinction, the type of resources these groups use is less likely to matter; it is the presence or absence of active rivalry that is critical to these armed actors. This book, then, sheds new light on why some insurgents become predatory, going beyond approaches that look to resource type as a primary explanation for insurgents' treatment of civilians whom they claim to represent.

The theory I propose in this book has a number of policy implications as well. I specify the conditions under which contemporary insurgent groups are likely to behave as social movements to reform states or make new ones. That is, I identify conditions under which these groups become more or less predatory toward local populations. This book also provides alternative frameworks with which to view insurgent operations. In a sense, the theory developed here places the analyst in an insurgent's shoes and reveals the constraints and motivations of such individuals. A broader understanding of the environments in which these groups operate, and the mode by which groups evaluate their options, may create the possibility for scholars and government officials to temper the most violent effects of internal conflicts.

2

Rivals and the
Logic of Insurgent Violence

So much is evident in itself, that this, like every other subject
which does not surpass our powers of understanding, may be
lighted up, and being made more or less plain in its inner relations
by an inquiring mind, and that alone is sufficient to realize the
idea of a theory.

—Von Clausewitz, *On War*

A foreign priest sits under an awning in the backyard of his home in Carta-
gena. He has lived in Colombia for twenty-four years, he says. Right now
he serves a neighborhood of people displaced by the civil war between the
FARC and the Colombian government. He talks about many issues, includ-
ing the paramilitary force in Colombia known simply as the "paras." There
was not as much violence that affected civilians before the paras, he says.
Now, though, the FARC seems more "blood thirsty," he tells me. At first a
person could distinguish between the FARC and the paras—they had differ-
ent modi operandi, he explains. However, today the two armed entities are
looking more and more similar.[1]

The FARC has its roots in peasant self-defense organizations, having supported—among other issues—better working conditions for agricultural
workers in the Tolima region of Colombia. On this basis the group enjoyed a measure of local support. However, the late 1980s saw the FARC
quickly evolve into a more violent and locally coercive insurgency with
resources stemming from drug trafficking and extortion.[2]

Why did the FARC transform into a coercive organization, having begun with the intent to serve and defend peasant communities in parts

of Colombia? More generally, why do some insurgent groups that share similar circumstances evolve in very different directions? Why, for example, did the SPLA become less coercive while the FARC grew increasingly violent against its constituent communities? Furthermore, why do groups that hold similar ideologies and operate within the same international environment (and are thus susceptible to the same international influences at relatively similar periods of time) change their treatment of local populations in opposing directions?

Several contemporary scholars and analysts have attempted to address insurgent violence. Some, for example, link insurgent violence to the unique types of conflicts being fought today. Others link control over geographical space and the notion of insurgent control to these actors' behavior. Still others, responding to resource-driven conflict studies, link resources to types of recruits. However, as I will explain, the problem with these various assemblies that attempt to explain insurgent violence is that they do not address the issue of *changing* behavior. This issue is important because, once the question of behavioral change is addressed, the role of resources, territory, and other unanswered questions can be resolved.

This chapter discusses some of the competing interpretations of insurgent violence toward civilians. For individuals who are unfamiliar with these theoretical arguments, the chapter should be a helpful introduction to the wider resource-conflict debate. Near the end of the chapter, I discuss the central hypotheses that frame the empirical chapters to follow.

Not-So-New Wars

A recent theme in conflict studies is the change that scholars ascribe to the wars of the past century. Some writers see the end of the Cold War as the close of an era when conflicts found or sought legitimacy through ideological platforms. Others view the conclusion of World War II as the point at which wars began to change. As opposed to conflicts of the past, which were often fought for universal principles such as socialism or democracy, these scholars characterize contemporary wars as lacking in broad political and social justifications. According to these theorists, participants in today's wars are driven by self-interest; they contest for resources that are more readily available than during previous times of war. This ease of access results from the expansion of global markets and the decline of state capacity to regulate commerce. Enzensberger goes so far as to argue that for parties involved in post–Cold War conflicts, there are no goals or ideas that bind participants together other than the need to plunder.[3] Holsti sees new wars as having little if any central control, and Snow views new wars as apolitical—that is, conflicts are autonomous activities separate from politics.[4] Kaldor highlights how new wars are distinct in their methods and targets and in how they are financed.[5] She thus emphasizes globalization: new wars characteristically thrive from global, mostly illicit markets.[6] Beckett claims that these wars are less ideologically driven than wars of the past.[7] As one scholar describes,

> No single crisis precipitates them, and they typically do not start at a particular date. There are no declarations of war, there are no seasons for campaigning, and few end with peace treaties. Decisive battles are few. Attrition, terror, psychology, and actions against civilians highlight "combat." Rather than highly organized armed forces based on a strict command hierarchy, wars are fought by loosely knit groups of regulars, irregulars, cells, and not infrequently by locally-based warlords under little or no central authority.[8]

Insurgent leaders of these new wars are often assigned the pejorative label "warlord."[9] Civilians, rather than opposing parties, are the targets of violence in these "new wars." Such violence is often linked to patronage-based politics under the aegis of warlords who take advantage of state collapse to enhance their positions of power in communities.

But using the concept of new wars as a rationalization for insurgent behavior is problematic. First, there are cases that do not fit this model of contemporary warfare. The PKK, for example, continues to issue Marxist rhetoric and to fight for a Kurdish homeland, just as it did during the Cold War.[10] Other groups use nationalism as an ideological device to guide individuals to the perspective that they share a common history.[11] Groups such as the Irish Fenians used nationalism to develop the Fenian Movement in both Ireland and the United States. Furthermore, Al Qaeda organizes itself around an ideology—a fundamentalist interpretation of Islam. Clearly ideology is alive and well.

According to some scholars, the motivation for the type of behavior that characterizes new wars lacks programmatic or broad political justifications. Although the new-wars motivation of conflict can reward insurgent-group members, the greed-driven motivation for war does not involve the promulgation of any significant contractual relationship with a particular community of supporters. New wars, then, are nonideological because they draw in the rural poor in ways that programmatic platforms have no effect in facilitating mobilization and control.

Yet, if we look closely, we find other factors that explain political violence. Many insurgent groups are extensions of earlier violent political programs. For example, politicians in Sierra Leone share responsibility for much of the violent behavior of youth after recruiting thugs and criminals into the country's security apparatuses. Doing so further detached these new "experts in violence" from social groups in whose name rebels previously fought.[12] Furthermore, despite the end of the Cold War, the subsequent termination of support for proxy conflicts, and the so-called end of international ideological battles, several insurgent organizations continue to follow—at least in name—the leftist ideas of that era. The FARC, for example, continues to refer to itself as a Marxist organization. Likewise, the Nepalese rebels (until they joined the government) carried the label "Maoist insurgents," as do other insurgent movements in Southeast Asia. This demonstrates that there exists a consistent ideological motivation among insurgent organizations. And like these actors themselves, their ideological motivations are diverse. New-war insurgents and less-coercive groups can exist in poor countries in the same historical period. The Zapatista Army of National Liberation (EZLN) claims to represent the poor and dispossessed of the Chiapas region of Mexico. Not only did this group have the popular support of much of the indigenous population in Chiapas and surrounding regions, it also attracted transnational NGO support for the rebels' defense of indigenous rights, human rights, and social justice.

There are other problems with the new-wars thesis. When seen through this lens, insurgent groups possess little if any agency. That is, under the new-wars rubric, insurgents are at the mercy of global economic and political forces. For example, one can argue quite convincingly that the end of the Cold War brought changes for states as well as for groups rebelling against them, as these latter entities found revenue and other forms of support drying up. This argument implies that armed actors fighting a state will operate under the thrall of criminal incentives, that is, that they are motivated by the profits and lifestyles that illicit industries can provide. This view also ignores the political nature of these armed actors' organizations and objectives. I argue that insurgent actions are much more autonomous and political than the new-wars thesis portrays them. Like states, insurgents operate in the international environment, and like states they, too, can take advantage of the dynamics this environment throws at them. If indeed such criminal incentives exist, one would expect them to have an overriding influence on insurgents' behavior, since these actors are at the whim of the global economy, and illicit activities offer fast ways to raise revenue.

However, contemporary history demonstrates that it does not happen this way. For example, the SPLA usually did not rely on criminal activities to fund new forms of warfare. Instead, the SPLA turned to foreign donors and Western governments for material support in its struggle. In attending international human-rights conferences, holding talks with USAID and government officials in Europe and the United States, the SPLA leadership filled a role that foreign donors deemed vital in southern Sudan. This group took advantage of foreign donors who were quick to provide resources for any actor that would stand up to the Islamic regime in the north and play a leading role in a region of Africa that seemed unmanageable. It was enough for the insurgent group to attend meetings and sign protocols in order to obtain foreign assistance.

Furthermore, illicit resources do not necessarily incite abusive treatment of civilians. The FARC demonstrated that a group can both involve itself in the production and trade of criminal resources *and* serve local communities. The FARC played this dual role when it enforced the taxation of drug traffickers and cartel owners while simultaneously ensuring that *campesinos* had access to food.[13]

In a fruitful divergence from the resource-focused accounts of conflict, particularly those that emphasize primary commodity exports, some scholars have begun to direct their attention to the micropolitics of conflict.[14] Much of this work focuses on explaining the use of violence against civilians during civil war. One study, by Stathis Kalyvas, examines civilian-targeted violence in the context of the constraints of irregular wars and attempts to explain why extreme violence takes place where no history of conflict exists. It concludes that the brutality of civil wars is a result not of the nature (greed) of the participants but of the interaction of forces in irregular warfare.[15]

Kalyvas's research systematizes the utility of violence by describing when combatants use selective and indiscriminate violence. Violence and the threat of future violence can allow a group to establish and maintain control by generating collaboration and deterring informers. To do this, the insurgents must use violence carefully. Indiscriminate violence is largely counterproductive, though it emerges at times because its use is less costly than its selective counterpart. The arbitrary targeting is more likely to occur where no single group has a monopoly of territorial control and where a stalemate does not exist. In such a situation, civilians have little incentive to cooperate. Because of the counterproductivity of such unsystematic types of coercion, insurgent groups prefer not to use it. Instead, groups target collaborators with the enemy for selective violence.

In this account, the key determinant of selective violence is the control of territory. In areas of total control, civilian cooperation is assured because the threat of violence exists. Denunciation of the insurgency is dangerous because the enemy of the controlling group is far away. Absent denunciations, the amount of selective violence is low. In zones where one side dominates but is contested by opposing forces, selective violence is high because the dominant side must eliminate people who help the enemy. In this territory-focused interpretation of insurgent-group violence, the alliance between civilian and combatant and central and peripheral actors determines how an insurgent group treats the local population. This dynamic is demonstrated most clearly in a zone where two parties to a conflict have balanced levels of control over territory. Where no single group exercises a monopoly of control, violence is low because civilians do not supply the necessary information to denounce one side's supporters for fear of retribution from the other side. Locals face an ambiguous structure of incentives to provide information. They will provide little or false information because they do not wish to be seen as favoring either side. Supporters coexist uneasily side by side.[16]

Eventually the balance of control shifts, and one side begins to dominate. Selective violence then increases as a stimulus to force the local populace to cooperate in an attempt to oust the weakened enemy. Thus, one party's dominant control of a certain area or town molds the community's willingness to collaborate with it, and violence is created in the interaction between political actors and civilians who will denounce others within the community.[17]

Several assumptions are embedded in this theory of irregular warfare. First, it unduly emphasizes the importance of territorial control. Although many conflicts are about the control over a specific territory (the Israeli-Palestinian conflict being perhaps the most obvious example), land for population dominance is not the only resource over which groups fight. The PKK, for example, acknowledges that it can no longer gain a Kurdish homeland for its people and fights instead for the recognition of Kurdish cultural rights. Second, according to the irregular-warfare view, civilians experience violence because the opposing forces fight for territorial dominance, which in turn leads to population dominance. However, if we unpack the appraisal of territory by groups and the state, we see that land may be valuable not only for population dominance but also for other reasons of strategic significance, such as access to rivers for transportation or to attack more valuable assets such as the provincial or national capital as an important step forward in conventional warfare. The relationship between resource extraction and territory can vary depending on the type of resource. For example, territorial control may not be necessary in acquiring recruits. Al Qaeda uses ideology to gather soldiers. The acquisition of arms may not necessarily depend on territorial control, whereas a continuous food source often does.

Furthermore, Kalyvas's territory-focused thesis provides little room for the influence of ideology on forces and civilians. For example, it does not account for civilians' political bias in favor of one side of a conflict. Furthermore, this approach does not allow the interests of locals to shape the conflict or the behavior of insurgents. Similarly, it fails to incorporate the micromotives of insurgents into the analysis and thus cannot account for how such interests shape the conflict. The personal interests of leaders are an important component in the study of political violence, as evidenced by individuals such as Jonas Savimbi, who led Angola's rebel force, UNITA. Savimbi's importance was highlighted when the group agreed to end the war only following his death. Furthermore, this thesis assumes that there is internal cohesion among armed forces and that such unity is constant. We know this is not the case in insurgent forces. Several groups existed during the early years of Guatemala's civil war, and a lack of unity was unmistakable. For example, the MR-13 was largely a Trotskyite group that was forced out of the mainstream insurgency. State repression of the Guatemalan Communist Party (PGT) during the 1960s facilitated internal splintering. Likewise, the SPLA was rife with factions following its formation in 1983. One splinter group, SPLA-Nasir, led by Riek Machar, eventually joined opposing forces.

Kalyvas's irregular-war approach also assumes that individuals can freely choose between conflicting groups that establish balanced levels of control. However, some communities may prefer to opt out of conflict by fleeing the scene. That has occurred in the war in Darfur. Many of the Sudanese civilians in western Sudan have fled to neighboring Chad to escape the violence from local militias. In Colombia, internally displaced persons (IDPs) flood cities such as Cartagena to escape the war in the countryside.

The territory-focused thesis further assumes that particular types of violence are displayed by certain sides to a conflict. How do we then account for instances when regular armies enforce measures violently? Why do some armed groups display restraint? Why, for example, did the FARC involve itself in drug trafficking much later than it could have done? In fact, initially following the exploitation of the narcotics economy, the FARC attempted to maintain its contractual relationship with locals, en suring civilian protection.[18] Likewise, the SPLA chose not to engage in the FARC's practice of kidnapping in order to raise funds. Kalyvas's school of thought also concentrates on selective violence. However, selective violence does not account for all deaths in civil war—some observers would even say today that it accounts for far fewer deaths than arbitrary violence does, though these numbers are difficult to verify. Nevertheless, though indiscriminate violence is difficult to predict theoretically, it still deserves attention. Arguably, this kind of violence deserves more attention because it is the kind that is misunderstood most—the kind labeled "senseless." For these reasons, the selective-violence approach detracts from an effective overall analysis of violence and order.

Nature's Folly

Since the 1990s, a great deal of attention has focused on greed-induced violence in the wider conduct and organization of conflict within states.[19] Some scholars link violence with the scramble for natural resources.[20] These scholars view the choices of insurgents in the context of individual incentives and the availability of resources easily wrested from the people. In such a context, insurgents fight largely for personal enrichment obtained through loot they seize in conflict.[21] This account of violence in modern wars survives in various forms throughout the conflict literature. Recent studies link recruitment to the type of resources; when an insurgent group uses material incentives for recruitment during times of conflict, high levels of civilian abuse are more likely to result. In this analysis, insurgents use violence to overcome the initial conditions of recruitment difficulty that leaders confront. In environments rich in natural resources or external support, insurgents are likely to commit higher levels of indiscriminate violence. Easily obtainable resources offer opportunities for looting, and those whose main motivation is to loot are poorly invested in the communities for which they fight.[22] Hence, these actors mistreat civilians. These opportunistic rebellions require indiscipline in the ranks to recruit and maintain membership. Otherwise, cadres are likely to abandon the group in pursuit of other options. In contrast, when resources are scarce, insurgents must earn acceptance by the local populace in return for public goods and security. Committed insurgents are more likely to exist in environments where natural resources are limited and when participation is risky.[23]

This opportunistic-insurgent theory has received a great deal of academic attention, though it also makes far too many assumptions to accord with on-the-ground reality. This theory assumes that the existence of local resources *determines* that insurgents will *inevitably* become violent predators. In doing so, it discredits the force of leadership. Instead of leading, the leaders of insurgencies are forced to accommodate the strategies inherent in the structure of incentives that they find. They cannot shape these incentives. Whereas the thesis discussed in the preceding section declares that the insurgent-state uses of violence shape the environment and noncombatant incentives, this second account of insurgent behavior has material goods doing the work.

There are several problems with this approach. The conduct of the SPLA and the FARC challenges these notions. According to the opportunistic insurgent thesis, the SPLA should have killed foreign aid workers and looted their stores much like the Lord's Resistance Army (LRA) did in northern Uganda. This theory, which is primarily promulgated by Jeremy Weinstein, does not account for shifts in resource endowments. Rather, it tacitly assumes that resources remain fixed. Yet, as I demonstrate in the analysis of the FARC, resources can and do change: the FARC went from depending on peasant support to relying on benefits from the illicit-drug industry. However, the group was able to maintain its early contractual conduct until the development of the paramilitaries. Where resources are easily gathered, they drive short-term predatory behavior because "opportunists" can dominate the micropolitics of these groups and their relations with locals.[24] This suggests that the failure to control key resources launches insurgents into path dependency of factionalism and violence.

Some people may suggest that an insurgent group's shift in behavior stems from its dependence on illicit industries in which it becomes involved. This would probably account for the FARC's behavior as it became involved in drug trafficking during the 1980s. With the onset of increased coca cultivation in the 1990s, much of it taxed by the insurgents, certain regions in Colombia became important strategic and financial bulwarks for the FARC. In an interview, a local farmer claimed that the insurgents had become profit oriented, and those who joined the FARC during recent years had done so merely for money. On its surface, the farmer's statement appears to support Weinstein's argument, which would view incentives to join the FARC as a result of the existence of material incentives rather than ideological ones. However, this account falls short. It inadequately explains the earlier shift in behavior of the insurgent groups toward civilians because it assumes that resources are constant. Furthermore, individuals claim that the paramilitaries (*parus*) in Colombia offer more to soldiers in terms of salary and looting.[25] According to the opportunistic thesis, we would expect FARC members to defect to the paramilitaries because of the incentives the latter offered. With these opportunistic individuals leaving the FARC, the group should have become more contractual toward civilians. However, this has not been the case. Colombia specialists confirm that the FARC engages in a wide variety of coercive activities and that in 2003 and 2004 the group appeared to have surpassed the paramilitaries in violence toward local residents.[26] The FARC has remained strong in numbers *and* practices violence toward civilians.[27] Furthermore, the opportunistic-insurgent thesis posits that outside patrons release insurgents from the long-term tasks of bargaining with and committing to local citizens.[28] If this is true, why were Cold War–era anticolonial liberation rebels and others who were heavily dependent on outside aid so keen to establish "liberated" zones? I present an argument and supporting information that suggests a different view.

Problems and Unanswered Questions

Like the new-wars thesis, typologizing insurgents as opportunists further depoliticizes insurgent violence. Just as many analyses of insurgent violence often perceive it as irrational, senseless, and hence apolitical, so too are many accounts of terrorist attacks laced with emotion or references to evil.[29] Yet counterinsurgency and counterterrorism are considered political in these same discourses. We can speculate that discourses that depoliticize do so with the aim of delegitimizing.[30] Rather than viewing violence as free of ideology, or as part of the new criminal enterprise of rebellion, I argue that violence is strategic and at times the only option left to armed groups. Insurgents use violence selectively to gather information among local populations. Leaders must allow insurgents to be violent and opportunistic when resources abound, or else the followers might abandon the fight. Either way, the behavior displayed by nonstate armed groups is a response to local dynamics.

This recent analysis of insurgent behavior also leaves several questions unanswered and a few issues underdeveloped. Although the recent resource-driven accounts of insurgent behavior illuminate several aspects of the political economy of war, they fall short in explaining how and why these groups change their treatment of civilians. In essence, they are narrow in their interpretations of political order. The questions that this new literature leaves unexplored do not concern why insurgents act the way they do, nor do they pertain to whether resources are important or not. The latter, I believe, has been established in this debate. Rather, the questions that remain concern why insurgents change their behavior and how other armed actors affect the relationship between insurgents and civilians.

First and foremost, recent analysis of insurgent violence does not help answer the question of why these groups—some with very similar ideologies and sharing similar resources—shift their treatment of civilians in very opposite directions. The opportunistic-insurgent thesis explains behavior by linking it to the scramble to obtain the resources necessary to fight foes. Yet in many contemporary insurgencies, behavior shifts independently of changes in resource endowments. That is, some groups shift from violent to solicitous behavior, even though resources appear to be constant. Likewise, shifts in resource availability do not correlate well with changes in insurgents' treatment of noncombatants whom they claim to represent.

Second, how important are resources to violent conflict? Although there have been myriad studies in support of or against the contention that resources drive conflict, particularly civilian violence in conflict, when one measures the evidence, the premise that resources are important is irrefutable. As I stated before, insurgent groups often operate in extreme environments where survival is rarely guaranteed on a day-to-day basis; for insurgents, resources are scarce, in part because of their status as illegal armed actors but also as a result of the conditions of the countries in which these groups operate.[31] Insurgents must have resources to operate. But are resources the instrument that drives behavior?

Third, how critical is the specific type of resource to insurgent behavior? That is, do illicit resources shape the behavior of armed groups?[32] I categorize resources as illicit if they are obtained illegally. More specifically, illicit resources refers to resources obtained through criminal networks such as drugs or arms trafficking.

Resources that insurgents require vary; different groups need different resources, at different times, and in different contexts. For example, the

FARC did not always benefit from participating in the illicit-drug indus-try. Rather, the relationship between civilian populations and insurgents varies depending on the level of competition a group faces. This relation-ship reflects a type of political order.

The fourth question left unanswered is how do some nonstate armed actors create political order in the context of the international environ-ment's reluctance to recognize new states? Questions regarding the in-teraction between insurgents and civilians and between insurgents and the state, as well as the importance of legitimate domination, are left un-answered. Recent studies of insurgent behavior forgo the analysis of the state's impact.

A Theory of Insurgent Behavior

The questions outlined in the preceding section are both empirical and theoretical in nature. They are empirical in that they concern local relationships and intergroup dynamics, which are difficult to assess unless one conducts research in these places. They are theoretical in the sense that we need hypotheses about insurgents and their shifts in behavior to answer our questions. Much of the remainder of this book is dedicated to generating and examining evidence to address these questions and evalu-ate the theory that I develop in response. Here I present summaries of the answers to the preceding questions, which will lead to a theory of insur-gent behavior.

Insurgent groups change their behavior toward noncombatants ac-cording to whether they face active rivalry. Competition in the insur-gent environment is the struggle among groups for a comparative ad-vantage in resources that will yield a position of competitive advantage, which in turn leads to enhanced capabilities and superior perfor-mance.[33] Without competition, insurgents can penetrate and centrally coordinate the activities of local communities through insurgents' own infrastructures. An increase in capabilities rests on low levels of rivalry. That is, a group can do more when it is not competing for resources. For example, it can adopt a contractual relationship with local popu-lations. With regard to establishing order, such a relationship means greater legitimacy because order through compliance and acceptance is cheaper and more effective than simple domination by force, though a contractual relationship also entails providing an administration that supplies public goods.

Why will insurgents necessarily respond with less violence toward civilians when there is little or no competition for resources from other armed entities? Arguably, these groups can act in whatever manner they choose when not faced with competition. However, insurgents have to operate under specific constraints in their relations with local populations. The scarcity of resources (either natural or those provided by the community such as taxes) in many conflict zones means that insurgents possess incentives to abide by contractual agreements, including the provision of such public goods as security. If they fail to provide such goods, civilians are likely to flee. Thus, it is a win-win situation for the insurgents to establish contractual relations with locals. If there is a single group, it can "afford" to enter a contractual relationship with civilians.[34] Under these conditions, insurgents can rely on a steady supply of resources without having to worry that these resources will dry up or be sold to others. For a very cheap price they win additional obedience from the population, which translates into increased order and capabilities for the insurgent group.

Competition changes the insurgent-civilian relationship and affects decision-making among these armed groups. A group becomes coercive when it faces competition from rival groups or states. In this circumstance, the previously singular insurgent group is forced to shift the logic of its priorities to the short term in order to guarantee its survival. The presence of rivals or competition means that already-scarce resources may become even scarcer. The priority of survival becomes preeminent, and the insurgent time horizon changes to the short term. If a group does not amass resources quickly, other groups will do so, driving the formerly singular group to extinction. The most efficient method of extracting resources quickly is through the use of force. Setting up contractual relations is a long-term investment, and focusing on this strategy in an environment of armed competition will lead to a speedy demise of cadres and perhaps the movement itself.

The state plays an interesting and idiosyncratic role in the insurgent-civilian dynamic because a government can become a rival to an insurgent group. Like an insurgent group, the state can be coercive toward a specific community or minority, or it can be contractual, treating all civilians relatively equally. When a repressive state begins to reform and establishes a reciprocal relationship with the civilian communities it formerly repressed, the insurgent group representing these civilians is likely to become violent toward the civilian population. The state becomes a competitor for the resources and obedience that citizens can provide. This means that when states and international organizations such as the United Nations recognize and grant various forms of group rights and encourage autonomy among communities where insurgents operate, the insurgents are likely to respond by increasing the level of violence toward civilians. The state, like other insurgent groups, becomes a rival for control over resources. The case of the PKK demonstrates what occurs when a state begins to reform. In particular, that case shows how popular support—an important resource—is affected by state reform.

The link between state institutions and political violence has been explored by scholars studying failed or collapsed states. In response to events of recent years—particularly in places such as Somalia, Liberia, and Sierra Leone—when the erosion of the central governing authority has helped instigate widespread political violence, analysts and scholars have discussed failed states and state collapse in their work on developing countries.[35] Although I would not classify Turkey as a failed or collapsed state, one could argue that there were pockets of collapse in Turkey that fueled the PKK's response to the government in Ankara. Although there is no standard definition of failed states, I understand them to be sovereign entities that are no longer able to provide basic services and that do not possess a monopoly over the means of violence.[36] The inclusion in this definition of the ability to provide services is the result of employing a Lockean definition of statehood, in which the state is defined in terms of service provision.[37] The function of a state's monopolization of violence is Weberian in origin. Again, there are debates on the precise definition of *failed state,* and there is much analysis of failed-state discourse.[38]

As demonstrated in the following case-based chapters, this study champions the influence of local dynamics. It does not, however, attempt to explain the complexities of all insurgent-group behavior. I am concerned primarily with the relationship between insurgents and civilians, with a focus on groups active during and after the Cold War. Although my analysis focuses here on a few cases, the theory that I develop can help in understanding behavior by other insurgencies today. However, in explaining behavior by other insurgencies, one must be aware of some limitations. For example, several elements are, admittedly, excluded from consideration in the model. Because the model emphasizes the dynamics at the local level, one may argue that it lends itself to reductionism and leaves questions unanswered. For example, do the actions and support of local populations actually help determine the strategy of insurgent groups that operate in the international arena? The tension between theoretical models and concrete developments is eternal. For the purposes of analysis, however, we must engage in some degree of reductionism, such as defining a band of rebels as a unit of analysis, as well as doing likewise for local populations and states. If we were to focus only on observable outcomes, the picture we present would become so complex that measurement, much less model building, would prove impossible. One could argue as well that this theory keeps certain key instrumentalities, such as the state, exogenous to the local dynamic. Indeed, this is true to a point. In nearly all the cases examined here, the state had little or no presence in the local communities in which the rebel groups operated at their inception. The state does, however, play a role in affecting insurgent-group behavior. Therefore, it is incorrect to say that the state continuously remains an exogenous force. Rather, the role of the state is case specific, though its effects appear to be similar across groups.

One area of contention in this study may be found in the ability to measure change. Indeed, the constraints in such measurements are a limitation to this model. For the skeptical (and often realistic) scholar, this limitation translates into a deep suspicion of insurgent-group intentions. How do we know, for example, that rebel groups' rhetoric of transformation actually implies change? Change is difficult to measure and may indicate not genuine transformation but rather lip service to those who demand it. However, just as we have recorded human-rights abuses, so too can we pinpoint periods of transformation. Although the declarations of insurgent groups may not correspond to their actual behavior, they are important data points of reference for this study. These declarations indicate that insurgent groups respond to an external audience.

Another area of debate that this book may bring up is that comparing such unique cases is unlikely to lead to broad generalizations because of differences in such aspects as culture. The findings from a study of insurgents in Latin America, one could argue, are not comparable to the results from a study of insurgents in Africa. However, I maintain that though cultures vary across cases, there is a thread—at times quite thick—that runs through them all and is an effect of human behavior. In other words, I argue very strongly that humans share a very common element: the desire for survival. I derive this argument from Abraham Maslow's needs-based framework of human motivation, in which humans are motivated by unsatisfied needs. Maslow's hierarchy consists of five levels of needs.

In order from higher to lower needs, they are self-actualization needs, esteem needs, social needs, safety needs, and physiological needs. According to Maslow, lower needs must be satisfied before other higher needs can be considered. For example, if fundamental needs (needs that sustain life) such as physiological and safety needs are not met, then a person or group of people will always be motivated to satisfy these basic needs. Higher needs such as social and esteem needs will not be recognized until a person or group of people satisfies those needs that are fundamental to existence.[39] Therefore, all humans will try to satisfy their most fundamental needs of survival before anything else. Thus, I think it quite possible to draw general statements about how humans create order and interact with one another in different societies and countries.

Collecting information for a study such as this often requires fieldwork in the communities being studied to truly understand local activities. Developments in Iraq, especially the U.S. failure to accurately identify local threats early in the invasion, throw into high relief the need to study the dynamics of local processes involved in competition.

Finally, this model does not account for certain intervening variables that intrude in the causal pathway, from the inner dynamics of rebel groups—the personal disputes and individual characteristics of leaders that can affect group behavior—to the actual military and economic strength of a state or the cultural and ethical baggage that armed insurgents bring with them. These issues lend a complexity to the model that make it difficult to assess the importance or effect of intervening variables. Again, herein lies the limitation of modeling human behavior: the inherent "cleanliness" that it creates out of actual events. Reality—particularly that which exists in conflict zones—is quite messy. Therefore, the model presented in this chapter and applied in the following case studies encompasses two contradictory themes: uniformity and elasticity.

3

"The Elephant Is Not Yet Dead"
The Reform of the SPLA

Yar works as a database officer for the SPLA. She is part of a contingent of female soldiers that make up a significant portion of the Sudanese insurgent group.[1] When she joined the group in 1984, like many others she was sent to Ethiopia for training. She then worked as a secretary for the insurgent leader, John Garang. In 1991 she left Ethiopia and went to the liberated areas of southern Sudan. She has five children and a husband, who is also a soldier in the SPLA.

As I have asked other soldiers of the SPLA I have interviewed, I ask her to talk about the group in its formative years and the group as it is today. In the beginning, she says, the movement was not as progressive or free—at least not as free as it is today. There were conflicts inside the group, she says, which led to human-rights atrocities. Yar looks up at me in a matter-of-fact manner. The SPLA was weak, she explains. To fight this weakness, she tells me, you must be democratic—everyone must be accommodated.

It took time, Yar explains further, but the SPLA realized it had problems. The SPLA became convinced that there was a need for democracy.

I ask Yar what caused this shift in the rebel group. She tells me that a lot contributed to this change. We learned our lesson, she says.[2]

This chapter details the changes in the behavior of the SPLA in southern Sudan. Following a description of this group's inception, I trace its evolution from a Marxist group supported by Ethiopian backers to a disunited faction-prone organization to a group with its own constitution and self-proclaimed democratic system of governance. That description is followed by an explanation for *why* these changes occurred and why the belief in this transformation by local citizens and the international community was important for the level of violence in the area as the SPLA evolved.

Sudan: The "Afro-Arab State"

Sudan is a diverse and distinctive place.[3] Physically, it is the largest country in Africa (see map 3.1), boasting a population of twenty-three to thirty million people, one-third of whom lives in the south. Sudan is roughly 65 percent African and 35 percent Arab.[4] Yet the percentages oversimplify the points of culture and identity. In actuality, Sudan is home to over five hundred tribes. In the south this number includes the Dinka and the Nuer tribes and numerous smaller tribes such as the Shulluk, Bari, Madi, Kakwa, Azende, Bagara, Toposa, and the Didinga, in addition to many others.[5] And, though Arab and Muslim identities dominate northern Sudan, and African and Christian identities prevail in the south, the distinctions between these two regions of the country are not so clear-cut.

Sudan: Northern Assimilation and Southern Resistance

The diversity found in Sudan means that it is inaccurate to speak of the north-south conflict in straightforward terms of culture, ethnicity, or religion. Indeed, religion, ethnicity, social rankings, and colonial legacies are all elements that have contributed to the conflict, which involves the government of Sudan in the north and the SPLA in the south. Yet, as noted by one well-known scholar of Sudanese history, Douglas H. Johnson, none of these elements by themselves can fully explain the conflict. Instead, the development of successive forms of political order and consequent regional inequities and underdevelopment, as well as ethnic and cultural enmity, all contribute to the conflict.[6]

Early establishments of political order along the Nile River and through eastern Sudan had a clearly defined relationship between their centers of power and their peripheries: manpower and food came from outlying regions. During the Muslim era, central power depended largely on standing armies made up of manpower (slaves) from the hinterland. Thus, these precursors to states were involved not only in domestic slave trading but also in international markets of slavery, which included slave trading and slave raiding. Each political unit maintained regions under its control from which it drew its slaves and other resources to fund its security.[7]

This market in and use of slaves was not unique to the Muslim era of Sudan. In fact, slavery dates back centuries in this region. The establishment of Egyptian Nile valley "states" probably was accomplished through

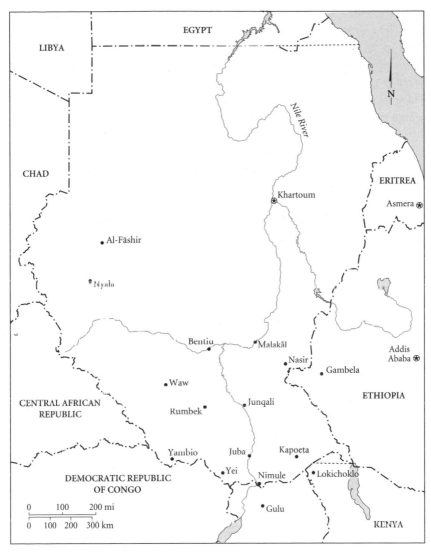

Map 3.1. Sudan 2008
(Perry-Castaneda Library Map Collection, University of Texas Libraries)

treaties and trade between groups, as well as through conquest and slave raids. The organization of a biennial delivery of "Ethiopian" slaves from Kush to the Persian dynasty located in Egypt was recorded by Herodotus.[8] Slaves probably did not come from the Nubian kingdom but were plundered from peripheral areas subject to its rule. Thus, the terms *Nubian, Nuba,* and *Sudanese* entered the colloquial Arabic of the river valley as synonyms for *slave.* Prior to the establishment of Muslim political units during the fourteenth century, then, pagan and Christian kingdoms had actively organized raids of their peripheries, partly because of the demand from external trade relations. Muslim rulers merely continued a tradition that had already been established by their pagan and Christian predecessors.[9]

It was the external trade relations with increasingly Muslim rulers that led to the development and entrenchment of Islam in the central Nile valley and to the political units of what today is Sudan. There were not only commercial reasons for conversions to Islam in Sudanic states. The states of Sennar, located along the Blue Nile, and in the sultanate of Darfur in western Sudan, were brought more in line with Islamic principles with their conversion to Islam. With Islam came literacy in Arabic and the introduction of Arabic legal texts. These books of law set forth "the principles of the Arabs." Furthermore, as Arab genealogies were introduced, rulers found new modes of political and spiritual legitimacy. For example, Sudanic kings uncovered Ummayid and Abbasid origins, and holy men discovered their descent from the family of the Prophet Muhammad.[10]

The adoption of Islam by Sudanic rulers began to sharpen the distinction between the centers and the hinterlands—between the individuals who had the opportunities and education to claim the protection of law and those who went without legal rights.[11] The exercise of the centers' powers within this new Muslim context, however, fostered ambiguities. People living closest to centers of power often gained more benefits by collaborating with rulers than did those who lived in outlying regions. However, as power increasingly rested on the size and strength of standing armies drawn from slaves (originating in the peripheries), free Muslim peasants often suffered coercion at the hands of high-ranking military slaves in the name of a Muslim ruler.

Yet the fact that many slave soldiers converted to Islam did not make them any more free. One's origin during this period defined one's social status. Coming from the hinterland usually meant that one was a part of the slave army. Territorial origins became an element of social stratification. Still, we must be careful not to read into the past the ethnic connotations of today. Even during the nineteenth century, certain terms that today have specific national or ethnic connotations then implied lowly origin or status. For example, *Nuba* were slaves in Sennar. *Sudanese* were slaves everywhere. According to the riverain populations between Dongola and Gezira, *Arabs* were considered to be uncivilized nomads.[12]

Up to this point in Sudan's history, the south remained largely unaffected by the succession of early political units in the north. Expansion into the south had been halted at the end of the eighteenth century by the Shilluk kingdom on the White Nile and by the Dinka peoples living along the Kiir, White Nile, and Sobat rivers. The Dinka even went so far as to offer refuge to Muslim pastoralists who were attempting to escape regimes in the north. Arab political dominance in the north came to an end at the hands of imperial forces. From 1820 to 1821, joint Turkish and Egyptian forces invaded Sudan and took control of northern regions. The Turko-Egyptian conquest of Sudan in the nineteenth century destabilized the regional balance. This new empire had more resources at its disposal and made far greater demands on those it ruled, for slaves and other forms of tribute, than had any empire that had come before. The northern Sudanese in Nubia, Sennar, Kordofan, and near the Red Sea were the first populations to fall to the Turko-Egyptians. These conquered people were soon coerced into collaborating with the ruling army in slave raids into the original hinterlands. Egyptian forces eventually penetrated the upper Nile basin. This opening eventually brought Europeans, Egyptians, and northern Sudanese merchants into the south. This period of the nineteenth century marks the beginning of the north-south divide in Sudan.[13]

Several developments contributed significantly to sharpening the north-south demarcation. The imposition of new forms of taxation and land ownership in northern Sudan began the impoverishment of the north and led to the expansion of slave raiding and slave owning further south. Furthermore, the tax and land reforms affected the northern economy as the need to increase crop productivity meant increasing the use of marginal plots. Farmers mortgaged their crops, and indebtedness rose. As a result, there was a large outpouring of people into the south to exploit new lands. Hardship in the north at the hands of the government led to subjugation and exploitation in the south.[14]

Prior to the Turko-Egyptian conquest, no orthodox, universally recognized religious authority was acknowledged in Sudan. Islam, up to that point in the country's history, was viewed and practiced quite differently by different people. The justification of the Turko-Egyptian conquest had been to claim Sudan for the Ottoman ruler of the Muslim word. As such, the new regime in Sudan was committed to Islamic law in place of tribal law and custom. For the Sudanese, though, such a version of Islam was foreign; they thought of their own laws and customs as Islamic in their own right, even though they were a fusion of pre-Islamic law and Islamic principles. A key point of conflict between the government and the Sudanese people was the government's attempt to suppress slavery. Pressure from the British government between 1863 and 1879 resulted in efforts to curtail slave raids. The challenge in suppressing the slave trade was largely an effect of the government's taxation policies, which actually increased the need for slaves. For northerners, it seemed irrational that taxation (which they described as unjustified) should be imposed on them while their main source of income (slave trading) was outlawed.[15]

In many ways, the invasion and conquest of Sudan by joint Turkish and Egyptian forces had a unifying effect on the country. The north and south united to resist foreign domination in a series of rebellions. The disintegrating economy in Egypt, which had led to the British occupation of that country, along with low morale of a poorly compensated Egyptian army in Sudan and the resentment by the Sudanese of that army, led to a revolution that was in essence a national movement. Muhammad Ahmed al-Mahdi—or al-Mahdi (the Islamic Messiah), as he came to be known—found his main source of support for the revolution to be the Arab Baggara tribes of southern Kordofan and Darfur. These tribes were known for their militancy and in particular their slave-raiding tendencies. In exchange for their support, the Mahdi promised the Baggara to restore the slave-trading industry if they successfully drove out the Turko-Egyptian regime. The Mahdi came to power in 1885, marking the establishment of the first independent Sudanese state. Khartoum in the north became the capital.[16]

Although the Mahdi did not live very long after his ascendancy, and the Mahdist era was cut short by foreign invasion, the effects of this period in Sudanese history were severe. The Mahdi espoused a strict, literal version of Islam, and his goal was to establish an Islamic kingdom over all other kingdoms. The Mahdiyya, both in its initial revolutionary campaigns and in its short sixteen-year life span, was also an extremely costly venture, both in terms of resources and its aftermath. The state itself saw a breakdown of law and order, famine due to drought, war, and inadequate central capacity to address the social and economic emergencies that prevailed. According to one scholar, the Mahdist state "would make the crises in Somalia and Bosnia look mild by comparison."[17] The result was devastating. Estimates cite that the population of Sudan fell from seven million before the Mahdist revolt to between two and three million after the end of the Mahdist era. The overall effect was in fact contradictory in nature. On the one hand, the Mahdi gave Sudan a common vision against foreign rule and the prospect of sovereignty. On the other hand, Mahdism also generated deep internal divisions, intertribal warfare, and general domestic turmoil.[18]

It is no wonder, then, that Anglo-Egyptian forces found it relatively simple to conquer Sudan in 1898 and put an end to the Mahdiyya. This British-dominated Anglo Egyptian Condominium government became a hybrid of shared sovereignty developed to acknowledge the Egyptians' former claims on Sudan and to accommodate British interests.[19] This new government took control of the north and defended itself from the threat of resurgent Mahdism in several ways. First, it reinstated tribal leaders who had been replaced by the Mahdi's agents. Second, the Anglo-Egyptian Condominium government supported orthodoxy against what it termed "fanaticism" in the constitution. Third, the new rulers attempted to quell Mahdiyya religious rivals.[20]

British and Egyptian settlement of southern Sudan, however, was not as smooth as it was in the north. The Mahdist state had had little if any control over the southern region of the country, aside from a few garrison villages. In a way, this was beneficial to the Anglo-Egyptian agenda, as they did not have to wean people from Mahdism. But because there was no need to offer rewards to people to win their loyalty to the new government, there was no way to ensure their patronage. Most populations of the south had viewed the Mahdist government as they had the Turko-Egyptian regime before: they rejected it. There was considerable continuity in the personnel who manned the garrison towns in the south under both regimes. Merchants from the north as well as administrators who had been a central part of the original colonial administrative and commercial outposts of the southern region of Sudan joined in the efforts to overthrow Egypt and then resumed their original posts. Likewise, Sudanese slave soldiers in the Egyptian garrisons were transitioned into the Mahdist army. Therefore, the inclusion of British soldiers in the returning Egyptian army of 1898 was scarcely a visible change to the structure of authority in the region. In fact, the majority of southerners categorized British officers as "Turks" along with Egyptians and the northern Sudanese.[21]

The return of Egyptian rule in Sudan presented the British with a dilemma. The British administrators saw that the Mahdist rebellion had in part been a response to Turko-Egyptian misrule, and they therefore tried to distance the new condominium government from that legacy. In doing so, however, the British were in a sense attempting to dissociate themselves from the authority they were trying to reassert. They frequently declared to southerners that the new government was not the same as the old Egyptian government, which had stolen southern cattle, burned villages, and conscripted captives for the army. Thus, the period of pacification in the south for the Anglo-Egyptian government was longer than that in the north.

As a whole, though, the south remained on the periphery of central government throughout the period of foreign rule. Southern Sudanese who were conscripted for Sudanese battalions of the Egyptian army were purposely separated from northern Sudanese, and the replenishment of these battalions was carried out in areas that coincided with old slave-raiding zones. Thus, the exploitive pattern of the nineteenth century continued—though on a lesser scale—under Anglo-Egyptian rule. Furthermore, the development of a more comprehensive administrative system throughout the south was prohibited by the central government's involvement in World War I and the continued demands that war made on personnel and resources.[22]

Despite the devastating effects of the Mahdi's rule both socially and economically, one element of that era endured: the Islamic agenda imposed by the state on the identity of nation. For the British Christian rulers, this was a point of concern. In an attempt to prevent Islam from spreading to the south between World Wars I and II, the condominium government administered the south under the Closed District Ordinance Act of 1920, which barred movement between the northern and southern provinces of Sudan.[23] This policy marked the beginning of the formal administration of Sudan as two separate entities. Resistance in the south, together with religious and cultural differences between this region of the country and the north, led colonial authorities to adopt distinct policies of administration for the two areas.

The balance in levels of economic, political, and educational development between the north and the south was severely disproportionate. The opening up of the south under pacification benefited commercial interests of merchants mainly from the north as well as the central government. For example, royalties collected from ivory sales went to the central government in Khartoum rather than to local provincial governments. Furthermore, religious leaders and merchants of the north benefited from this administrative system that allowed them to obtain rights to labor and land. For example, the Mahdi's son accumulated considerable wealth by participating in government contracts for wood, fuel, and meat. In the south, however, commerce continued to be in the hands of northerners or foreigners.[24]

There were also disparities between the north and the south in the development of educational institutions. The lower echelons of the Sudanese civil service, for example, were recruited from schools in areas of Equatoria, where the minority Fartit and Jur peoples resided, rather than from areas where the majority Dinka lived. The Equatorians were also recruited as police to replace the army in the rural outposts. Thus, they were co-opted early on into the colonial security system. The pacification of the majority Dinka and the large Nuer populations in the south was actually carried out by the Equatorial Corps.[25] The policies of the British and Egyptians therefore supported divisions among the various groups of people in the south. By the end of the condominium, more than three-quarters of state expenditure went into the northern cotton-growing scheme; all government and higher-education facilities were located in Khartoum and its surrounding towns.[26] The result was the emergence of urban elites and a landed aristocracy in the north, which subsequently excluded the south from their struggle for independence. Sudan was structured to resist organization as a unified political unit.

On the eve of Sudan's independence, following elections to the first self-governing parliament, members of the Liberal Party (to which most southerners belonged) campaigned for the separate administrative status of the south. Federalism, they claimed, should be the constitutional solution between the disparate entities of the north and the south. Meanwhile, a commission announced that northerners would be appointed to all the senior-level positions in the south. Southern Sudanese leadership convened a conference in Juba in the south to discuss the political future of the country as a whole. It was at this conference of 1954 that it was decided to vote for independence of Sudan from Egypt on the condition that a federal system for the entire country was adopted. The south would be an autonomous state. Failing the passing of this resolution, the conference declared its right to self-determination, including the option of complete independence from the north. Within the national parliament, however, no consensus on the issue of the south emerged.[27]

In response to the marginalization of the south, with the increase of northerners taking over southern administrative positions, as well as positions in the police and as teachers in government schools, southern fears of northern domination increased. Soldiers of the southern Equatorial Corps, whose British officers had recently been replaced by northern Sudanese officers, feared they would be forced to disarm and be transferred to the north. After several weeks of mounting tension in the summer of 1955, a mutiny broke out in the southern town of Torit, the headquarters of the Equatorial Corps. Though not well organized, this mutiny spread to other southern garrison towns. Many mutineers fled with their families south to Uganda. Others were tried and executed by the Sudanese Army.[28]

Following Sudanese independence in 1956, there was a small though unfocused military campaign to find the remaining mutineers and bring them to trial. On a larger scale there were more repressive activities in the south by the military, as the army began burning villages to punish increasing opposition to the government, especially among educated southerners. Several leading southern political figures and a number of students fled to the bush and to neighboring countries, where they joined with the remaining exiled mutineers and formed a political movement and the core of an insurgent army known colloquially as Anya-Nya— named after a type of poison.[29] It is this point that marks the beginning of the first of Sudan's two civil wars—a response to the economic, political, psychological, educational, and cultural ostracism of the south by the north.

The first Sudanese civil war lasted until 1972, ending with the Addis Ababa Agreement, which established the south as an autonomous region with a parliament and a High Executive Council. Yet the relative peace that the agreement effected was fleeting. In June 1983, under pressure from conservative and radical elements and in an effort to eliminate growing liberal democracy in the south (which was incongruous with a national system with an authoritarian presidency), President Nimeiri issued "Republican Order Number One."[30] This order called for the redivision of the south into three regions—Equatoria, Bahr el Ghazal, and Upper Nile— and enabled the central government to deal with each region separately, using tribalism to foment intertribal fighting.[31] The result was increased community division and factionalism. The government's repressive measures succeeded even though they increased the insurgent groups' appeal by comparison. Furthermore, when the north sponsored other factions, it created rivalries and competition for resources in the south. State repression and intergroup rivalry was high; no single insurgent group dominated control over resources.

Amid this violence, Nimeiri eroded southern autonomy. In September 1983, he declared a revision of the penal code, linking it "organically and spiritually" to Islam. This made Islamic law the single force behind Sudanese law.[32] Although one-third of the country's population was non-Muslim, *Shari'a* was imposed on all Sudanese.[33]

Civil War and the Genesis of the SPLA

Sudan's second civil war began following the SPLA's formation in 1983, with the compounding of various events including the discovery of oil in the central and southern regions of the country.[34] The government's breaking of the Addis Ababa Agreement only intensified southern grievances. In January 1983, southern troops belonging to the 105th Battalion refused orders to abandon their weapons and transfer to the north. These soldiers feared that they would be sent to Iraq to join with another Sudanese contingent fighting Iraq's war against Iran, a condition that would leave the south open to an all-northern unit and increase its vulnerability. Following failed negotiations with this southern unit, President Nimeiri ordered an attack on the soldiers, which inspired a succession of mutinies throughout the south.

Deserters and mutineers found refuge in Ethiopia, where they came together to form the SPLA.[35] Many southern Sudanese rallied around the SPLA, some in protest over the abrogation of the Addis Ababa Agreement, while others expressed a rejection of consistent inequalities instituted by the north against the south. John Garang de Mabior, a Twic Dinka, emerged as the group's leader. Garang was a former officer in the Sudanese Army and a U.S.-educated agricultural economist. Under him, the SPLA broadly defined its objectives, claiming that Sudan needed to transform as a whole into a multiracial, multireligious, and multiethnic democratic state.[36] Garang's new goal for the SPLA was a marked difference from that of southern autonomy expressed by the Anya-Nya following Sudan's independence.

The SPLA saw the war as a struggle for liberation built on a socialist base. Therefore, during the insurgent group's formative years, the struggle against oppression and subjugation by the north dominated SPLA rhetoric. The group declared in its manifesto, the main task of the SPLA/SPLM is to transform the southern movement from a reactionary movement led by reactionaries and concerned with the south, jobs and self interest to a progressive movement led by revolutionaries and dedicated to the socialist transformation of the whole country. It must be reiterated that the principal objective of the SPLA/SPLM is not separation for the south. The south is an integral and inseparable part of the Sudan. Africa has been fragmented sufficiently enough by colonialism and neocolonialism and its further fragmentation can only be in the interests of her enemies.[37]

The SPLA viewed liberation as the separation between religion and the state, *not* the creation of a separate state; it called for a "New Sudan" that encompassed a unique cultural order. In following the preferences of Mengistu, the president of Ethiopia, Garang demonstrated the constraints of the Cold War: Mengistu did not want a separatist SPLA as an ally while Ethiopia's military fought its own separatist movement.

While the SPLA attempted to consolidate forces in Ethiopia, Nimeiri confronted growing opposition in the north, and before long an *intifada* led to his political downfall. The transitional government that took Nimeiri's place was unable to reach an agreement with the SPLA, and the war in the south moved north into the Nuba Mountains in southern Kordofan and the southern Blue Nile. During this period, a radical religious organization known as the Muslim Brotherhood restructured itself into a broad-based political party called the National Islamic Front (NIF). When it appeared there was sufficient will behind the peace process, popular opinion in the north shifted to favor the religious right in Khartoum, which viewed any compromise with the SPLA as a threat to the Islamic trend. This suspicion among conservatives in the government of Sudan resulted in another coup, and in 1989 Sadiq el Mahdi's government was overthrown by General Omar Hassan Ahmad al-Bashir in alliance with the NIF.

Bashir endorsed the NIF's national agenda of Arabization and the deepening of divisions between the government and the SPLA. Under his leadership, a Command Council was drawn up to rein in opposition, and in so doing it suspended the constitution and dissolved the parliament and all political parties. At the end of 1989, the regime announced that *Shari'a* law was to be implemented throughout the entire country. Furthermore, the government of Sudan stepped up offensives in the south.[38] During this period, the government of Sudan was backed by the United States. Like many U.S. choices of allies during the Cold War, the alliance with Sudan was strictly ideological (at least in the view of the United States). At the time, the NIF was at war with an insurgent group allied with USSR-supported Ethiopia, which in turn garnered Khartoum support from countries battling the Soviet Union and the "communist threat." Thus, issues confronting the nation affected not only Sudanese civilians but also the foreign policies of other states, which heightened the sensitive nature of Sudanese domestic policies. Religion became a critical force in widening the division between the north and the south in a manner that reignited calls for southern secession.[39] As the Sudanese government became increasingly coercive toward southerners, the appeal for independence from the north surfaced with more force. The question of independence, however, proved to be a divisive factor within the SPLA.

When I first met SPLA commander Edward Abyei Lino, he was the acting representative of the SPLA in Kenya. Tall, lanky, and extremely personable, he was also calm and had a quieting effect on those with whom he spoke. With graying hair and dressed in a fine suit, he sat down with me in Nairobi in a local café, our first of several meetings.

"The movement wants to be a state ultimately," he says, describing the end goal of the insurgent group. Yet, he continues, the group has had to deal with several elements that are often at odds with one another. For example, the group has had to fight the government of Sudan while at the same time providing for the needs of southerners.

The SPLA has also had to deal with foreign NGOs, he tells me. "There is a difference of philosophy" between the SPLA and foreign aid organizations. The NGOs claim neutrality, but they must recognize, he tells me, that they have resources and must deal with the appropriate authority on the ground. The SPLA on the ground will be the one to allow civil society to develop, to allow the delivery of services, which in turn can facilitate better governance in the south. Essentially, the SPLA faces many challenges. "No liberation movement has gone unchallenged," he reminds me, speaking as though such bumps in the road to statehood are par for the course. The elephant, he tells me, is not yet dead.[40]

Fractious Politics

Some scholars have characterized intragroup fighting in southern Sudan as the extension of tribal enmities, though a more accurate explanation for tensions within the SPLA should also include ideological and personal differences among the leadership. Conflicts within the insurgent group arose over its Ethiopian-backed objective of unification, while complaints of dictatorial behavior also arose among high-level SPLA officials. The result of this discord was a severe lack of unity within the group, but its most intense impacts were felt by civilian populations who found themselves caught in the middle of conflicts between the north and south as well as those between SPLA factions. Because a rivalry for southern resources had arisen, levels of violence in the south climbed and hit civilians hardest.

In an effort to understand the SPLA's fractious nature during its development, one southerner and former SPLA member explained that the group did not have the advantage of undergoing a period of political incubation that would have allowed it to develop a distinct political ideology. From the start, it was primarily a military-focused insurgency, influenced by its Marxist backers in Mengistu-led Ethiopia.[41] In fact, Ethiopian support and a militaristic focus arguably impeded the development of a clear political program in the SPLA's infancy. Thus, from its beginning the insurgent group lacked a dogma that represented the ideology of the dominant social forces in its region. In other words, it is possible that had the SPLA begun with backers other than Ethiopia, it would have called for southern secession. Unification had not appeared in the rhetoric of the south's political struggle prior to 1983, and many individuals within the SPLA criticized its leadership for what they perceived as a fundamentally flawed objective. To further emphasize this point, several people I interviewed, as well as scholars, argued that the group's socialist beginnings were merely exercises in "sloganeering" and were intended to motivate the masses.[42] Paul, the former governor of Lakes County in southern Sudan, remarked that the original source of the SPLA's resources did not necessarily confirm a communist framework for the insurgent group. Paul was attending the University of Juba in the south of Sudan when he left "to go to the bush" and join the SPLA. He trained as a solider in 1987 and worked for a time for the insurgent group's humanitarian wing, the Sudan Relief and Rehabilitation Association (SRRA).[43] Another man, David, a former county commissioner of Rumbek and an attorney by trade, said that he joined the SPLA in 1985, two years after its formation. Claiming he was being "frank" with me, David said that just because the insurgents took arms and obtained resources from communist Ethiopia did not mean that the group had a communist foundation. The group went where the resources were, he explained.[44]

Indeed, other southerners like Paul and David who joined the SPLA voluntarily were not motivated to rally behind the group for the communist agenda but rather because of nationalist ideals. That notwithstanding, Garang continued to push for unification, citing the deterioration of Sudan and southern grievances in particular as the country's most pressing problems. In a radio announcement that Garang gave over Radio SPLA, broadcast from Ethiopia, he reiterated much of the insurgent group's manifesto but addressed a broader audience without using ideological jargon. Nimeiri's abrogation of the Addis Ababa Agreement was one theme among many. As Garang explained, the resumption of civil war was the result of the general deterioration of social services throughout Sudan and the oppression by the country's security apparatus. He proposed the foundation of a "New Sudan," with a federal government for the regions and a restructuring of the central government to reflect the federal system.[45]

The SPLA was hardly a month old when cracks in its veneer materialized. Several Anya-Nya veterans, to retain their former seniority, proposed that the military and political wings of the SPLA be separated. These individuals suggested that two men, Samuel Gai Tut and Akwot Atem, head these two bodies and offered Garang the position of deputy commander of the group. Tut was a Nuer officer, and Atem, like Garang, was Twic Dinka.[46] Not surprisingly, the Anya-Nya members also preferred the south's original (postindependence) objective of separation from the north.[47] However, the SPLA's stated goal of a united Sudan was directly in line with the policy of Mengistu-led Ethiopia, which was battling its own separatist groups and was therefore mostly interested in meeting its need for resources. Thus, support from the Ethiopian regime was not dictated by its ideological solidarity with the SPLA but by its national interests. These interests inhibited Ethiopia from backing a secessionist insurgent group such as Anya-Nya. Support for the SPLA's call for a New Sudan was a far more palatable cause for Mengistu because it did not threaten a diplomatic backlash for the Ethiopian regime in the Organization of African Unity (OAU) and within other international forums.[48] At the same time, Ethiopian support garnered Garang more resources against an already weakened Anya-Nya movement, tipping the scale in his favor. But other divisions deepened within the SPLA, as several elite members began forming separate units outside the group's main body.

There were also divisions in the group relating to complaints about Garang's leadership of the SPLA. Some officers were dissatisfied with his qualifications to lead an insurgency. Garang was an educated southerner with an advanced degree from an American university, but his time in the field was limited to a few months serving in the original Anya-Nya after the completion of his military training. In military matters, his background forced him to rely heavily on veterans of the organization during his early years as leader of the SPLA. This was a source of tension in his relations with field commanders, many of whom, though lacking in formal education, had spent several years in combat with the Anya-Nya and had advanced to high levels.[49] Several of these veteran field commanders argued that the SPLA had become a group that served a few high-level and mid-level southern elites.[50]

The Impact of Militias

Though the imposition of *Shari'a* became a driving force for the war, ethnic issues soon surfaced and became another element in the instability and underdevelopment in the south.[51] The government of Sudan was largely responsible for fostering this feature of the war. The impending threat of southern insurgents and the desire to clear the upper-Nile regions for oil exploration by interested foreign corporations spurred Khartoum to implement its plan of raising a Nuer army to fight the SPLA.[52] The government of Sudan supported several militia groups for that purpose.

Normally, militias pay allegiance to an ethnic group or a nationality that views its political and physical security as independent of the state. The fact that Khartoum was supporting these armed and mobile groups did not necessarily mean that they were loyal to the north and supported its cause. Many of these militias were composed of the rural populace and used the war to pursue their own objectives, which often differed from the government's goals. Some militia members went to war to settle enmities with neighboring ethnic groups under the guise of a religious war.[53] In an effort to bring these groups under more centralized control, Sudan legalized militias under the Popular Defense Act in 1989.[54] So began what one SPLA commander referred to as the "balkanization of tribes."[55] While some Nuer tribes remained allied with the SPLA, a large portion of militias drew their support from the Bul Nuer, Lak Nuer, and various Lou Nuer sections and from former Anya-Nya soldiers. These militias as a group became known as Anya-Nya II.

Yet the impact of Khartoum's divide-and-rule tactic fell most directly on the southern civilian population. The Anya-Nya II's strategy was to make civilians in SPLA districts targets, spurring SPLA retaliation. The

SPLA struck back—often indiscriminately—against the Lou, Gaajak, and other Jikany Nuer and did so particularly violently against civilians they believed to be supporting the militia. Here we see coercion as a response to the presence of rivals. Although one can argue that some of these attacks were motivated by revenge, many were induced by a need to replace supplies lost in attacks, demonstrating the impact that the need for resources has in shaping the overall environment in which insurgents operate.[56] Yet it was because the SPLA faced several rivals at this point that the need for resources became more pressing; active rivalry increased competition and forced the group to extract resources as quickly and efficiently as possible in order to ensure its survival. Civilians thus became entangled in the SPLA's and the government of Sudan's personal vendettas, as well as in the SPLA's need to do away with competition over resources in areas where resources were scarce.

The government of Sudan's strategy of supplying tribal militias continued for several years. In general, the effects were twofold. It gave the war the trappings of a tribal conflict with little relation to national policies. And by making war through surrogates, the government of Sudan could claim with little opposing evidence that it was not fighting a civil war.[57]

Adapting to this change of government strategy, the SPLA began to get the upper hand over the government-backed militias as early as 1987, by adopting a more mobile strategy. Eventually some of the militias began to make peace with the SPLA and limited abuses on civilians. Some civilians found it in their interest to negotiate with the insurgents, for example, in order to return their livestock to pastures formerly denied them. Garang encouraged this kind of negotiation but insisted that the civilians use Dinka chiefs as intermediaries, which embedded the group's position in the south and strengthened the control the SPLA attained over resources.[58]

The Split of 1991

The SPLA came more or less to control the insurgency under Garang, though there were limits to this domination. The nature of southern geography limited widespread control in many ways, and though the use of two-way radios between headquarters and the field improved matters, local commanders often carried out their duties in their own ways and with a great deal of autonomy. For example, though all death sentences imposed by SPLA courts were referred to the high command for confirmation, in practice they were imposed and carried out by local commanders.[59] Several high-level commanders, for example, were said to have performed summary executions of their own troops and, according to one member of the movement, were never held accountable.[60] Hence, any notion of chain of command was often more theoretical than practical.

During the SPLA's formation, a number of individuals and groups denounced Garang's leadership for the lack of transparency and the dictatorial style in which he led the group. To demonstrate these authoritarian holds on power one need only look at the group's institutions and their opaqueness in this early period. For example, the SPLA held its first national convention in 1983, but it did not hold another until 1994. The central organizing body, the Political-Military High Command (PMHC), whose members Garang appointed, was not fully convened between 1986 and 1991. In fact, in 1987 the body became a double-tiered structure of permanent members and alternating commanders, the latter of whom had only limited voting rights. Civilian figures had little role in the creation and implementation of policy, and there was no regular forum where questions of accountability could be raised on political, military, and financial matters.

The lack of transparency in the SPLA was a part of the group's early *modus operandi*. Internal purges of individuals whom the group suspected of being government spies were also common and reached high levels, including several members of the PMHC and culminating in the arrest and detention of various commanders. Some individuals accused of military indiscipline were executed; others were held in prisons without being formally charged.[61] One man, speaking on condition of anonymity, told me that Garang had "physically liquidated" individuals whom he saw as a threat to his power.[62]

Two commanders in particular spoke out against the lack of transparency within the movement: Riek Machar and Lam Akol. These two high-level officers were involved in a number of diplomatic missions with Garang on behalf of the SPLA, yet by the end of 1990, they had been reassigned to field positions. The geographic shift of the group's military focus from the northern part of southern Sudan to the southern portion, in towns such as Juba, left the two men politically and militarily marginalized. Stationed at Nasir, the SPLA's rear base near refugee camps and training areas in Ethiopia, Akol and Machar had direct access to potential recruits for their cause as well as the option of receiving assistance—in whatever form—from Khartoum. There they found strong support among the Sudanese Nuer in the region and even among Ethiopian Nuer authorities for the removal of SPLA leadership, while others who were sympathetic to the Nasir cause supported structural reform of the insurgent group.

The split in the SPLA began with an attempted coup by Akol, Machar, and Gordon Kong, all SPLA commanders. In a paper entitled "Why John Garang Must Go Now," the three men protested Garang's leadership style and demanded independence for the south.[63] This offshoot of the SPLA became known as the SPLA-Nasir faction.[64] The split was not surprising. Within most movements that challenge a ruling regime and link a radical intelligentsia to the peasantry, there can exist a "revolution within a revolution," a movement with divergent visions of legitimate political order and justice.[65] These movements, seen from the insurgent perspective as unruliness or outright rivalry, can promote disunity and encourage factionalizing. The split also offered an exploitable division to Khartoum. The practical implication of the division was that the SPLA once again faced active rivalry.

Initially SPLA-Nasir did not have an overwhelming level of support, though that soon changed. Since the start of the war in 1983, a large Sudanese refugee population had settled around three camps in western Ethiopia: Itang, Fungyido, and Dimma. Official estimates put the number of refugees from Sudan in Ethiopia in 2003 at nearly ninety-five thousand.[66] Most of these refugees arrived in 1983 and during the 1990s.[67] By the end of the 1980s, there had not been any large-scale return of this displaced population. Traveling great distances meant that refugees and IDPs had few if any ties with the local communities through which they passed and thus were utterly dependent on the relief agencies for food. During the early months of 1991, anticipating the fall of Mengistu, international donor agencies began to plan and prepare for repatriation. To assess the refugee situation, many of these donor agencies sent staff to Nasir, where a majority of the refugees had settled. Because Akol and Machar were stationed in this region, they found themselves in a position to negotiate with relief groups and speak directly to UN agency staff and representatives of foreign governments. Of greater significance, though, was the link established between SPLA-Nasir and the government of Sudan. Machar's brother-in-law, recently appointed head of the SRRA, the relief wing of the SPLA, was the faction's main link with the north. Direct contact was established, and by August 1991, SPLA-Nasir had secured military support from Khartoum for the overthrow of Garang.

The intra-SPLA coup was announced via radio to SPLA commanders in the south during late August 1991. SPLA-Nasir announced the new objective as the independence of southern Sudan. Although support on the ground for this initiative was at first sparing, it did spur Garang to retaliate. Thus began a period of tactical conflicts between the two factions, encouraging the formation of further offshoots and increasing competition for scarce resources. The populations that bore the brunt of this division were the local communities in which these groups traveled and at times based themselves.[68] Coercion of southerners included obstruction of relief efforts, raiding and looting southern towns, and seizing food from rural civilians.[69] In 1991, for example, the perceived inequality in aid distribution among Dinka and Nuer led to several devastating raids by Nuer in which twelve thousand civilians in Dinka Bor County were killed.[70]

The SPLA's attitude toward the relief community was uncompromisingly hostile. The famine can be laid largely at the feet of the government of Sudan and the SPLA, which adopted deliberate policies that denied food to civilians and obstructed relief supplies. The two sides also prevented starving populations from carrying out coping strategies such as collecting food from the bush.[71] The diversion of aid—an act that I consider coercive or violent against civilians—has been widely documented by scholars and aid organizations and has been confirmed by southerners themselves. One man, Marko, made a particularly lasting impression on me. Marko had heard that I wanted to talk to people about the SPLA. Under the intense noontime heat, dressed in neatly pressed trousers and button-down collared shirt, and wearing rubber flip-flops, Marko walked several kilometers to meet with me. Sitting up straight and with an air of dignity about him, Marko told me how food that was meant for civilians had wound up in the hands of SPLA soldiers. Relief, he explained, first passed through the hands of the SPLA, which used it for its own consumption. Many commanders took advantage of their position. They diverted food allocated to civilians and then sold it to the few southerners who could afford to buy it.[72] To further demonstrate the impact of the war on civilians, between 1983 and 2002, approximately two million deaths were reported to have resulted from the war. Only 3 percent of these deaths were battle related. The remainder of deaths were caused by attacks on civilians, malnutrition, and disease.[73]

The split within the SPLA, along with Khartoum's role as main supplier to the Nasir faction, enabled the government to direct and regain military dominance in the south. As time progressed, SPLA-Nasir went through further iterations. In 1993, the group dropped its SPLA-Nasir label and became SPLA-United when it combined with other ethnic groups in the south. In 1994, it went through another branding following a Nuer reconciliation meeting, when it adopted the title the South Sudan Independence Movement/Army (SSIM/A).[74] This rebranding occurred after a small gain by the SPLA within the south. In 1997 the SSIM went through a final organizational transformation when it became the South Sudan Defence Force (SSDF), an army formed under the Khartoum Peace Agreement composed of ex-insurgent forces including those from SSIA. The changes in name highlight the irony of a regime aiding a separatist movement in its own national territory and demonstrate the primacy of the state-insurgent relationship over considerations of ideology in determining insurgent strategies and behavior. What was supremely important for the government of Sudan was the demise of the SPLA. Likewise, the collapse of the SPLA would benefit Machar's faction because not only would it expand his power in the north as a result of his government alliance, but it would also broaden his reach in the south. The ease with which factions such as the SSDF changed sides highlighted for the SPLA the priority of doing away with rivals over the importance of promoting an ideology.

Throughout this period, these splinter factions remained under the thumb of Khartoum, an affiliation that lasted until January 2000, when Machar left the government and once more took up arms against the north, forming the Sudan People's Democratic Front (SPDF). As I will outline in greater detail, the factionalizing among the SPLA during the 1980s and early 1990s contributed to the insurgent group's coercive behavior toward civilians in the south.

Santino sits in the meager shade of a tree underneath the bright sun of northern Kenya. He is a refugee in Kakuma Camp outside Lokichokio, where there are approximately eighty thousand refugees from Sudan and surrounding countries. Each nationality is housed in its own neighborhood, and each family within these neighborhoods is given a shelter of sorts made from such trees as the one under which we try to find shade. The area where Kakuma is located is dry and dusty, and the temperatures hover in the low 100s. It is not uncommon for it to reach 115 degrees at mid-day.

Despite the meager surroundings, Santino is optimistic. A former soldier in the SPLA, he tells me that the insurgent group has gone through many much-needed changes. The SPLA was an army from 1983 to 1994, he tells me. Now, he says, it is a new entity. I ask him if there is democracy in the areas where the SPLA has control. "There is a lot of it, shining," he responds, smiling. Now a civilian has a say in how the south is governed.[75]

Change

By the mid-1990s the SPLA had perceptibly changed its way of treating civilians, with a marked decline in its coercive behavior toward them. The SPLA acknowledged the need for democratic institutions and addressed the immediate needs of southerners, a population that it had previously overlooked and harassed. What caused the SPLA to change its behavior toward noncombatants? Does the reason lie in the disappearance of significant rivals? Did the shift from relying on communist resources to Western ones affect the group's behavior?

The explanation for such a sea change in SPLA actions lies primarily with the absence of rivals, which in turn led the group to pay heed to the resources that Western donors brought and the normative stipulations they levied. The SPLA decreased its human-rights abuses, expanded local participation in the governance of southern "liberated" zones, and markedly changed its character.

Transforming Structures of Governance: The 1994 National Convention

Because the SPLA's initial goal was complete reformation of a unified Sudan rather than outright secession, the SPLA did not initially try to establish a quasi-state in the areas that came into its control; leadership did not focus on constructing institutions that would address the needs only of southerners. During the early years of its development, the SPLA focused at the local level primarily on negotiating disputes and administering law through local traditional courts. Local administration from 1983 to 1991 was rudimentary at best.[76] At the onset of its governing experience, the SPLA relied on a system of indirect rule for governing the civilian populations and displayed a reluctance to cooperate with civilian organizations and churches (though cooperation improved with the United Nations' establishment of Operation Lifeline Sudan, or OLS). Some local traditions were recognized, but many chiefs found themselves subordinated to the SPLA, losing much of their autonomy in the process.[77] This situation, in addition to the SPLA's general feeling of unaccountability for the southerners it claimed to represent in "liberated" zones—as well as its killing of several humanitarian aid workers—spurred numerous complaints about the group both within the movement and among external observers.[78]

The development of formal democratic institutions, even if it is done superficially, appears to be antithetical to the growing dominance of one group. Indeed, for a time the SPLA leadership found itself in a classic dilemma. The insurgents claimed to be democratizing, and while they carried on as a military regime engaged in war, southern Sudanese civilians began to expect further participatory rights in the administration of the south. Concerned with the perception of being a functioning legitimate authority while choosing to develop democratic structures, the SPLA found itself confronted with the contradictory nature of liberalism and winning a war. We can compare the situation to that of a state attempting to increase control while confronted with strongmen—local ethnic or political party leaders who hold significant amounts of political support. In the presence of these strongmen, states find that they can marshal only a limited amount of political support. Leaders find that they must have strong state agencies to substantiate their own strategies of survival in the midst of growing civil strength. However, the state must also mobilize enough support from the population so that these agencies do not threaten leaders' political longevity. Here, then, is the paradox: political mobilization cannot be achieved without establishing channels to the local populations to induce political support; strong agencies are necessary in the first place.[79]

Many rebel groups have revolutionary legitimacy—power obtained by capturing the state. Yet with such legitimacy comes immense pressure to live up to and maintain the ideals of the insurgency. Many groups have "prelegitimacy."[80] These groups often thrive on the laurels of revolutionary legitimacy and quickly find it difficult to develop the liberal institutions for which they rallied.[81]

Amid criticism from international and local actors, the SPLA held its second national convention. The 1994 national convention served several functions. First, it signified a political rebirth of the SPLA by promulgating a political program with the objective of equipping the group and the "liberated" zones with participatory structures. Resolution 7 prescribed the development of autonomous local administrative units at traditional authority levels—the *payam*,[82] the village, and the county. The resolution also stated that civilians could become members of the SPLA without undergoing military training—a significant step toward decreasing the SPLA's militaristic culture.[83] This resolution signified the group's intention to open participation to civilians. Furthermore, the national convention promoted renewal and promised southerners a chance to voice their opinions and grievances to the SPLA without fear of retribution. For the first time in the history of the SPLA, the national convention oversaw elections for top positions within the group itself, as well as in the newly formed Civil Administration of New Sudan (CANS).

The primary product of the convention was the Watershed, a document that spelled out policies for a civil administration and for the development of structures that would foster democracy. The Watershed formally separated the military from the civilian administration and established a political and administrative entity in the Nuba Mountains, presided over by a National Executive Council (NEC) and a newly created National Liberation Council (NLC). The latter was a legislature made up of approximately two hundred members. A final result of the convention was the reaffirmation of Garang as chairman of both the NEC and the NLC. Garang modeled the need to reform Sudan on the legacies of such African insurgent leaders turned presidents as Uganda's Yoweri Museveni and Rwanda's Paul Kagame.[84] The Ugandan leader's influence on the SPLA cadre is palpable, even today. Many of the southerners who took up arms and joined the movement in 1983 were schooled at such Ugandan universities as Makerere. In fact, Garang and Museveni were classmates at school in Tanzania.

A number of liberal institutions based on traditional forms of rule were established. Using entities such as the *boma* and *payam,* the SPLA facilitated the building of a new hierarchy of customary courts, from the village to the county level.[85] In other words, the SPLA was providing public goods amid disorder.[86] The immediate effect was to expand the degree of local participation in governance. For example, the SPLA strengthened the role of chiefs in matters of appeal and made an effort to reflect the legal history of the south, dealing with issues such as water supply, the lack of infrastructure, education, and road maintenance.[87] Furthermore, officials who served in these branches of the government were elected and dealt directly with local populations.[88]

Many of these new structures inspired changes in the relationship between local communities and the insurgents. The SPLA extended opportunities to participate in local decision-making to traditionally underrepresented groups of southerners. For example, 25 percent of the local leadership positions were designated for women, though admittedly this mandate was difficult to implement because of the tradition of reserving formal education for males.[89] The First Equatoria Regional Congress of 2002 proclaimed that there should be a basic law (constitution) for the new Sudan to "guarantee all the rights of citizens and their obligations" and that "women['s] representation in the government, executive, legislative, judiciary and all parastatal bodies shall be proportionate to the women['s] population."[90] This change toward gender equality reflected the norm among the foreign staffs of international organizations and thus was probably an adroit method of acquiring additional international attention and resources from donors.

While significant changes occurred at the historically neglected local level, radical changes took place in the SPLA's rhetoric as well, as it put an increasing emphasis on democracy and civil society.[91] For example, the SPLA held a conference for high-level officers and relayed the need to stop the harassment of civilians by soldiers and other military personnel. One conference organized following the national convention was the 1996 Conference on Civil Society and the Organization of Civil Authority in New Cush. The main goal of this meeting was to "deliberate thoroughly and pass resolutions and recommendations that [would] help strengthen civil society and encourage the establishment of effective and accountable civil authority in the New Sudan."[92]

Walking through the center of Rumbek in southern Sudan, I am approached by a man. He tells me to follow him. I hesitate, and he motions for me to come forward. I am hot, thirsty, and just a little bit nervous about this turn of events. Reluctantly, I follow this man into a compound with a makeshift fence around it. Once inside, I am led to a huge tree under which are several chairs. Judge Reuben Madol Arol sits in one.

I have met Judge Reuben once before, and found him extremely amenable to talking. He was an older man, a lawyer by training, and seemed quite esteemed in local Sudanese society. At the sight of him I let out a huge sigh of relief. He motions for me to join him under the tree for a cup of tea.

Reuben speaks with much authority on the SPLA. Having been a local judge in the area for several years, he has seen the changes the insurgent group has experienced. He says that in 1994, "for the first time the ordinary Sudanese were given a chance to say something about the government and the liberation struggle."

Today, this liberalization of the group continues. "Military tribunals are now giving room for judiciary structures. This is a positive step forward," he says.[93]

The SPLA's newly found legitimacy among southerners reflected its freedom to administer without rival competition and explained why the group intentionally changed its behavior beginning in the mid-1990s rather than 1991, after Machar broke away. Individuals and groups in several towns in the south confirmed the changed relationship with civilians during the 1990s. Many people I interviewed acknowledged a distinct contrast between the SPLA prior to 1994 and afterward. A former village administrator claimed that earlier in the group's history the organization was purely a military one: judges were military people, as were the administrators and the policemen.[94] Furthermore, civil society groups did not exist in the south prior to that time, at least not as formal participants in SPLA affairs.[95]

Following 1994, local communities were—in theory—allowed to participate in local governing institutions involving "every sector of society."[96] The group established guidelines that dictated that governance was to be centered on civil society. As one southerner maintained, "In the beginning it was tough because it was a military government—there were no laws. Now, when the [group] captures a city, it establishes a civil structure. Leaders are elected and appointed."[97]

A prominent local judge in Rumbek confirmed that, following 1994, "ordinary Sudanese were given the chance to say something about governance and the liberation struggle." The courts and the local commissioners were more accessible than in the past, and people were allowed to speak openly without fear.[98] Rebecca, a tall and very self-assured-looking southerner who identified herself as a member of a local women's group called Kony-rot (Help Yourself), said that people participated in local decision-making and that the SPLA authorities asked the community to participate. Rebecca proudly added that she was the only woman in the village who rode a bicycle.[99] Mary and Priscilla, who had been displaced from Bor County due to the war, stated that they were able to vote for leaders within the Episcopal Church. The SPLA, they claimed, provided the opportunity for local citizens to elect women to the local *payam*.[100]

This broadening of political participation within the SPLA reflected a new working relationship between civil society in the south and the insurgent group. According to one southerner I interviewed, at first this relationship was difficult to maintain because the insurgents were governed by the military. But following the transformation in the group's behavior, when the SPLA captured a town, it would establish a civil structure with elected leaders. For example, civilians described how the position of commissioner was filled through an appointment with community input: civilians recommended five names for the post, and one person out of the five was appointed by the High Command.[101] Isaac, the commissioner of Rumbek at the time, told me that the civilian population participated in governance and that that demonstrated the application of democratic principles in the south. Since the insurgent group had liberalized, he said, people have had representation.[102] Monica, who called herself the deputy community leader of Rumbek, remarked that local communities in the south were modifying old laws throughout "liberated" zones to make their societies strong bases from which democracy could grow.[103]

The monopoly over resources that the SPLA gained through this community outreach in turn allowed the group to choose policies that garnered it additional local and international resources. One of the more significant elements of the 1994 Watershed was the modification of the SPLA's original charter to include the right to self-determination. This provision acknowledged that the southern Sudanese should be guaranteed the ability to decide through elections whether to remain a part of Sudan led by the north or to form their own state following liberation. The SPLA's choice to adopt this agenda, a result of the decreasing presence of rivals, represented a major *volte face* from the goal expressed by the SPLA during its early years, when the insurgents had largely ignored sovereignty: they would pick and choose the rules by which they wanted to abide.

In spite of this rhetorical democratization, in truth the SPLA enacted reforms selectively, and much of the change did not reach the inner workings of the group itself. The draft constitution created in 1994, for example, was never legally enacted.[104] This document introduced the idea that the SPLA consisted of two separate entities: the SPLA, or military side, and the civil authority structure. Even though the draft constitution never had formal force, it was significant because it was intended to formalize the regulation of the south by a civil authority taking on responsibilities that were normally the prerogative of a state.[105]

Yet the lack of implementation meant that the political bodies it created were still firmly in the hands of the military arm of the SPLA, specifically John Garang. One significant incident that reinforced the level of personal domination that Garang had over the SPLA (and consequently over the area), and that perhaps demonstrated the fear Garang had that this domination would slip from his hands, was the 1999 dissolution of the NLC. In December 1999, Garang, who possessed the power to call this governing body to session, dismissed the entire council. The following month, in an act that violated resolution 5.2.0 of the Watershed that deemed the NLC to be the highest legislative and decision-making body of the rebel group, Garang dissolved the council, stripping it of its powers and declaring that its duties were to be assumed by a newly developed Leadership Council. The new Leadership Council would act as the highest legislative, administrative, and military body in southern Sudan. In a letter sent to SPLA officials, Garang wrote,

> I Comdr/Dr John Garang de Mabior, chairman and C-in-C, SPLM/SPLA, issue the following order: 1) the NEC is here dissolved with effect from 7th January 2000, and all NEC secretaries and deputy secretaries are here relieved of their duties . . . ; 2) the former NEC secretariats shall be restructured and reconstituted under seven commissions . . . ; 3) an SPLM Leadership Council (SPLM-LC) is here formed with effect from 07/01/2000, and it shall be the highest political organ of the movement under which the reconstituted NEC shall fall . . . ; 4) the titles of regional governor and deputy governor are here abolished, . . . and all regional governors and deputy governors are here relieved of their duties.[106]

This action on the part of the commander in chief of the SPLA solidified his control over the movement while at the same time putting forth a picture of the group as democratizers with the southern Sudanese interests at heart. It also allowed him to legitimately eliminate potential rivals. Therefore, with the help of the international community (in the form of donor assistance, capacity-building activities, and overall concurrence on the rights of the south to secede from the northern regime), the SPLA, under Garang's authoritarian rule, was able to consolidate its monopoly of control over local populations upon entering the twenty-first century.

The changes *would* have had a significant impact, namely by redistributing power, if the chairman's decisions had been subject to the approval of a congress. Arguably, the omission of such a check on Garang's authority represents an unwillingness within the SPLA to give form to its rhetoric.[107] However, it is possible to break down the SPLA's motivations even further. To the extent to which the leadership was successful in its monopoly of control, the SPLA found itself obliged to administer to the civilians living in the "liberated" zones. Once a liberation group becomes involved in extracting resources, distributing goods and services, and settling disputes, it creates interests that run counter to war.[108] This dynamic appeared to be the case with the SPLA, which found that if it was to dictate behavior and mobilize local populations without resorting to coercive measures that were reprehensible in the eyes of the international community, it had to deliver the components for viable governance and even development to southern Sudanese populations. However, the SPLA leadership made sure it had its finger on the pulse of events in the south. During the period 1994–2000, the SPLA used the wartime situation to justify its interference in civilian matters and its channeling of resources to the military effort.[109]

By integrating itself into the democratic structures, the SPLA accomplished two feats. First, it appeared to be democratizing to the international diplomatic and aid community, which in turn guaranteed the group more Western funding and support for its fight against the northern Islamic regime. Second, it allowed the insurgent group to retain control over the management of the south.

The fact that some reforms were carried out at the local level indicates that the SPLA was comfortable allowing local structures to administer to the populations in "liberated" areas. These structures were manned by SPLA officers who appeared to possess certain degrees of autonomy, often to their personal financial advantage. The possibility of such personal enrichment cemented the loyalties of these individuals to the SPLA. This strategy hindered the development of further rivals as it allowed the SPLA to monitor the flow of resources. Thus, although the leadership was not willing to surrender central control to the populace by instituting a parliamentary democracy, it allowed "liberated" areas to govern themselves in most respects, as long as there was an SPLA presence within the local administration.

The visas that the SPLA issued for travel in southern Sudan highlight the group's control over resources. In order to get into southern Sudan and travel between towns and villages, visitors obtained a visa issued by the insurgent group, not by the government of Sudan. Each time an individual entered a village, the visa was handed over to the insurgent group's relief wing, the SRRA. That allowed the SPLA to know and control who was coming in and out of its territories. It was also a revenue-generating activity, as most visa applicants had to pay a fee to obtain the SPLA document.

Human-Rights Abuses and the SPLA

While the SPLA was seemingly transforming its structures of governance, it also improved its human-rights record. The SPLA had committed numerous human-rights abuses during earlier phases of the war, including summary executions and disappearances, torture, holding prisoners in harsh conditions, pillaging civilian assets (mainly cattle and grain), capturing civilians including women and minors, and denying minors the opportunity to be reunited with their families.[110] Forced recruitment was also common among SPLA units: boys brought to or lured to Ethiopian refugee camps for educational opportunities were separated from their families, trained, and deployed as soldiers in the organization.[111] Most national laws permit recruitment into national armies at the age of eighteen. International law, including humanitarian and human-rights law, offers protection to children in areas of conflict through a variety of devices drafted since World War II. The most significant of these instruments for protection of children combatants are Protocols I and II of the Geneva Conventions of 1949 and the Convention on the Rights of the Child.[112] The SPLA organized a "Red Army," a force consisting of fourteen- to sixteen-year-old boys. Former SPLA officers claimed that these boys initially were used for fighting. During the early years of the war, the Red Army experienced continuous losses.[113] Despite these reports, the SPLA continually denied the recruitment of underage soldiers. In addition, the SPLA also abducted females as fighters and for sexual purposes.[114] Interviews with civilians and soldiers alike confirmed the shift in the SPLA's tactics and policies in regard to its human-rights record. During the early days of the insurgent group, one southern Sudanese reported, civil society was not safe in the face of the SPLA.[115]

Over several years in and around southern Sudan, I interviewed approximately fifty-five people, including civilians, SPLA personnel, religious officials, soldiers, and foreigners. Each individual, regardless of his or her position, noted a change in the SPLA's relations with noncombatants and local communities. Although no one directly commented on the mechanism for this change, it appears that the SPLA slowly began to address many of the social issues that arose among local populations as a result of the war. One female civilian noted that many women in the south had to live without their husbands because of the war and consequently had to make ends meet by themselves. Since the group's transformation, she said, the SPLA had taught women how to provide for themselves.[116]

The Transformation of the SPLA's Legitimacy

There is no singular definition for *legitimacy*. In a political sense, however, I use the term here to describe a state that has approval among the general population of those being governed. Like John Locke, I view legitimacy to be linked to the idea of consent. As Locke states, "the government is not legitimate unless it is carried on with the consent of the governed."[117] The SPLA initially had difficulty being recognized as legitimate by southerners because of its coercive treatment of civilians. Because from its very origin its main task was waging guerrilla warfare and hence stressed military over civic needs, the SPLA did not experience a smooth transition into an authority that southerners readily took to be their legitimate representatives.

By the late 1990s, the SPLA had made progress in institutionalizing its legitimacy in the region through both military and civic means. The lack of infrastructure in the south and the SPLA's own dearth of resources meant that most development was paid for by foreign entities. With the support of USAID and other foreign donors, development activities were launched in the south, enabling the SPLA to enhance its legitimacy both locally with southerners and throughout the West.

Support from the United States, for example, was significant. By the mid-1990s, nearly 80 percent of U.S. aid to Sudan went to southern insurgent-controlled areas. One report claims, "On humanitarian grounds USAID committed to supporting the SPLA/M in the south and Garang said the aid agency committed US $42.5m over the next five years."[118] The SPLA's initiative, formerly called "Peace through Development," facilitated microenterprise and fostered income-generating and food-security projects. In November 1999, President Clinton signed Public Law 106-113, the government budget for fiscal year 2000, which included, in section 592, a line item that appropriated aid from the United States to the SPLA: "providing humanitarian assistance, including food, directly to National Democratic Alliance participants and the Sudanese People's Liberation Movement operating outside of the United Nations' Operation Lifeline Sudan structure."[119]

In the first five months of 2002, the United States designated over $26 million in foreign assistance to the southern sector of Sudan. This money was officially allocated to health-care services, food relief, infrastructure development, and water and sanitation services.[120] However, the SPLA was able to control much of the distribution of these resources because any entity, individual, or organization working in the "liberated" zones of the south had to pass through the SRRA. This arrangement allowed the SPLA to take credit for services provided to local communities; foreign assistance facilitated the good name that the SPLA won for overseeing the distribution of public goods, resulting in an increase in the group's civic legitimacy. Interviews I conducted in 2001, toward the end of the war, indicated that international donors were well aware of the SPLA's power in the area and more specifically of its monopoly on the distribution of resources. This arrangement was to both parties' benefit. Cooperation for the donors meant fewer civilian deaths, as they were able to distribute more humanitarian relief. For the SPLA, cooperation meant a more constant supply of donor financing.[121]

Gideon Mathai is all smiles. Wearing a long-sleeve shirt and white pants, he looks comfortable and at ease in the north Kenyan heat. I sit with him in Kakuma, as he explains the changes that have occurred in the SPLA. Gideon, unlike the majority of SPLA members, is a member of the Nuer tribe. He tells me that he is the representative of the Nuer community in the refugee camp.

His story, he says, is not unlike many others' from Sudan. He worked in Khartoum after finishing university. But he was then forced to join the Sudanese military. Eventually, he says, he escaped and went south to Kakuma.

The SPLA has been through many changes, he tells me. The movement fell apart after the split of 1991. Many entities in the south were under the direct control of the insurgents. Not now. The churches, for example, are more independent—"freer than before," he tells me. Explaining further, he says that before 1994, when you met a Sudanese pastor in the south, he was probably part of the SPLA military. Today, Gideon says, if you are a pastor, then you are just that—a pastor.[122]

Development initiatives augmented the SPLA's legitimacy and control among southern communities. In the town of Nimule, a County Development Committee was partially responsible for implementing development at the community level. According to Joseph and George, the committee's chairman and secretary, respectively, the program—with USAID monies—helped them establish income-generating and food-security projects in the community. Local civilians, Joseph and George said, felt empowered by such projects.[123] In the same town, Mary and Priscilla, members of the Mothers' Union in the Episcopal Church of Sudan (a group they said met every Tuesday to discuss family issues), maintained that they were able to go openly to a local administrator with funding problems for a soap-making project. Women gained more skills, and many began to obtain an education. According to one woman, since 1994 women have gained more power within their families and community.[124]

The role of women in the SPLA expanded greatly with the transformation of the insurgent group. Monica in Rumbek, who called herself a deputy community leader and said that she was part of a "regional liberation council," explained that women have the opportunity to be self-reliant, using as an example the fact that they could trade in the market independently. From the village to the county level, she said, women can now contest for a place in parliament and vote. In addition to her membership on the regional liberation council, in 2001, three women were elected to the National Liberation Council.[125] The growth of women's opportunities signifies that the SPLA is aware of international liberal norms that emphasize female rights and equality.

By obtaining legitimacy among local citizens, the SPLA increased its dominance in the south without having to revert to coercion. It learned that by granting at least a minimum of services, it could more efficiently and effectively obtain the support it needed to acquire resources; it did not need to expend additional resources on forcibly extracting from local communities, nor did it have to spend resources on the provision of public goods, since it could claim credit for the foreign provision of such goods. The SPLA could do this because it did not face rivals and thus could dedicate energy to establishing contractual relations with locals. Since the group saw that this arrangement was a way to keep donor finances flowing, it was happy to acquiesce.

Another indicator of the change in the SPLA's local legitimacy was the freedom of movement it allowed local populations in the "liberated" zones, particularly in later years. An ability to move freely in an area meant that individuals could increase the operation of independent economic activities, which was often necessary for survival. Engaging in independent economic activities such as trading goods in markets allowed southerners to obtain a wider range of basic goods. By allowing a degree of movement from town to town, or from rural village to town market, the insurgent group was perceived as increasingly representative of the people, which further facilitated the group's control over resources. One southerner claimed that prior to 1994 the military ruled the "liberated" areas, restricting movements between villages—a necessity of control amid competitors. After 1994, people could move freely and were released from the burdens that came with supporting a military regime.[126]

The SPLA was also gaining recognition in the international arena. Shedding its military fatigues, the group established a frequent presence in the United States and Europe. The group also became a signatory to a number of international treaties. For example, the SPLA signed the 1997 Geneva treaty banning the use of land mines. It also agreed to demobilize child soldiers and signed the Maputo Declaration on the rights of the child in 1999.[127] By attending international human-rights conferences and holding talks with USAID and government officials in the United States, the SPLA leadership played a role that foreign donors needed filled in southern Sudan. The SPLA took advantage of foreign donors, who were quick to provide resources for any actor that would stand up to the Islamic regime in the north and take the lead in a region of Africa that appeared to be unendingly messy. It was enough for the SPLA simply to attend meetings and sign protocols in order to obtain foreign assistance.

Following the terrorist attacks of September 11, 2001, the SPLA further improved its status in the international community. Khartoum, in particular President Bashir, felt mounting pressure to sit at the negotiating table with the SPLA. Having formerly harbored international terrorist Osama bin Laden, the government of Sudan was not in a position to negotiate as far as the international community was concerned. International awareness of Sudan and its conflicts was heightened by events in Darfur in the western part of the country. The unfolding tragedy in Darfur placed the idea of a peace deal (and the SPLA's legitimate part in the peace process) on international political agendas and squarely in the sights of the general public.

Although the veracity of many interviewees' statements can be questioned, the fact that similar statements in different towns were made in and out of the presence of the SPLA indicates that there was a general consensus about the legitimacy of the SPLA and its leadership of civilians. One could argue that the views of these people did not reflect reality, that civilians instead were expressing their biased perceptions rather than factually recounting actual events. Perhaps civilians only believed that they could move with more freedom; perhaps they only thought their level of participation in their own governance had increased. Even though some analysts may argue that the change in the SPLA was mostly about the perception of civilians, the fact that southerners even *perceived* a change is important. Their perception facilitated the SPLA's ability to maintain

FIGURE 3.1.
Estimated Civilian Fatalities Perpetrated by the SPLA

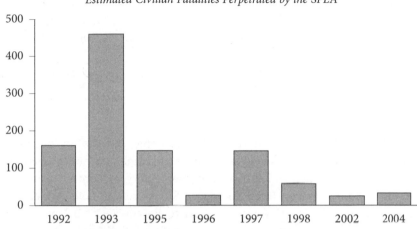

Source: Uppsala Conflict Data Program 2008.

control in the region once rivalry decreased because it led civilians to accept the SPLA's authority willingly.

However, there is substantial evidence that the civilians' statements do reflect actual, empirical change. Figure 3.1 graphically depicts this trend, showing one-sided violence by the SPLA toward civilians during the bulk of the war years. Just as the qualitative information presented in this chapter tells us, the SPLA permitted considerable coercion against civilians in its earlier years, but the practice gradually decreased.[128]

Explaining Change

There are several explanations for the SPLA's transformation in behavior that lie outside the immediate insurgent environment. Some scholars claim that the group's vulnerability to externalities, such as its dependence on Ethiopia during the Cold War and Ethiopia's subsequent termination of military support, forced reform within the SPLA. The end of the Cold War also resulted in the loss of the SPLA's rear bases on the Ethiopian border and its political headquarters in Addis, forcing it to face the realities that accompanied over 130,000 refugees who were forced to evacuate from Ethiopian camps.[129] Yet another reason lies in the ever-repressive nature of the regime in Khartoum, which could easily have spurred reticent southerners to lend support to the SPLA.

TABLE 3.1
TABLE 3.1
Measuring Rivalry, Illicit Resources, and Coercion throughout Three SPLA Periods

Period	Active Rivalry	Use of Illicit Resources	Coercive Behavior toward Civilians
SPLA1: 1983–1993	High	Low	High
SPLA2: 1994–2000	Medium	Low	Medium
SPLA3: 2001–2005	Low	Low	Low

Although these explanations are all reasonable, they do not deal with the key mechanism for change in the SPLA's treatment of noncombatants: lack of active rivalry and the concomitant ability to control resources. As the following pages demonstrate, the SPLA's role as sole extractor of resources was significantly more critical to its change of behavior than were the type of resources and new wars. The SPLA's ability to control resources in the south during the late 1990s and early twenty-first century was inextricably linked to the decrease in the number of rivals it faced— the weakening of factions and the decision of northern political parties to support the SPLA. It was this set of circumstances that enabled the SPLA's new strategy of allowing more access to external donors and adopting international norms of democracy and human rights.

Using the data collected in the field, detailed in the preceding sections, I separate the SPLA's activities over three periods of time, which are presented in table 3.1. This division allows me to better trace the process through which the SPLA changed its treatment of civilians. The first period, SPLA1 (1983–1993), began in 1983 with the group's inception. The SPLA was not guaranteed resources from its constituent population because of the intense rivalry among several groups, which increased the competition for scare goods. This was also a time when the SPLA was highly disorganized and not unified, thus making access to resources within Sudan uncertain at best. The behavior of the SPLA toward noncombatants, as we have seen, was extremely coercive at this time and included such atrocities as forced starvation, rape, summary execution, looting, and the kidnapping of children for use as soldiers.

During the SPLA's second period, SPLA2 (1994–2000), active rivalry decreased. Although most rival groups fell apart or merged into the main SPLA, Machar's SPDF maintained a separate identity during this period, though by the end of SPLA2 it was fighting the government of Sudan once again. Machar decided to terminate cooperation with Khartoum but found himself in the minority among his commanders. The fissiparous tendency within these groups was a clear sign that rival factions were fast becoming less of a threat to the SPLA. Once Machar left the government, many of these south-versus-south struggles decreased.

The formation of the New Sudan Council of Churches (NSCC) also aided the SPLA's grip on resources in the south during this period. Formed in January 1990, in part with the support of the SPLA "to strengthen the churches to better serve the suffering people in the SPLA/M-held areas," the organization represented the Catholic and Episcopal Churches in SPLA-controlled areas.[130] The NSCC, despite its ties to the SPLA, was accepted by several international organizations as an independent body.

The development of similar Sudanese indigenous NGOs (SINGOs) lessened rivalry and increased the SPLA's control over southern resources during the SPLA2 period. "In early 1993, the [SPLA] allowed the establishment of the first SINGO."[131] These organizations were financed by external donors and undertook activities that outside sources funded, such as providing services to local populations and attracting further donor monies. These were the only activities in which they could safely engage without posing a threat to the SPLA.[132] Thus, although SINGOs were a positive step for southern civil society and may have appeared as a further move toward the development of democratic reforms in the south, the activities of these locally operated organizations remained firmly under the watch of the SPLA.

Support from the international community, in this case foreign NGOs and donors, helped the SPLA gain further control at this time. Warring parties in 1994 signed an agreement that formalized the tripartite principle of the Operation Lifeline Sudan (OLS) operation. As long as the NIF regime in the north remained hostile toward relief operations, it was in the interest of OLS and foreign donors to encourage the SPLA to establish an explicit claim for the right to administer the "liberated" zones in the south. "A quasi-autonomous region in the south would make the humanitarian apparatus less dependent on approvals from Khartoum. . . . At the operational level, inside the southern Sudan, the guerrilla factions had the last say in the never-ending discussion on access, security and abuse of the humanitarian organizations and their assistance."[133] The increasing ability of foreign NGOs and other external donors to work in the south demonstrated the SPLA's concern for the well-being of civilians, which in turn increased the SPLA's legitimacy among many international agencies and foreign states, as well as among the local Sudanese communities. The

SPLA thus established its position as sole extractor of resources and legitimate force in the south.

While Western donors began bringing resources into the south, the SPLA tried to recover from the loss of eastern-bloc resources following the end of the Cold War. The group reevaluated its strategy as a result of the rapid end of the Cold War; it had not yet reconciled itself to the democratic norms that many Western donors required. The cessation of aid from Ethiopia following the end of the Cold War and the presence of factions in the south made maintaining a monopoly over foreign and local resources much more important because increasing competition placed a higher premium on resources and support. As the SPLA began establishing theoretically democratic structures, it gained popularity, thus increasing its local support. This support allowed the group to extract resources such as food and recruits legitimately from the population. However, it still participated in forms of looting and skimmed resources off many of the programs that humanitarian and development assistance organizations operated in their region.

Another element that helped solidify the SPLA's control over the southern populace and resources was the breakthrough made in 1993 vis-à-vis the northern opposition. The SPLA forged linkages with northern political parties through the National Democratic Alliance (NDA), which included the Umma party and the Democratic Unionist Party.[134] This step was important because it allowed the SPLA to broaden its support base. The NDA agreed to participate actively in the fighting against the government of Sudan and for the first time recognized southerners' right to self-determination. The NDA, which needed SPLA firepower in order to force the NIF out of its position, agreed to establish a secular constitution after NIF dominance in the government ended.[135] For the SPLA, this was a major concession. By the mid-1990s, this alliance further won the "hearts and minds" of many southerners, who saw that the SPLA leadership had the support of northern parties and was serious in pursuing what the majority of southern Sudanese wanted—self-determination. Winning the support of local citizens meant increased control over resources; the SPLA came very close to embodying state builders.

The SPLA also enhanced its control over resources in the south as a byproduct of facilitating access to international assistance activities for southerners. The SPLA increased and maintained dominance over resources by ensuring that financial transactions were filtered through its own hands via the SPLA relief arm. Though nominally independent, the SRRA was responsible for distributing food to needy southerners in the "liberated" zones. The SPLA would routinely skim off food and distribute it to soldiers instead.[136] This was not surprising since most of the SRRA personnel were SPLA officers drawn from the security unit.[137] The SRRA operated on two levels, central and local. The former concerned itself with interactions with foreign NGOs and OLS. The latter focused on local issues, and its staff was mainly made up of officers stationed within SPLA "liberated" zones. The SPLA solidified its position as sole legitimate force in the south when, in January 2000, it issued a "Memorandum of Understanding" that announced that it alone possessed governmental authority in dealing with aid organizations operating in areas under its control. In order for assistance agencies and organizations to operate in the southern insurgent-held areas, they had to agree to the SPLA's terms.[138] Specifically, the insurgent group issued an ultimatum to the thirty-nine humanitarian-aid agencies active within SPLA-controlled areas of southern Sudan and demanded that these NGOs sign an SPLA-drafted Memorandum of Understanding that controlled their activities and essentially dictated their relationship with the SRRA. If these organizations failed to comply with these demands, they would be forced by the insurgent group to leave southern Sudan by 1 March 2000. The memorandum included the demand that an NGO must seek SPLA permission before interacting with local communities. It also demanded control over the distribution of humanitarian assistance, required NGOs to work in line with the objectives of the SRRA rather than solely humanitarian principles, declared that the SPLA would control whom NGOs could hire as local Sudanese staff, required the payment of "security fees" and a number of additional taxes and charges including charges for the landing of aircraft carrying humanitarian aid and for NGO movement within SPLA-held areas. Furthermore, the memorandum stated that the SPLA would be entitled to the use of NGO transport on occasions and that aid agencies had to submit their budgets to the SPLA for approval. The SPLA also stipulated that any NGO assets would have to be left to the insurgent group if there were any interruptions in the aid organizations' work, which the SPLA reserved the right to order.[139]

Mark Duffield and colleagues have written that the SRRA was "completely under the control of the SPLA leadership."[140] African Rights, a nongovernmental organization based in the United Kingdom, also confirms that:

The SRRA officials were all named from amongst the soldiers anyway. . . .
They received no salary and usually no instruction from the head office.
Without supplies, they had nothing to do except other military duties. If
aid did not materialize, the first human needs to be served would naturally tend to be those close to the army.[141]

The SPLA made money by participating in several economic activities
within the zones it controlled. An example is the practice of buying back
slaves from tribal militias, a practice that dates back several centuries in
Sudan. During the period under study here, slave raids directed by tribal
militias against Dinka civilians came to the attention of several religious
and human-rights groups. Investigation by these organizations revealed
that those selling individuals back were not the only ones profiting from
the practice. Some local SPLA authorities in the south were found to be
participating in fraudulent buy-backs, as transactions for the freeing of
some slaves were achieved not through Arab middlemen but through
SPLA soldiers posing as Arab middlemen. The SPLA funneled all slave-
redemption activities through its administrative offices in the south after
Garang wrote several foreign organizations engaged in slave buy-backs
demanding that these religious organizations and human-rights groups
channel their activities through the SRRA. This activity closely resembled
the one that the Eritreans and Tigrayans pioneered in the 1980s.[142]

The SPLA exploited its monopoly over local resources to gain the con-
fidence of NGO outsiders. Such strategies are not new and have been
noted in prior studies about other regions. For example, during the conflict between Eritrean insurgents and the Ethiopian government during
the 1980s, the Eritrean People's Liberation Front (EPLF) and the Tigray
People's Liberation Front (TPLF) developed fake NGOs to channel foreign aid into their organizations. However, they only did so once they
were certain that they could control the distribution of services (if not all
local communities) and use the aid as a tool to attract followers and make
the Ethiopian government seem "nonhumanitarian."[143]

The period of SPLA3 (2001–2005) was dominated by peace negotiations. The SPLA had an unfettered monopoly over local and aid resources
because it had no rivals. Moreover, the SPLA established its automatic re-
ceipt of a portion of the Western resources flowing into the south, as well
as of local support. The sources of these materials were, again, Western donors that required attention to international norms of democracy, or they
were local civilians. During SPLA3, the SPLA's behavior toward civilians

became fully contractual. It did not face competition for resources from rivals and could thus attend to the norms that donors required. The SPLA thus firmly established itself as the legitimate representative of southern Sudan. During this period, an international task force facilitated peace talks, ending with the signing of the Comprehensive Peace Agreement (CPA) in 2005. John Garang became vice president of Sudan, and Bashir remained head of government. The decision on self-determination was scheduled for resolution by plebiscite in 2011.

The Role of Rivals

The setbacks that the SPLA experienced during the early 1990s, in particular the increasing competition for resources and support following the split of 1991, forced the SPLA to reexamine its strategy. Toward the end of the 1990s, Nuer commanders and soldiers returned to the insurgent group.[144] In January 2002, Machar and Garang signed a peace agreement between the SPDF and the SPLA. The agreement appeared to further SPLA interests with a merger of the two groups under the name SPLM/ SPLA. It also confirmed the SPLA's objectives as the fight for a united secular democratic "New Sudan" during an interim period, leading to self-determination for the south and other marginalized areas. The agreement officially ended hostilities between the two insurgent groups and called for the establishment of several technical committees to propose ways to integrate military forces and political and governance structures so that the combined unit could intensify the struggle against the north. This merger was a major blow to the government of Sudan's *divide et imperia* tactic and further enhanced the SPLA's military strength as well as its image both in the south among civilians and throughout the international community. With the reintegration of Machar and the SPDF into the insurgent group, the SPLA no longer faced credible local competition, and it was able to attain a nearly complete dominance over the southern regions of Sudan.

The SPLA's heightened legitimacy in the south and among the international community helped it become an acceptable interlocutor as the United States pressured Khartoum to be party to the Machakos Protocol of 2002, the first of the peace talks between the SPLA and the government of Sudan. On the surface, the SPLA ensured protection of society from external foes and guaranteed internal order and security in daily life. In some places, the SPLA adopted a neutral role as mediator in community affairs, whereas in other "liberated" regions there was little SPLA local participation or representation in the structures of administration.[145]

While the SPLA leadership was successful in monopolizing control, it found itself obliged to administer governmental entities for the civilians living in the "liberated" zones. The SPLA, which found that if it was to dictate behavior and mobilize local populations without resorting to coercive measures that were reprehensible in the eyes of the international community, it had to deliver the policies for viable strategies of survival and even development to southern Sudanese populations. However, the SPLA leadership made sure it kept its finger on the pulse of events in the south. During the period 1994–2000, the SPLA used the wartime situation to justify its interference in civilian matters.[146] Thus, by integrating itself into the local democratic structures the SPLA retained control over the management of the south. That is not to imply that the SPLA did not display a semblance of concern for the local populations. On the contrary, because foreign donors highlighted the welfare of civilians, this matter became a common part of SPLA rhetoric as well as its behavior following the national convention. In this sense, democratization killed two birds with one stone. It increased the already rising support that the SPLA enjoyed among local citizens, and it demonstrated to donors and the West that it was reforming its ways and adopting the norm of democracy. However, this reform would not have been accomplished if the SPLA had not been confident in its ability to control local populations and the flow of resources, that is, if the SPLA had not been able to integrate itself into the very structures it established.

An Uncertain Peace

Of the three insurgent groups analyzed in this book, the SPLA is perhaps the one that has had the most "success"—if one were to measure success by ending conflicts in a negotiated peace. The conflict between the north and the south, which since 1983 had killed more than two million people, uprooted more than four million, and made refugees of over six hundred thousand Sudanese individuals, came to an end in January 2005. Beginning in 2002, the insurgent group and the government of Sudan signed a series of six agreements, culminating in the Comprehensive Peace Agreement (CPA) in 2005 that officially ended the war. Yet clashes between the north and the south have not been absent from Sudan.

The CPA consists of several major provisions, each addressing a major theme of the conflict: autonomy, oil wealth, economic issues, the armed forces, administration, and Islamic law. Regarding the first, the peace agreement maintains that the south will have autonomy for six years, after which in 2011 Sudanese will vote on a referendum regarding self-determination. The vote for self-determination is a significant part of the SPLA's retention of legitimacy among southerners. My research in the field indicates that most southern Sudanese define legitimacy in terms of an independent state. For example, in a 2003 statement, the Funj peoples of the southern Blue Nile region in Sudan expressed their "entitlement to a self-autonomous and representative government, accountable and elected by Funj people. This government would fall administratively under the SPLM government."[147] This statement indicates that the Funj are willing to accept the SPLA as the legitimate authority if it can maintain its promise to hold a vote on self-determination. If this vote proves impossible to hold, come 2011, clashes among southerners is not unthinkable.

Oil wealth was and continues to be a major point of contention in Sudan. The CPA dictates that revenues from oil, located largely in the Abyei region, are to be shared between the Khartoum government and the SPLA on a 50/42 basis. Small percentages will be allocated to other regions and ethnic groups. Situated in the central part of the country, Abyei is a particularly contentious area because it has not been clearly defined, and thus it is unclear as to which area—the north or the south—it belongs. The CPA prescribes that Abyei be accorded special administrative status during the interim period. During this time, the area has representation in the legislature of Southern Kordofan and Warap states in the north. At the end of the six-year interim period in 2011, Abyei residents will vote in a referendum to maintain special administrative status in the north or to become part of Bahr al-Ghazal state in the south.[148]

Although the future status of southern Sudan at this point remains unknown, many of the provisions in the CPA seem to support the bifurcation of Sudan. For example, the agreement maintains that two separate currencies are to be used within a dual banking system. The north retains the Sudanese pound, while the south now uses the Sudanese dinar. Militarily, the north and south retain separate armed forces. The government was mandated to withdraw its approximately ninety-one thousand troops from the south by mid-2008. Integration of troops is also outlined in the CPA, allowing for the creation of a force of twenty-one thousand soldiers, of which half will be government and half will be SPLA forces.

These troops are deployed to disputed areas, and though they are commonly stationed, they maintain separate command and control structures. The CPA outlines that if, following 2011, the south decides not to secede, the two sides of this force will unify.[149]

The distinction between the north and the south also extends to the creation of a separate administration for the southern region. The SPLA created a government of southern Sudan with John Garang as president and his second in command, Salva Kiir Mayardit, serving as vice president. However, the overall governing of Sudan is split in a government of national unity. The CPA dictates that positions in the central, transitional government be split 70/30 in favor of the government in the north, and the proportion of positions between north and south in contentious areas such as Abyei are split 55/45. Garang's time in office, however, was cut short when he was killed in a plane crash in July 2005. Salva Kiir took over Garang's position as vice president of Sudan and president of the government of southern Sudan, but the longtime leadership and charisma of Garang was mourned, and his death arguably placed added tension on the diplomatic environment between the north and the south.

The final provision of the CPA addresses the issue of Islamic law. The agreement dictates that *Shari'a* remains applicable in the north, yet part of the constitution was to be rewritten so that it did not apply to non-Muslims throughout the country.[150]

Although the CPA stood for a model of "good governance in the Sudan [to] create a solid basis to preserve peace and make unity attractive," several incidents have occurred since 2005 that signal the frustration of the agreement and its dubious force to bring change. For example, in October 2007, the SPLA temporarily suspended its participation in the government of national unity, citing Khartoum's failure to honor the peace agreement. The south's governing body resumed participation in the national unity government in December 2007, but this incident raised several warning signs regarding the strength of the agreement and the willingness of the parties, particularly the north, to follow through on the provisions outlined in 2005. To further frustrate efforts to maintain peace in Sudan, clashes between northern and southern Sudanese forces broke out in Abyei in May 2008. Unconfirmed rumors circulate that southern Sudanese forces are attempting to stockpile weapons in an arms race with the north.[151]

Although the war in the Darfur region of western Sudan is not directly related to the north-south issue, it affects the strength of the CPA. One of the major insurgent groups involved in the Darfur conflict—the Sudan Liberation Army (SLA)—received political and military support from the SPLA in 2003–2004. The SPLA attempted to open up a Darfur front during peace negotiations leading up to the CPA, in an effort to keep the north negotiating in good faith, an endeavor that ultimately failed when it was overtaken by the Darfur agenda. Still, there was optimism for a time in different national and international circles that the signing of the CPA and the entry of the SPLA into the government of Sudan would facilitate an end to the fighting in Darfur. This hope, however, was dampened after the death of Garang and several missteps by the government.[152]

The SPLA case reveals several important points that are connected but not central to the significance of insurgent-group monopoly of resources and control. First, even if an insurgent group uses democracy as a foil to hide its true motives, sooner or later people in the local and the international communities will expect it. Once local communities begin to expect to have a role in their own governance, the insurgent group has two options. It may no longer perceive civilians as a viable base of resources, as the following chapter on the FARC demonstrates. Instead, insurgents will treat civilians as rivals in the struggle for local and regional political control. On the other hand, as in the case of the SPLA, if insurgents retain their monopoly of resource control, levels of violence are likely to decrease. As the study of the PKK shows, when insurgents face rivalry, especially from the state, they are likely to increase violence against civilians. Yet, as the study of the SPLA demonstrates, if insurgents maintain the monopoly over resources, they are likely to consider favorably the appeals for democratization. This type of democracy can be identified as *dependent* democracy, a type of democratic governance in which the level of democracy depends on the level of control held by the ruling party or group, much like South Korea during the 1980s, when authoritarians knew that a certain number of opposition members in positions of power would not fundamentally change the system or threaten the power of the old elite.

This subject leads to the second important point that arises from the study of the SPLA: the quality of the state is a necessary but not a sufficient condition in determining insurgent-group behavior. The fact that the Sudanese state was consistently oppressive gave the SPLA the impetus to act less coercively toward civilians, because the insurgents did not have to fear that the regime would co-opt local communities by providing them with political channels for participation in governance. In fact, as Machar and the ever-evolving SPLA-Nasir demonstrated, elements of the state's opposition *do* get co-opted by regimes, but it is not the result of the state's provision of avenues of participation. Rather, the regime can co-opt only the elite element of society, which means that in any democratic movement in which the state is seen as consistently oppressive, insurgent groups should have little to fear from community co-optation. What groups such as the SPLA should fear is elite co-optation. In many ways, we see this dynamic in the PKK case, where Turkey's liberal reforms have swung Kurdish moderates to join more conventional channels of addressing politics. In fact, Kurdish elites now populate parts of Turkey's parliament.[153]

The change in strategy that the SPLA made was not a spontaneous event; rather, the change took place after several years of fighting between the insurgents and the ruling regime in the north, as well as within the SPLA itself. In the group's early years, because the SPLA faced serious rivals and dissatisfaction with its objectives and leadership style, Garang found it difficult to maintain a firm grip over all elements of the movement. That meant that in its earlier history, the SPLA was not assured a monopoly over the southern regions. As a result, the group adopted coercive tactics. As more rival factions emerged and engaged in the conflict, the SPLA's dominance in the south decreased further, and levels of violence against civilians (as documented in human-rights reports) increased.

In many ways, the contemporary international environment provides insurgent groups with a framework from which to operate. Following the Cold War and the fall of Ethiopian leader Mengistu, the SPLA lost its external financiers. The group faced pressure from Western countries to democratize and followed accordingly—at least on the surface. From an external point of view, this evolution in the group's relationship to outside forces (and their possible financial support) is highly rational. Like the FARC, which turned to bigger sources of revenue to facilitate the expansion of its fronts, the SPLA had to find a link to fresh resources and thus reformed its ways to suit the presumed predispositions of foreign backers. Indeed, it was the SPLA's ability to become the sole recipient of resources—to be without active rivalry—and thus to exercise control over the flow of resources and donor agencies that gave the SPLA the impetus to reduce strong-arm tactics against civilians. Still, in light of the SPLA's early record of human-rights abuses and violence toward southerners, it is remarkable not only that the insurgents weathered the shift but that they made the change at all.

The explanation for the SPLA's transformation from a fractious and co-ercive movement to a contractual nascent state lies not in the pressure that may have been generated by the international environment and its democratic agenda. Rather, the SPLA's varying policy toward southern Sudanese reflects the presence or absence of rivals within the insurgent group's own environment. The SPLA confronted resource problems but did not base its decision to reform on the presence or absence of resources or on the international community's normative wish list. Rather, the SPLA made its choices in the context of its overall concern for being accepted as the sole armed entity using resources in southern Sudan. Shifting alliances and the history of factionalizing in the region led to the adoption of coercive behavior during the 1980s and 1990s throughout regions of the south. Once rival factions either dissolved or were absorbed by the SPLA, the insurgency transformed itself (though strictly on its own terms) into an entity that developed reciprocal relations with its host populations, enforcing rules, policing, and acting as intermediary between NGOs and local populations. As a result, violence against southerners decreased.

The changes the SPLA made between 1991 and the signing of the peace agreement with the north in 2005 were dramatic considering the southern environment, the history of factionalizing, and the ideological and personal differences among elites within the SPLA. The SPLA improved its human-rights record and increased its level of legitimacy both locally among southerners and internationally among states and donor organizations. In direct contrast to the FARC and the PKK, which found their active rivalry increasing, the diminishing number of rivals in the case of the SPLA reduced the level of coercion that the group practiced or condoned. Furthermore, the SPLA reduced its coercion against civilians in a highly volatile and ever-changing environment. The international pressure to adopt democratic norms would not have influenced the SPLA leadership if rivals had remained. The lack of rivals permitted the SPLA to control resources, which in turn gave the SPLA room to develop local institutions and structures of governance.

4

From Jekyll to Hyde

The Transformation of the FARC

The woman I am speaking with in the small village located in north-central Colombia tells a disturbing story. It is clear, though, that she has told it several times. She does not cry. She does not ask for assistance. She merely talks. She tells me her name, but I will call her Maria. She was a pastor with her husband in the village of —— for eight years. In 2002, she tells me, her husband was assassinated, and she had to leave the area with her nine-year-old daughter. She thinks it was the FARC that had her husband killed. Informants that lived in the village had seen that her husband was not acting under the authority of the insurgents.

This behavior of the FARC's was different than it had been in years past. In 1994, she tells me, the FARC in the region were extremely disciplined. They would even investigate human-rights abuses. I ask her when the FARC's behavior began to change. Their behavior changed, she says, when the paramilitaries arrived in the area.[1]

The FARC began as a mediating force in rural Colombia, representing peasant communities in the southeastern region of the country. The FARC initially maximized its legitimacy among its targeted membership by providing services for peasants, such as protection against the harsh policies of some large landowners and education in exchange for food and supplies. The group investigated human-rights abuses perpetrated by its own cadres against the local communities it served. At the end of the 1980s, despite its involvement in the illicit-drug industry, the FARC continued to have a contractual relationship with local residents. The group even came close to modeling itself as an alternative to the central government in specific regions when the government agreed to create a demilitarized zone—*zona de despeje*—for the FARC in 1998. This geographically defined area was to be the starting point for the evolution of further peace talks between the group and the government.

Unlike the SPLA, as discussed in the preceding chapter, however, the FARC became more coercive rather than more contractual in its behavior. By the late 1990s, this peasant-based insurgent group had become extremely violent in its treatment of the rural population it had previously protected. What explains this dramatic change in behavior toward noncombatants? Does the source of resources—in this case, drug trafficking—determine the type of behavior, an argument that parallels Weinstein's thesis?[2] As I argued previously, illicit economies do not always correlate positively with the nature of insurgent behavior. This chapter delves deeper into insurgent treatment of noncombatants and specifically dwells on the resource-violence nexus. The change that occurred in the FARC's relationship with civilians contrasts directly with the transformation that the SPLA's relationship underwent. Moreover, both changes occurred at relatively similar periods of time and in the same international environment. Despite the different circumstances and the opposing directions in which the FARC and the SPLA changed, the reason for the FARC's transformation springs from the same causal mechanism as the SPLA's: active rivalry.

This chapter traces the development of the FARC, from a group that found its roots in peasant self-defense organizations that supported better working conditions for peasant farmers to its growth as an independent insurgency with resources springing from drug trafficking and extortion.[3] I examine the process of the FARC's transformation and in doing so demonstrate the multiple events, circumstances, and forces that led to the FARC's recent coercive behavior toward the very population it initially set out to protect. As the evidence detailed here shows, the presence of active rivalry in the form of paramilitaries shaped how other variables such as resources influenced the changes in the behavior of the insurgents.

"A Project of Exclusion"

Colombia is a large country, roughly three times the size of Iraq (see map 4.1). Three vast mountain ranges split the country into several distinct regions. Each of these regions is unique in climate, population, and economy. The cattle and coca-growing area of the eastern plains makes up nearly one-third of the country's territory, but it contains just a small portion of Colombia's forty million residents. The Middle Magdalena Valley

CARIBBEAN SEA

Ríohacha

Santa Marta

Barranquilla
ATLANTICO   LA GUAJIRA

Cartagena   MAGDALENA

Valledupar

CESAR

VENEZUELA

Sincelejo

PANAMA

SUCRE   NORTE DE
SANTANDER

Montería

CORDOBA   BOLIVAR

Cúcuta

PACIFIC
OCEAN

Arauca

Bucaramanga

ANTIOQUIA   SANTANDER   ARAUCA

Medellín

Meta River

Puerto
Carreño

Quibdó

CHOCO

CALDAS

Manizales

CASANARE

El Yopal

BOYACA

CUNDINAMARCA

Meta River

VICHADA

Oronco River

RISARALDA

Pereira

Ibagué   Santa Fe
de Bogotá

Armenia

QUINDIO   TOLIMA

VALLE
DEL
CAUCA

Cali

META

Puerto
Inírida

Neiva

HUILA

GUAINIA

CAUCA

Popayán   San José del Guaviare

GUAVIARE

NARIÑO   Florencia

Pasto   Mitú

Mocoa   CAQUETA   VAUPES

PUTUMAYO

BRAZIL

ECUADOR   Puerto
Santander

AMAZONAS

PERU   Amazone River

Leticia

0   50   100   150 mi

0   100   200 km

Map 4.1. Colombia 2008
(Perry-Castaneda Library Map Collection, University of Texas Libraries)

is the core of the country's oil industry and accommodates portions of its illegal drug economy as well. Urabá to the west and on the coast is also known for accommodating various elements of the narco-trafficking industry, namely, drug and arms trafficking, though it is most known for its banana plantations. With such a geography and, as I will describe, a history riddled with dissension and internal fragmentation, unity in Colombia has been ephemeral.

Colombian officials tout their country as being the longest lasting democracy in Latin America.[4] It is also one of the few countries in Latin America with nearly consistent positive economic growth since the 1940s.[5] Colombia avoided much of the debt crisis that affected the region during the 1970s and 1980s. Some scholars claim this political stability reflects the durability of the country's political party system, as the historical dominance of the Liberal and Conservative parties has lent Colombian politics an air of certainty.[6]

There is, however, tremendous room for social and political ferment notwithstanding these durable democratic institutions. Colombia has one of the most inequitable distributions of wealth in the Western Hemisphere, next to Brazil.[7] Between 60 and 68 percent of the country's population lived at or below the poverty line in 2004. Rural poverty levels rise as high as 85 percent. The country is also strongly divided along ethnic and racial lines, which is not surprising, in light of the history of inequality established by the Spaniards who conquered the country and by later laws that institutionalized inequity.[8] The deep social divisions reflect the proportion of individuals of European descent living in urban areas compared to those classified as *campesinos,* or peasant farmers.

These divisions helped lead to the formation of the FARC and the longest lasting civil conflict on the South American continent, a conflict that has displaced two to three million people and has been responsible for more than forty thousand deaths (most of them civilian) since 1999 alone. In recent years, various armed groups—which appear to favor action against civilians rather than direct military confrontation—have increasingly targeted local indigenous communities.[9]

The human-rights lawyer is bursting with energy. He is slender, always on the move, and well dressed. In one of several interviews I have with him, he tells me he has been threatened by both the government of Colombia and the FARC, though he says he is not dissuaded from fighting for human rights by these modes of intimidation.

Describing the history of Colombia, he tells me that the Spanish period was one of war-maintained hatred between the classes. There was no attempt at accommodating anyone aside from the hijos de españoles *(children of the Spanish). To vote, he says, one had to have land. Only the Spanish had land. "The Republic of Colombia is a project of exclusion."*[10]

Class Struggle and Land Reform

As in Sudan, the sources of modern conflict in Colombia lie largely in the country's historical inequalities. Spanish colonialism left indelible social and political structures in this Latin American country that set the scene for generations of disparity. The class divisions were in part shaped by topography and further reinforced by political divides and the patterns of Spanish conquest. Under colonialism, a peasant population thrived in the agricultural sectors of the country in the east, while in the west along the Caribbean coast the legacies of the slave-colonizer relationship, beginning with the arrival of African slaves, largely shaped the economy. Following the conquest of what the Spaniards called New Granada, the colonizers controlled only portions of the territory. They occupied frontier cities in the north and portions of the eastern highlands but had little control of the countryside around them. In areas where the Spanish had complete military control, regions outside the Hispanic cities were inhabited almost exclusively by indigenous populations. While the larger cities of these early Spanish settlements rose up where there were dense pockets of indigenous people that could be used as labor, colonial settlements also were established because of the presence of precious minerals, namely, gold.[11]

In the course of "settling" and "civilizing" the indigenous populations, Spanish administrators found the populations' dispersion problematic. Indian peasants living in small communities were difficult to acculturate and control religiously and politically. The solution in many areas was to merge smaller indigenous communities into larger ones. For example, in 1601, 83 indigenous communities in the jurisdiction of Santafé de Bogotá were combined into 23, and in 1602 another 104 Indian communities were merged into 41 larger ones. This combination of indigenous towns also had the benefit of removing them from the plots of land they had occupied, thus freeing up large areas for the Spanish to claim. Moving the indigenous to concentrated areas generated a greater supply of labor for Spaniards. The Spanish authorities imposed several overlapping labor obligations on the Indian communities to ensure that indigenous labor was used for their desired purposes. In Santafé de Bogotá, for example, Indians had to supply designated terms of service to cities and residents, work in silver mines in Mariquita, and provide labor to Spanish farmers. This meant that Indian adult males would spend up to half a year away from their homes and thus could not effectively farm their plots.[12]

One of the major social changes that took place among the indigenous communities as a result of Spanish conquest, particularly in the eastern part of the country, was the decline of the Indian population. Over time, a large Indian population evolved into a predominantly *mestizo* (mixed) one. In contrast, in the southwestern region, populations held on to their indigenous identities for a longer period of time. In the west, Indian communities also declined, replaced largely by African slaves and their descendants. Local and provincial identities remained strong even after independence.[13]

Colombia won its independence from Spain in 1819 after fighting for several years with the colonialists.[14] These wars of independence, initiated largely by Creole elites, brought significant social changes to the country. Most notably, Afro-Colombians who were once slaves gained their freedom. These individuals filled out the military ranks during wartime, having been promised freedom in exchange for their service. Yet the Creole elite retained a largely unchallenged monopoly on power following independence, and therefore self-determination did not end the inequities among the various sectors of society. Conflicts emerged between clergy, a historically conservative and powerful part of Colombian society, and the university-educated liberals. The military also came into conflict with these liberal civilians.[15] These conflicts placed Colombia on a path for future inequities, disagreements, and war.

During the struggle for independence, two major political sectors had emerged as a result of political fragmentation. Some historians depict the emergence of these political factions—what became the Conservative and Liberal parties—as a sequel to an earlier conflict between liberals and Bolivarians in 1826–1830.[16] It was the civil war from 1840 to 1842, however, that created a nearly irresolvable rift between the moderates, who founded a coalition with the Bolivarians, and the Liberals, who sought to exclude them.[17] Although the conflict between the parties was largely ideological, its consequence was the development of a deep division that became inherent within Colombian politics and society.

The conflict between the parties also involved the struggle for land. During the late nineteenth and early twentieth centuries, the Colombian government began a major land-reform effort, which furthered the acquisition of public lands and stimulated the development of small- and medium-sized farms. The subservience of local government officials to large landowners facilitated the privatization of public land. When the Colombian government passed legislation in 1874 (and again in 1882) to reform public land policy and urge settlers to resist the misappropriation by large landowners, many of these pioneers felt they had to petition the government to protect them from the growth of *latifundios*—the owners of great landed estates. These reforms represented a response to improvements in transportation and technology, which had led to an increase in demand for Colombia's agricultural products in the industrialized world.[18] Prior to this time, minerals—particularly gold—had constituted most of Colombia's exports; however, by the end of the nineteenth century, coffee had become one of the country's largest agricultural exports, and the number of coffee haciendas was in the hundreds.[19] These large estates were located mainly in Northern Santander, Santander, Cundinamarca, Tolima, and southwestern areas of Antioquia. This agrarian boom led to a period of confrontations between collective groups of settlers and the landowners and their allies, and it set the stage for further battles between the two dominant political parties.

The land reforms benefited large estate owners and worked against the interests of peasant farmers. To facilitate the huge local and global demand for agricultural products, large landowners needed a greater labor force. One of the quickest methods of creating a large labor pool was through land seizures or the assertion of the rights of private-property owners over those peasants living on the land.[20] The estate owners—*hacendados*—planted crops primarily on land for which they had title. Their possession of titles enabled these landowners to create a frontier of closed resources, as opposed to the previous one of open resources, in which merely occupying the land had entitled one to ownership.[21] Thus, many peasants became tenant farmers. The effect was the alienation of territory for peasants and the growth of disgruntled would-be small landholders.[22]

Much of this peasant labor force initially lived in the highland regions, far from areas of export agriculture cultivation. The land-reform effort, which led to private land tenure, forced these people to migrate from the highlands to lower elevations for work. This migration created a small-holder sector in the midlands and lowlands that was made up largely of peasants. These individuals traveled to "frontier regions"—unsettled public lands—to farm and earn money in the cash economy. The settlement of these public lands in the mid- and low-level regions continued the original labor problems for large estate owners who relied on hired labor. Migrating peasants were less willing to accept work as wage laborers when they had access to public land. Large landowners sought to resolve this problem by enacting enclosures, which allowed for the commercialization of agriculture while eroding peasant property.[23]

Enclosures in Colombia meant the privatization of property by a small percentage of society and tied labor to these large estates. Property titles were not, at this time, functional in Colombia, and by law frontier settlers were allowed to claim title to land that they farmed. However, many of those who worked smaller plots of land could not afford the costs of surveying and thus could not acquire title. Moreover, the land that the estate owners chose to enclose or privatize was not public land in the sense that it was unoccupied. Peasant farmers resided on this land and did not have the resources to fight for it through legal channels.[24]

Colombia's privatization of public land benefited several sectors of society. Merchants and politicians often appropriated land through patronage networks. "The cumulative effect was to block the peasants from access to the most desirable land, thus encouraging them to sell their labor power."[25] Government reports confirm this effect. One congressional committee reporting in 1882 claimed, "it is generally through the dispossession of the poor settlers that rich people acquire large landholdings. . . . Many . . . obtain immense extensions of territory which they hoard with the sole purpose of excluding settlers from those areas or else reducing them to serf-like conditions."[26] A statement from the Municipal Council of Cauca in 1907 was quite clear about the meaning and effects of these land acquisitions: "In Cauca, the majority of the *hacendados* have taken over vast zones of public lands . . . which they neither work themselves nor allow others to work. By monopolizing the land, they aim only to undermine the position of the independent cultivators so as to form from their ranks groups of dependent laborers."[27]

While the agricultural boom strengthened the large landowners' hold on state politics, the majority of the Colombian people who worked the land found themselves shut out of the benefits of the new agricultural prosperity. Thus, the potential "coffee middle class," the would-be sturdy foundation for Colombian democracy and economic prosperity initially envisioned in the reforms, did not find itself much better off than it had been prior to the agricultural boom. A survey during the mid-1930s in several coffee regions found that average farm families numbered seven members, all of whom lived and slept in a single room; all dwellings lacked running water, and 97 percent were without proper latrines.[28] Agrarian conflict became a common occurrence. Between 1875 and 1930, more than 450 conflicts occurred in the frontier regions.[29] The agrarian struggle that eventually gave rise to the FARC and other armed groups had commenced.

Changes in the political system during the late 1920s provided *campesinos* with the outlet through which to channel their animosity and to renew their struggles against the large landowners. In 1926, the Colombian Supreme Court ruled that the only method by which to distinguish private from public land was with an original land title. Most peasants were aware that the estate owners had appropriated land illegally and possessed no such title. The *colonos,* or settlers, attempted legal avenues of protest and contestation. They challenged property rights and took cases to court. Usually, however, litigation lasted for several years and led to the imposition of a compromise that was unacceptable to the peasants. These periods of litigation were characterized by assassinations, imprisonments, and dispossessions.[30] Therefore, many peasants declared the land they occupied as their own and settled on lands of alleged proprietors. Several *colonos* of an estate claimed that if the law did not protect their property rights, then they would either migrate or resort to crime.[31] The state's response was to send in police forces to stop the settlers. Incrementally, then, the path of legal action was replaced by violence as a mode of resistance.[32]

La Violencia and the Precursors to the FARC

While land-reform issues ignited violence in rural areas, politics in Bogotá saw the two dominant political parties constantly at odds with each other. The Conservatives identified with large landowners and the Catholic Church; the Liberals were considered to be reform minded, though they also reflected some conservative economic interests. In 1930, a split in the Conservative party facilitated the Liberal party's capture of the executive branch, ending a half century of Conservative political dominance. The Liberal party's victory deprived the Conservatives of central control and patronage networks on the local level.

The period of time in Colombia's political history from 1930 to 1946 is known as the "Liberal Republic." As the label suggests, during these sixteen years, the head of state was a Liberal party member.[33] The Liberal Republic ushered in a wave of state centralization and direct intervention in the economy. Several ruling statesmen of this period, such as Eduardo Santos, advocated for the "social function" of property, a philosophy that many conservatives found alarmingly radical, bordering on communist. In 1932, an agrarian-reform proposal began to develop in government whereby individuals could acquire legal ownership of public lands merely by working the land.[34] The social agenda instituted and supported by many Liberals during this period thus met with unwavering Conservative resistance and increased the tension between Conservative and Liberal partisans.[35] These tensions finally erupted as *La Violencia* (The Violence).

The beginning of *La Violencia* is associated with the April 1948 assassination of Liberal party member and populist leader Jorge Eliécer Gaitán, who had created a social and political force that swept across party lines. His populist movement, known as Gaitanismo, emerged amid the urban growth and economic inflation of the 1940s, conditions that were propitious for mass mobilization.[36] Gaitán's organization, La Unión Nacional Izquierdista Revolucionaria (UNIR), advocated economic redistribution, which threatened the social, political, and economic structure that ruling elites and their allies had created. The UNIR condemned "the exaggerated maldistribution of wealth in the country as well as the concentration of political power in the hands of a minuscule oligarchy."[37] Gaitán's assassination in Bogotá launched two weeks of social and political protest in the capital, which quickly spread to the rural regions.[38] As violence increased, an estimated twenty thousand Liberal and Conservative partisans armed themselves and set out to settle old political scores. Not only did they fight over land, but they also faced off for political power, since power at the local level was critical to acquiring land.

During the period 1948–1966, *La Violencia* resulted in over two hundred thousand deaths.[39] A scholar describes this period:

> prisoners imprisoned or executed their guards; those individuals previously persecuted now exercised power in many localities; judges incited subversion; pulpits were silenced and priests either imprisoned, held incommunicado, or killed (principally in Tolima and Cundinamarca); peasants invaded haciendas, expropriated cattle, and gave orders to landowners.[40]

Order was eventually restored in the capital, and the elite oligarchy that had ruled Colombia once again took control of the country. Leaders soon took measures to ensure that what had taken place in Bogotá would not occur elsewhere in Colombia.[41] Conservatives ensured that militant workers were fired; they purged and imprisoned union leaders as well, attacking the use of the strike as a legitimate form of protest. In Antioquia, for example, there was general harassment of workers and government employees, as described by the historian Mary Roldán. And Conservative authorities emphasized the popular insurrections occurring in some towns and claimed they were proof of a communist plot to seize control of Colombia.[42] The clergy, historically a part of the Conservative backbone, gave tacit support for the killing of those involved in the uprisings following April 1948.

As violence overtook the countryside, conflict between the dominant parties continued in the urban areas. Liberal politicians refused to accept defeat in places where the party previously had control, and Conservatives, who dominated the army, politicized the armed forces and replaced Liberal officers whenever possible, turning the armed forces into a partisan political instrument.[43] It soon became clear that bipartisan cooperation in resolving the countrywide conflict was not possible, a supposition that became reality when the Liberal party left the Cabinet in June 1949.

These two decades in Colombia stand out in history for one unfortunate reason: the barbarity of the period. It has been described as a time of "nihilistic or self-destructive re-creation of the colossal orgy of power."[44] Although relative order was eventually restored in urban areas, the countryside became an environment of chaos, a reflection of the partisan conflict. Yet the violence that developed in *el campo,* or rural regions, was a part of several distinct developments that influenced the formation of the FARC. The most evident of these developments was the increased use of state-sanctioned terror. Torture, murder, and agrarian intimidation such as the use of a scorched-earth policy were common. Conflicts were often resolved through murder by people who used their political affiliations to claim the assistance or complicity of the local authorities. *Pájaros* (murderers) had extensive networks of protection and were often rewarded according to the importance of their victims.[45] The Colombian-born historian Gonzalo Sánchez describes the period:

The extreme modality of this process was, of course, murder. Extreme not only for the number of victims but also because of the indescribable torture that surrounded these murders and marked for life the entire generation that witnessed them. . . . Conflicts—between neighbors, between rural laborers and employers, between squatters and landlords . . . were resolved in bloodshed by those who, by virtue of their political affiliation, could count on the complicity of the authorities.[46]

The response to state-condoned terrorism was the creation of insurgent groups. This resistance emerged during the violence because the leaders of the Liberal party proved unable to stop the increasing terror. Insurgent groups were the offspring of peasant self-defense leagues that identified with leftist political parties such as the UNIR and the Colombian Communist Party (PCC), which emerged from the Revolutionary Socialist Party of the 1920s. The self-defense organizations grew out of the tradition of the struggle for land and thus were loyal to the peasant population. Originally they were located in Marquetalia, Riochiquito, El Pato, and Guayabero, remote areas south of Bogotá. These organizations were traditionally more defensive than they were offensive. Their strategies did not include such tactics as terrorism or ambushes of military or police forces. Nor did these organizations initially defend themselves against the state. Rather, the self-defense organizations from which the FARC emerged protected peasant communities from the private security forces of other peasant communities.

During *La Violencia,* as the government stepped up peasant-targeted attacks, the self-defense organizations evolved. They became more mobile and offensive.[47] Word of insurgency spread during the years of the violence as displaced persons migrated to regions where these groups based themselves, particularly in Tolima. Peasants arrived from elsewhere to fight for the Liberal doctrine along with Communist peasants. Many of these peasants, including Manuel Marulanda Vélez ("Sure-shot"), were the founding members of the FARC.

Insurgent centers became refuges and soon were barriers to the imposition of state authority. These groups were not only the means of resistance to the state, but they often acted as the replacement of the government. Initially, Colombia lacked the military muscle in insurgent-controlled areas to address rebellion. In the state's absence, guerrilla groups set up parallel government structures, providing food, security, and other sources of social support to local populations.

At the beginning of the thirties, the agricultural workers who put into effect the Communist slogan of "the revolutionary taking of the land" by occupying the large estates and establishing agricultural settlements on public lands in several departments [Colombian equivalent to a U.S. state], employed self-defense to protect their conquests. . . . Self-defense organizations, such as the "Guardia Roja," the "Correo Rojo," the Litigation Commissions effectively combined three fronts of struggle: defense against aggression, using arms if necessary; solidarity; and the search for "legal" solutions.[48]

Self-defense communities became linked to the communist presence in nearby countries such as Cuba. These groups were highly organized, with codes of revolutionary morality that enforced respect for women, children, and the elderly, as well as laws that prohibited torture and scorched-earth tactics. Women had a key role in areas of resistance, serving as lookouts for peasant fighters in southeastern Antioquia, for example.[49]

A critical element of *La Violencia* was the breakdown of social order, which affected the structure of property holding in rural areas, as thousands of peasants abandoned their land or were forced to sell it to flee or as a result of extortion. Landless groups migrated to distant colonization zones or urban areas. Other displaced peasants joined self-defense leagues turned guerrilla or rebel groups. Large landholders in areas of violence and displacement could (and often did) take over peasant lands, as did a new group of shopkeepers and merchants. However, the large estate owners had more options, and many also moved to urban areas to wait for the situation in the countryside to improve.[50]

By 1952, these insurgents became a serious threat to the government and the military. In one case, a commander and his soldiers destroyed an entire Colombian army column of one hundred men, considered a surprising feat by largely peasant-led fighters.[51] Key insurgent leaders approached their governing body, the Liberal Directorate, with a choice: either help the insurgents by leading a general revolt against the government, the military, and the ruling Conservative party, or else they would do so on their own.

The insurgents then convened a conference attended by representatives from the country's most important insurgent groups. This meeting became known as the First National Conference of the Popular Movement of National Liberation. Its national coordinating commission facilitated the organization of a judicial system and allocated duties to civil and military commanders as well as public officials. It guaranteed civil rights, established conditions and limits to land use, and began establishing agricultural colonies that it claimed belonged to the Revolution. "The law of the *llano* was, in effect, the most complete democratic project proposed by the armed movement to counter the fascistic project of [the government]."[52] During *La Violencia*, the *llanos* referred to the plains of the eastern slope of the Eastern Cordillera, Casanare and Meta, Sumapaz, the Antioqueño regions of Urrao, the Lower Cauca, and the Middle Magdalena, to Tolima. After the departments of Nariño, the Santanders, Boyacá, and the Cauca Valley were pacified during the 1950s, violence moved to this area of the country.[53]

Meanwhile, on December 1, 1957, a caretaker government led by a military junta oversaw a plebiscite that established what came to be known as the National Front. The National Front was the result of a 1956 pact wherein the Liberals and the Conservatives agreed to form a bipartisan government, alternating the presidency and sharing multilevel government positions.[54] When a fissure in the Conservative party developed in 1957 and a military junta seized power, Conservatives and Liberals realized they needed a rigid agreement between themselves to preserve civilian rule. In July 1957, they drew up the Pact of Sitges, which provided for parity in Congress and the Cabinet for a period of twelve years. Under the National Front, the parties received mutual political guarantees; the party leaders agreed that there was no viable alternative to a constitutionally mandated agreement for equally shared power in Colombia.[55] The inauguration of the National Front, which in theory was meant to be a negotiated path out of the previous years of terror, in fact launched a new phase of the violence.[56]

The Evolution of the FARC

In this section, I trace the formation of the FARC and other insurgent groups in Colombia. I also examine the significance of the 1984 Uribe Agreement, which facilitated the legalization of the FARC's political entity known as the Patriotic Union, and I detail that party's subsequent decimation by political rivals. Finally, I explain how the closure of that political path for the FARC left it with the sole option of enhancing its military capabilities by using proceeds from the drug trade.

The FARC Forms

The National Front instituted a limited democracy that espoused an exclusive bipartisan monopoly over the government, the autonomy of the military in the management of public order, and the centralization of state decisions in the executive office rather than in the congress.[57] This arrangement resulted in intense military aggression, under Guillermo León Valencia from 1962 to 1966, against the renegade peasant regions.

In 1955, under the Rojas Pinilla administration, the government stepped up violence in the Communist-influenced regions in response to the purported existence of "sixteen independent republics" (as these groups labeled themselves). Militants from the zones that were affected by these state military offensives held a meeting in 1964 and began calling themselves the "Southern Bloc." Two years later, at the second national conference of guerrilla groups, the FARC was born.[58] The peasant leagues of the 1950s, operating in fixed areas, became an armed movement that combined agrarian reform experiments with the organization and military experience of the Communist Party.[59]

Inspired by the leftist thought that had gained widespread acceptance in Latin America during this period of Cold War rivalry, two types of insurgent groups emerged during this era: agrarian communist and *foquista*.[60] *Foquista* is a type of militia. The word itself is derived from the *foco* theory of revolution. The major element of this type of revolution is guerrilla warfare, also known as *foquismo*, or focalism. Inspired by Che Guevara, the central principle of *foco* theory is that small, quick moving militia groups that place themselves at the center of a movement can provide a focus for popular discontent against a regime and thereby spark insurrection.[61]

Many of these groups were inspired by the Cuban Revolution and followed its pattern by indoctrinating the local populations and communities, from which they developed networks of resources. The National Liberation Army (ELN) officially formed in 1962 and began operations with minor terrorist acts in urban areas, but it also gained strength with bases in the rural regions of Santander and Antioquia during the 1970s.[62] The ELN traditionally operated in Aruaca, a department near the Colombian border with Venezuela, in the northeast. Another group, the M-19, also developed during this period. That group, which formed in 1974, based itself and operated primarily in urban areas and followed the example of the Montoneros in Argentina and the Tupamaros in Uruguay. After the success of the Sandinistas in Nicaragua in 1979, the M-19 reoriented its strategy toward the rural sectors. The group's demise came shortly after it seized the Palace of Justice in 1985, an act that resulted in a strong reaction of Colombian armed force and the subsequent death of numerous civilians, government officials, and the group's leadership. The M-19 was forced to demobilize following that incident.[63]

Unlike most of the Latin American guerrilla movements of the twentieth century, the FARC's social-class composition was largely of peasant origins. The group's leadership, made up of individuals such as Manuel Marulanda Vélez, Rigoberto Lozada, Carmelo López, José de Jesús Rivas, and Ciro Trujillo, was all of lower-class, peasant origins.[64] The FARC drew less substantial support from intellectuals and urbanites, which is the result of several factors. First, the FARC's peasant makeup is a reflection of its historical foundations, which were in the peasant self-defense leagues. The organizational divisions between the Communist Party and the FARC also contributed to its makeup. The Communist Party consisted mainly of urban intellectuals, students, and working-class individuals. This division was institutionalized when the Communist Party and the FARC severed ties during the late 1980s. Furthermore, the FARC's political tactics did not address the concerns of the middle class.[65]

The FARC Establishes Political Legitimacy

Many antigovernment groups organized during the 1960s and mounted insurgencies in Venezuela, Bolivia, Argentina, and Brazil.[66] In contrast to the vanguard *foquista* guerrillas, inspired by Che Guevara and the Cuban Revolution and starting among urban educated classes, the FARC had its origins among the peasantry and operated within an agrarian-communist framework.[67] In establishing ties to local populations, the FARC ensured its differentiation from "bandits"—groups it claimed committed criminal acts against the local peasant population.[68]

Initially, the FARC responded to local situations in which rural workers and small landholders came together to defend themselves against violence from the military and large landowners. The FARC thus began as part of a regional structure of social warfare that highlighted individual as well as collective survival. However, as peasants cooperated for their mutual defense, the FARC's goal came to include the transformation of the government through political, economic, and social proposals that demanded a broad system of protection for the lower classes.[69] Its objective was to mobilize the disaffected and the dispossessed population to form an alternative society.[70]

"In Colombia, democracy has its limits," says anthropologist Wilder Guerra. From his office in Cartagena, he speaks broadly of the state and its reach in Colombia. "Democracy is not constant" in all areas of the country, he

continues. "Look at Bogotá. It is similar to Western Europe," he remarks. Yet there are places outside Bogotá where people are displaced and exist without rights.

Colombia has a strange situation, he explains. There is a wide scale of illegalities—it is very complex. There are armed groups and armies replacing the functions of the state. People are under the control of these armed groups. "Life is controlled by them," he says.[71]

Alongside the Communist Party and agrarian organizations, the FARC became part of a structure of local power.[72] The FARC relied on local resources—resources from the community—which shaped its responsive character in its early years. The group's relatively small size and its deep roots in the areas where it operated meant that it had relatively easy access to food, shelter, protection, and information in the peasant communities. The FARC became a readily acceptable alternative to the Colombian government, particularly in frontier areas, where state officials were few. In areas where coca became the primary agricultural crop, the FARC established both a police and a judicial system.

The state's weakness where the FARC formed ensured that the FARC could act as the legitimate organizing body for peasants. For example, one of the FARC's duties was to defend *colonos* and protect the subsistence economy of the peasants. These insurgents also adjudicated local disputes and social conflicts. The FARC policed areas under its control by investigating criminal activity and weapons possession.[73] The FARC also focused on working with communities to create cooperatives and provide political education to the peasants.[74] According to one man who joined the FARC while he was still a university student, FARC commanders saw his intellectual talents and made him a teacher.

> They soon got him a small chalkboard, which he carried around with him wherever he went. When they stopped to rest . . . he would take the board out to give the peasant soldiers mini-lessons in math, science, English, and anything else he could remember from college. He also organized soldiers to perform plays and write poetry.[75]

In exchange for the services the FARC rendered, it imposed what it called a "progressive income tax." Many poorer peasants were exempt from paying this tax.[76] The FARC also raised money by taxing beer. The revenues supported schools and local community projects. Elected committees of local residents oversaw the disbursement of the taxes collected. As the longtime Colombia correspondent Stephen Dudley claims, "The guerrillas punished drunks, adulterers, and murderers. They also protected villagers from aggressive drug traffickers and forbade the use of dangerously addictive coca derivatives. The FARC was becoming a virtual state."[77]

As evidenced by the FARC's history and my own field research, it is clear that the FARC limited violence and coercion against peasants during its early years. When the FARC began taking money and arms from the drug industry, it maintained—at least for a time—its contractual relationship with local civilian populations despite the fact that the drug industry was already widely associated with rent seeking and violence.[78]

The FARC also made moves to become independent of the PCC. Although the FARC's behavior and rhetoric remained Marxist and socialist, the leaders made it clear that the forms of these political philosophies that originated in Europe were not particularly suited to Latin America in general and to Colombia in particular. Rather, the FARC wanted to use the socialist experiences of the Soviet Union and Cuba merely as a guideline in order to develop its own system of governance.[79] According to Dudley, this was one reason for the FARC's participation in the kidnapping industry.[80] There is some indication that the FARC was kidnapping and holding people, in particular ranchers and large farmers, early in its history. Although ransom resources from kidnapping were illicit, these early kidnappings happened far more rarely than the indiscriminate kidnapping that occurred in later years and only targeted people whom the FARC and most of its supporters considered ideologically legitimate targets. Thus, though the FARC did kidnap during this period, it did so discriminatingly.

The FARC was not the first organization in Colombia to use strategic kidnapping. During *La Violencia,* guerrillas and bandits kidnapped people to exert pressure on political rivals and to secure financing. The ELN and the M-19 ransomed business executives and wealthy landowners in order to extract hefty ransoms. Thus, the FARC followed suit, to secure its independence and to further strengthen its movement. It was notorious for kidnapping government officials and others working with the Colombian state. The FARC's "retentions" included diplomats, large estate owners, and businesspeople, particularly those working at petroleum extraction in the countryside. Though the PCC condemned such acts, the FARC's governing structure formally accepted the legitimacy of the practice of kidnapping for political reasons at its Sixth Conference in 1978.[81] The money extorted by means of this strategy for a time funded the FARC's expansion into urban areas. As the FARC grew and began re-focusing its strategies, it posed a larger challenge to the state. The fact that powerful elites were at an ever-increasing risk of being kidnapped meant that state officials risked losing their patrons. As a result, the government heightened its counterinsurgency efforts.

Following a harsh military campaign against the PCC and the FARC in the early 1980s, President Betancur initiated exploratory efforts toward a peace deal with the insurgents. The result was the 1984 Uribe Agreement, named after the municipality where it was signed. The FARC agreed to condemn kidnapping, blackmail, and terrorism, and Betancur promised that the state would make continuous efforts to improve the education, health, and employment levels for all Colombians. Through the Uribe Agreement, the government of Colombia gave the FARC a modicum of legitimacy and allowed it to reorganize its political structure. The state recognized FARC leaders as political actors, a status they had not been afforded under the PCC. Thus, one of the major effects of this agreement was to alienate the PCC, for the FARC had not included the PCC in its negotiations with the government.[82]

The divide between the PCC and the FARC widened further when, as an effect of the agreement, the FARC formed a political wing called the Unión Patriótica, or Patriotic Union (UP). Some in the Communist Party viewed this move as a betrayal, as it signified the joining of main-stream capitalist politics and the loss of the socialist ideal that the FARC had espoused from its very beginning. However, to many more within the FARC the move was a political one that allowed the insurgent group to address peasant grievances through negotiation and political processes as opposed to resorting to violence.

The legitimacy that the Colombian state accorded to the FARC pro-vided the impetus for the group to apply its political strategy. Within a short period of time, the FARC had extended its influence to urban areas of the country under the banner of the UP. The UP officially began in 1985, under the auspices of such political leaders as Marulanda, Jacobo Arenas, Raúl Reyes, Alfonso Cano, Jaime Guaraca, and Timochenco, and it en-compassed the FARC, the PCC, and other left-wing groups. This impor-tant step signified a turn in political events. With the creation of the UP, the FARC entered mainstream national politics. According to high-level commander Simon Trinidad, the UP was important because it allowed the FARC to draw up a strategic plan. Prior to its formation, he said, there were only somewhat vague plans regarding the group's strategy to take power. The strategic plan defined the FARC's tactics and military strategy in great detail. Much of this expansion sprang from the Seventh Conference of the FARC of 1982, where the group's leaders decided to end the FARC's isolation from the urban populace and move into the cities. This expansion also necessitated more resources, and the FARC, no longer able to ignore the ease with which the cocaine trade garnered money, began its official involvement in that industry.[83] At the Seventh Conference, the group developed an eighteen-year plan to win the war against the Colombian government. The plan was simple: build an army and eventually surround the major urban areas. The FARC's plan necessitated approximately twenty-eight thousand troops by 1990 and a larger budget. To emphasize the new plan, the leaders of the FARC added the words *ejército del pueblo* (army of the people) to the organization's name. The FARC became the FARC-EP. The group had turned offensive.[84]

Meanwhile, in the cities, the FARC embedded itself through the UP and established Juntas Patrióticas—"solidarity cells"—small groups of followers linked to unions, student groups, and peasant leagues. Working for the UP, these cells came out into the open, advertising the FARC's ideas, organizing political rallies, and recruiting new members. The FARC soon attracted another section of the urban class, university students.[85] Those who joined the cells went into the *barrios* and spoke with people about the problems of the urban poor, gathering information on the political and social stances of the peasantry who had migrated to the cities.

Between 1984 and 1988, the UP was quite successful at rallying support. For example, the party did well at the polls, and several UP candidates won elections as mayors in FARC-controlled areas. As one UP member described, "We achieved the highest number of votes ever for a leftist party. We got more congressional reps than ever before. In less than a year, the UP got two leaders who had a national profile."[86] In 1986, the UP participated in elections and won 350 local council seats, 23 deputy positions, 9 seats in the House, and 6 seats in the Senate. UP president Bernardo Jaramillo won a seat in the Senate in 1990. In record time the UP had organized the Colombian left (the insurgents, progressives, democrats, and regional sectors of the Liberal and Conservative parties). In a subsequent important move, the UP broke up the bipartisan consensus that the two main political parties had tacitly used to wield power. This accomplishment, however, threatened the Colombian ruling parties and provoked a violent reaction in more militaristic sectors of the Colombian oligarchy.[87]

Although the UP entered the Colombian political arena with a peaceful political strategy, it did not leave that way. The UP was driven out of politics amid a barrage of violence. Between 1986 and 1990, more than four thousand members of the UP and the Communist Party were assassinated.[88] The party's first president, Jaime Pardo, was brutally murdered in 1987. That same year, 111 militants were said to have been killed. The following year, the number of murdered members rose to nearly 300. In 1989, one large landowner had 400 UP militants murdered. In the midst of the UP's apparently grand successes—such as the election of sixteen mayors and the 1990 election of Jaramillo to the Colombian Senate— party members were quickly disappearing. When Jaramillo took over as UP president following the death of Pardo, a journalist asked him how he thought he would die. "They're going to kill me," he responded without hesitation, "on any corner, at any moment. It could even be in my house. I know they're going to kill me."[89]

During this time, the government attempted to distance itself from the numerous assassinations and the decimation of the UP by claiming that the killing was the sole responsibility of the major drug traffickers, many of whom had begun to employ defense groups in the wake of FARC taxation and kidnappings.[90]

Following Jaramillo's death, there was a massive exodus from the UP. It became clear that the party had been crushed.[91] The annihilation of the UP signaled that the political door had been shut tight against the FARC.[92] For FARC members, this development stressed the importance of intensifying their focus on a military strategy as the appropriate means to bring their political goals to fruition.[93]

Coca, *los Campesinos*, and the FARC: The Intersection

With the door to politics tightly closed to the FARC with the decimation of the UP, the group focused its efforts on its military arm. In order to strengthen this realm of the insurgent group, the FARC became more involved in drug trafficking. Although the drug industry blossomed during the 1980s, the industry was not new to Colombia. Historians and others have noted the presence of coca and its importance as a cash crop since the 1500s.[94] Marijuana became the main cash crop during the 1970s in Colombia as the result of a crisis in the cotton market. In fact, marijuana plantations received technical support from U.S. agronomists.[95] Many large landowners shifted to producing marijuana, and by 1974 nearly 80 percent of farmers in the Colombian region of Guajira grew the plant. During the 1970s, the FARC denounced drug trafficking under orders from the Communist Party, which claimed that it did not represent communist ideals.[96]

The production and trafficking of cocaine moved heavily into Colombia when the United States put pressure on Bolivia and Peru to eradicate coca, which had been grown there for centuries. Cocaine production and trafficking had begun in Colombia before the FARC became deeply involved in politics through the UP. The FARC's involvement in cocaine production and trafficking gathered steam when the Colombian economy took a downturn in the 1980s. With the increase in industrial exports and manufactured goods, along with higher export taxes, production of Colombia's hitherto major agricultural moneymaker—coffee—declined. Many farmers then turned to growing coca. As Colombia became an important producer of coca, more and more peasants who had originally cultivated other crops moved to outlying regions of the country where the coca leaf was grown. Workers who lost their jobs because of commercial liberalization or because of the declining prices of coffee, wheat, or barley found employment on the drug frontier.[97] Some people moved to the coca frontier attracted by the opportunity, but others went to Meta, Caquetá, and Putumayo because of the unavailability of sufficient agricultural land elsewhere. At the time, coca was the most lucrative crop these migrants could grow. After the downfall of the UP, FARC leaders realized that in order to expand its military forces expeditiously, they could no longer ignore such a facile source of funding.[98] The FARC's involvement in the coca-producing and trafficking industry facilitated a huge growth in its forces, from approximately two thousand soldiers in 1982 to more than eighteen thousand by 2001.[99]

As I have emphasized, the FARC's initial involvement in the drug industry was as a collector of rents. Moreover, the "official" nature of its collective decision to get involved in this industry highlights the organized and self-regulated character of its behavior. These were not competitive warlords, driven by the desire for personal gain, who chose to become involved in drug trafficking. In the richest coca-producing regions, the FARC secured a stable economic foundation for the peasants by regulating market relations and prices. As more traffickers flooded into the region, the FARC struck a deal with them: pay taxes and the group would leave their businesses alone. The FARC taxed all parts of the drug business within its reach, including the protection of shipments, the use of the jungle to establish labs, and the use of land as clandestine airstrips to export the product.[100] The FARC forced the narco-traffickers to pay the peasants the market price for coca leaves and provided financial and technical assistance and protection to *colonos*.[101] FARC commander Yazid Arteta claimed that the FARC urged peasants to set aside a portion of their land for raising food and to keep a smaller section of the land for growing coca.[102] Where the FARC tended to have substantial influence, it protected the peasant economy by battling the large landowners and what it labeled the "narco-bourgeoisie." This action prevented the large landowners from expanding their holdings at the expense of the *colonos*.[103] Under conditions of relative market stability and protection, the FARC made it possible for peasants who depended on the subsistence economy to join international markets with little personal economic disorder, which contrasted strongly with the experience of those who remained subject to the legal economy's market forces.[104]

The economic circumstances of the peasants, the increase in the inventory in the FARC's armory thanks to the influx of tax revenues, and the weakness of the state in these regions played an important role in determining the position that the FARC had in these zones. Its economic and military strength allowed it to secure positions of power in the rural regions.

[The FARC] extended services in the areas of credit, education, health, justice, registry, public works and ecological and cultural programs. Consequently, the insurrectionaries not only were the recognized local government but also were a civilizing agent in an environment that otherwise would have been, as one local priest put it, a "veritable vortex."[105]

Some accounts of the FARC's involvement in the drug industry claim that the group was nearly forced to join the coca trade because the peasants turned to it as a result of the downturn in the agriculture sector and the economic reforms imposed on them for legal crops. And so, in protecting its peasant base of support, the FARC was obliged to support the peasants' shift to illicit agriculture as a supplementary income. Thus, in this interpretation, the FARC—with its limited resources—still needed to manage peasants in areas under its control.[106] These developments in turn transformed the dynamic of the conflict, adding dimensions of organized crime and getting the government and self-defense forces involved. Such accounts blame these factors for causing the increase in wartime violence. Others argue that the FARC, under orders from the Communist Party, initially denounced drug trafficking,[107] but when the FARC began to break away from the Party, it needed the income from coca to finance its expanded military strategy.

These interpretations could both be correct, since the two views are not necessarily antithetical. The FARC's estimated budget for expanding its force to eighteen thousand was approximately $56 million, which enabled it to extend its struggle from twenty-seven fronts in 1989 to sixty fronts by 1999.[108] Members of the FARC purposely chose the military and drug route as opposed to the political one because it was the more lucrative. "The political thing didn't work," the journalist Dudley told me. "War works," he said. Nevertheless, I argue that despite the apparent greed of a few people in the FARC's leadership, the behavior exhibited in recent years by the insurgents is a result not of that greed but of other local forces—namely, the presence of significant rivals, including other insurgent groups, the military, local community organizations, and the state. In the same interview, Dudley seemed to imply as much when he said, "the FARC is like an animal stuck in a corner."[109] Narco-traffickers establishing niches in the FARC-controlled areas settled under the protection of the insurgents. The government, under pressure from foreigners to eradicate the trafficking of coca, first fought the drug industry. The drug industry in turn looked to the insurgents for security[110] and then was obliged to accept the insurgents' conditions. These conditions included according the FARC a monopoly of arms and, of course, paying taxes to the FARC. Paying taxes to the FARC meant accepting FARC authority in the region.[111]

The entente between the FARC and the cartels soon soured as drug traffickers wearied of paying rising protection taxes.[112] Furthermore, as the FARC presence grew in areas such as Montes de Maria in the north of the country, FARC members began to kidnap drug traffickers and their relatives, as well as large landowners. In response, the traffickers created and financed a group called MAS—Muerto a los Secuestroseros (Death to Kidnappers). Working closely with the military, MAS struck back at the insurgents and anyone else suspected of associating or sympathizing with them.[113] MAS and other similar groups grew into what became the paramilitary forces, or *paras,* which have worked with the Colombian armed forces to fight the insurgent groups in the country, in particular the FARC.[114]

The human-rights lawyer is almost poetic in his descriptions. I ask him to tell me what happened when the FARC and the paramilitaries operated at the same time. "A whirlpool of violence," he says, shaking his head.

The FARC supported the farmers, he recalls, describing the group in its earlier years. People from all parties became part of the movement known as the FARC. The insurgent presence grew into areas of the north, such as Montes de Maria. As that happened, a group called MAS developed into self-defense forces, he says. They united with the Colombian army and became the paras.

Most campesinos *supported the FARC, he continues, but the paramilitaries attacked the peasant farmers to get at the support base of the insurgents. Farmers would provide food and shelter to insurgents, and the* paras *would massacre them for doing so. The FARC began planting land mines to protect themselves from the* paras *and the Colombian military. But that hurt the civilian population the most, he says. Soon, he says, it became difficult to distinguish between the insurgents and the paramilitary forces.*[115]

Las Paras and the FARC

Ironically, the paramilitaries like the FARC—began as self-defense groups steeped in the tradition of the rural societies. The origin of paramilitary groups in Colombia dates back to Decree 3398 and Law 48 (1965 and 1968, respectively), which provided the legal basis for the creation of civil defense organizations. These laws sprang from Cold War counterinsurgency doctrine as taught by the U.S. government in the School of the Americas. This doctrine required a mixture of military, paramilitary, political, psychological, and economic resources to fight insurgent groups. Like many Latin American countries allied with the United States during the Cold War, Colombia incorporated this doctrine into its own national military strategies.[116]

The growth of the paramilitaries during the 1980s was a manifestation of the Colombian military's, ranchers', landowners', and drug traffickers' counterinsurgency strategy under the Betancur administration.[117] The decisions of these various parties to take up arms underlined the lack of state capacity in the rural regions during this period. It also suggests fear on the part of the drug traffickers and landowners that the FARC's involvement in the drug industry was threatening not only the cartel's profits but also the individual profits of state and military officials.[118] The *paras* were organized to stop the FARC's inroads. Paramilitary units developed in several departments of the country. Several units were led by Fidel and (later) Carlos Castaño, whose motivations were not purely financial. These two brothers wanted to exact revenge for the kidnapping and murder of their father by the FARC.[119] The paramilitaries enjoyed support and training by various Western states, including Israel and the United States. However, most of their resources came from the narco-traffickers, who were in a prime position to direct these groups because of the traffickers' relative autonomy and financial independence from the central government.[120]

Paramilitaries worked in collusion with the Colombian military, local government officials, and the police.[121] Evidence of this collusion appeared in the testimony of local civilians and NGO leaders and was confirmed by human-rights groups. A Human Rights Watch report maintained that several military officers were on the payroll of the Autodefensas Unidas de Colombia (AUC; United Self-Defense Forces of Colombia)—one of the most prominent paramilitary groups—and received salaries based on rank.[122] During several interviews I conducted, individuals displaced by the war stated that they feared reporting their circumstances to local authorities because police and other officials were under the control of the *paras*. Human-rights organizations confirm this fear, and it is reported in the United Nations' *State of the World's Refugees 2006*. Many displaced people do not register for fear of being attacked, stigmatized, or displaced again.[123]

The collusion between the Colombian military and the *paras* has been well established. In 1995, for example, the Castaño units issued a manifesto that declared their support of the military in their fight against the insurgents. The document stated that the paramilitaries received logistical and material support from the armed forces, and from some large landowners, cattle ranchers, and businesses.[124] As one scholar of Colombia notes, "Many high-ranking military officers are collaborating and fomenting paramilitarism."[125] This collaboration had a clear rationale. With the paramilitaries doing the dirty work, it was possible for the military to disclaim responsibility. As long as the paramilitaries fought the Colombian state's enemy, there was little interest for the military in battling the insurgents themselves. The armed forces responded to the Castaño manifesto with a clear statement of disapproval of these military links with the *paras*. Captain Garcia-Marquez, the newly appointed head of the navy in Cartagena reiterated this disapproval: "The AUC," he said, "was legal originally, but it degenerated. Any person in the military with connections to the AUC is thus illegal."[126]

Fueled by a vast amount of resources, the AUC set out to extinguish the guerrilla threat in the country. During the late 1980s, these units spread throughout the Colombian countryside. In 1987, the minister of government claimed that there were at least 140 AUC units.[127] In 1996, Castaño claimed that the AUC included 2,000 armed fighters.[128] The number rose to 11,200 by 2000, an increase of 460 percent in only four years.[129] In 2001, the AUC was estimated to have an armed presence in 40 percent of Colombian municipalities, and it is reported that over 70 percent of its resources comes from the drug industry.[130]

Paramilitaries infiltrate the ranks of local functionaries, bribe them, and subordinate them to their own plans.[131] They influence politics by using violence and intimidation and by replacing local officials.[132] They also station armed units throughout rural areas to maintain control over who enters and leaves those zones. Forces acting under the name AUC maintain numerous bases and roadblocks throughout the Colombian countryside. They "move with apparent ease. They employ faxes, the Internet, sport utility vehicles and pick-up trucks, radios, helicopters, laptops, and cellular and satellite telephones to disseminate threats, identify targets, prepare death lists, and coordinate massacres."[133]

Like the FARC, the *paras* aim to expand their control of local governments throughout the country. However, unlike the insurgents, the paramilitaries espouse no political or social ideology other than to protect incumbent political groups. These groups' common goal is to stop the insurgents (with a particular focus on the FARC) from developing their revolutionary projects.[134] Soon after the entrance of the *paras* into the Colombian conflict, it became clear that these counterinsurgency groups did not aim merely to annihilate the FARC. Rather, they wanted to eradicate the idea that the Colombian state had opposition.[135]

In one village, a group of farmers breaks bread together at tables set up in a communal area. Upon finishing their meal, a few of them stay to talk with me. The families of this village, they tell me, were displaced in the year 2000. The trouble began, one says, with a bomb going off in a local police station. People did not know who was responsible for planting the bomb, though the rumor around the village was that the paramilitaries had staged it to make it look like the FARC. Soon, after the bombing incident, the paramilitaries came to their houses and said they could not ensure their safety or the safety of their families—that the farmers should leave.

The farmers tell me the paramilitaries forced them to leave because they wanted the fertile land for themselves. Land is one of the resources the insurgents and the paramilitaries are fighting over, a younger-looking farmer tells me. Before the arrival of the paramilitaries, the locals in the region did

*not have many problems with the FARC. The insurgents came to their vil-
lage in 1995. "They were disciplined," the young man says. If people were
suspected of being against the FARC then, the insurgents would investigate
the claim. Today, however, they just kill you.*

*I ask the young farmer to tell me why he thinks things changed, why the
FARC changed the way it interacted with the members of his village. He
simply says that when the paramilitaries came into the area there was confusion as to who supported whom. The presence of the* paras, *he says, made
the FARC defend itself.*[136]

The impact of the *paras* has been extensive, both for Colombian rural
society and for the insurgents. The paramilitaries have reportedly killed
more than two times as many civilians in attacks as have the insurgents,
and more than three-quarters of these killings were conducted during
large-scale massacres.[137] In February 2001, in the village of Chengue, one
group of paramilitaries marched into the village and pulled the men into
the main square. "Then, one by one, they killed the men by crushing
their heads with heavy stones and a sledgehammer."[138] Between 1998 and
2002, the paramilitaries became some of the most well-stocked and largest nonstate armed groups in the world. They used U.S.-made weapons
such as the AR-15 assault rifle and the M60 machine gun, accumulated
large amounts of ammunition, and demonstrated extremely low firing
discipline.[139]

The AUC entered into peace talks with the government in July 2003
under the pretext of agreeing on and mapping out a plan for disarming
over the coming years. However, rather than diminishing, the paramilitaries have grown in strength.[140] Furthermore, evidence exists that paramilitary groups continue to form in areas where demobilization has occurred.[141] Their finances, the majority from the trafficking of drugs, have
also increased sharply. One explanation for the increase in finances is that
prior to the negotiated amnesty, the *paras* exported massive quantities
of stockpiled cocaine, knowing that what was sold prior to the start of
the amnesty with the government would be pardoned.[142] However, much
of this activity has gone on with no discernable effort by the Colombian
government to limit or halt it.

Another reason for the huge rise in paramilitary forces in recent years
has been their links to the Colombian military and their financing from
programs of the U.S. government, as well as from some foreign business
interests and large landowners who tired of threats from the FARC.[143] One

of the greatest potential sources of paramilitary funding is Plan Colombia, a "pro-democracy" drug-war package from the United States to Colombia. Funds from the package are dedicated largely to strengthening the armed services, the main source of support for the paramilitaries throughout the 1980s and 1990s.[144] With the money earmarked for Plan Colombia, the administration of George W. Bush expanded the package's goal to defeating the insurgents. The Bush administration justified this component by calling it a method of fighting "narco-terrorism."[145] Since 2000, nearly $4.7 billion has been given to Colombia to fund the war on terror and drugs. Much of this money goes to bolster the Colombian military in its fight against the insurgents. However, with links between the military and the *paras* clearly established, it is inevitable that some of this money found its way into AUC hands. Foreign companies operating in Colombia also contributed to the funding of the paramilitaries. For example, Cincinnati-based Chiquita, the banana grower, admitted to paying illegal armed groups in Colombia for security purposes. U.S. court documents indicate that the Justice Department knew about the Chiquita-paramilitary link since April 2003, yet the banana growers continued payments for another ten months.[146]

The paramilitaries' political power was reflected in the 2005 Justice and Peace Law, passed by the Colombian government, which—after earlier failed attempts at demobilizing the paramilitaries—called once more for these groups to hand in their weapons. This agreement between the AUC and the government placed a statute of limitations on prosecuting individuals, required lighter sentences than courts had normally been imposing, and blocked extradition for those wanted by the United States. The Bush administration supported this law despite numerous extradition requests by the U.S. Justice Department that were pending and subsequently made void. This agreement left paramilitary drug traders immune, while FARC leaders continued to be extradited and charged in the United States on trafficking charges. The *paras'* immunity increased the militia's strength, heightening the level of competition between the *paras* and the FARC.

The FARC Changes Its Behavior toward Noncombatants

With the advent of the paramilitary forces and the added complexity they imposed on the conflict, the dynamic that had cast the FARC as protector of peasants was bound to change. During the late 1990s, the FARC began to change its tactics in dealing with the local populations, from contractual to increasingly coercive.

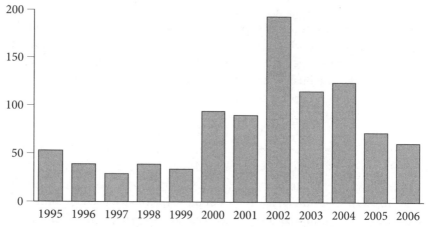

FIGURE 4.1.
Estimated Civilian Fatalities Perpetrated by the FARC

Source: Uppsala Conflict Data Program 2008.

Information in human-rights reports and data that I collected in the field outlines major changes that occurred in the FARC's treatment of noncombatants. In 2000, several human-rights groups reported that the FARC killed 496 civilians nationwide, employing methods that resulted in avoidable noncombatant casualties.[147] Witnesses reported that in March 1999, the FARC left a town in Antioquia in virtual ruin and were responsible for numerous civilian casualties there. According to witnesses, the FARC executed twenty-one police, several of whom had been seeking medical assistance at a local hospital.[148] Researchers at the Conflict Analysis Resource Center (CERAC) in Bogotá confirm that the FARC engaged in a wide variety of coercive activities that included the intimidation of civilians. In 2003 and 2004, the insurgents surpassed the paramilitaries in this behavior.[149] Figure 4.1 displays data collected on one-sided violence perpetrated by the FARC between 1994 and 2005. Although the numbers are estimates, and thus are quite low, the chart demonstrates the relative pattern of FARC behavior toward civilians.[150]

The FARC was responsible for repeated breaches of international humanitarian law as well, including killing and kidnapping civilians.[151] For example, in June 2004, the FARC killed thirty-four coca gatherers in the northern department of Santander.[152] The FARC dismissed such claims and argued that international humanitarian law was "a bourgeois concept," suggesting that it was not something the FARC had to obey.[153]

Not only did the FARC step up its coercive behavior toward local populations, but it did so indiscriminately and disproportionately. On September 19, 2004, four civilians were killed and seventeen injured, including ten children, when the FARC detonated a mine and opened fire on a civilian vehicle in the San Carlos municipality in Antioquia.[154] According to a human-rights lawyer, the paramilitaries and the FARC took turns committing massacres in a village located in the department of Sucre to "see who the better artist was."[155] The FARC, according to a farmer, traveled through villages and towns, burning and killing people, even without using guns.[156]

The FARC in its early years maintained considerable legitimacy and support among the peasant populations in which it operated, representing peasant interests as a political and military organization.[157] However, as the FARC gained power, it became caught in the dynamic of war.[158] It is this dynamic—namely, the presence of paramilitary forces and the subsequent threat to the FARC's resources and survival—that transformed the group's behavior toward local populations. Several individuals in the northern village of Chinulito told me that when the FARC entered the region in 1995, they were friendly and helpful to the people. Jorge, a peasant farmer in Chinulito, told me that the FARC soldiers were quite disciplined. Now, he continued, they just kill without asking questions.[159]

The FARC not only did an about-face in its treatment of those it claimed to represent, but it also changed its former juridical process in handling misconduct within its ranks. The FARC had formerly punished misconduct, particularly in interactions with civilians, but the insurgents apparently chose to stop enforcing this commitment. Jorge told me the FARC stopped investigating human-rights abuses perpetrated by its own soldiers against local civilians, something the insurgents had done in the past.[160] Furthermore, now the FARC reportedly does not allow independent judges or prosecutors to administer justice and has rigid control over the local media in the areas under its command.[161] FARC officials scrutinize the judges' actions and impose control in areas in which they operate through kidnappings and assassinations.[162]

In the past, members of the FARC denounced the forced recruitment of children for use in soldiering. According to Article 38 of the 1989 UN Convention on the Rights of the Child, it is a violation of human rights to recruit children less than fifteen years of age.[163] However, reports indicate that today the FARC forcibly recruits children. In 2000, the office of the Public Advocate reported sixteen cases of missing minors who had been forcibly recruited, killed, or forced to flee from their homes by the FARC.[164] The insurgents, as well as the paramilitaries, use children in urban areas as informants. For example, gang members in a particularly poor area of Cartagena called *La Popa* are paid by both the paramilitaries and the insurgents to be informants. The ages of these individuals range from fourteen to twenty-two years.[165] A 2006 news article claimed that children as young as eight years old continue to be recruited by the FARC.[166] Children, the article states, are occasionally forced to join the ranks of the insurgents, but some are attracted to the status of wearing a uniform and carrying a weapon. Female children suffer the most abuse, with over half reporting that they are raped or forced to have sexual relations with other soldiers, often commanders. Furthermore, like the conflicts in Sierra Leone and Liberia in western Africa, these children carry out violent acts, including killing, mutilation, and torture.[167] Nevertheless, the FARC has claimed that the children's actions are voluntary.

Carmen is dressed in long sleeves despite the intense Colombian heat. She tells the story of how, in years past, when the FARC—las guerrillas—moved into the area of Montes de Maria, villagers did not experience any trouble with them. "We would see the guerrillas, and they would not bother the people." Within the past decade, though, the FARC changed its treatment of local populations. As Carmen recounts, "In 2002 the guerrillas took my son, and since then I have not known what has become of him. . . . I know that they took him because the Red Cross told a chief that the guerrillas had him, and also some workers said that the guerrillas took him to use as a servant."[168]

When I ask Carmen to explain the FARC's radical change in behavior, she simply states that the FARC was not as violent before the paramilitaries arrived in the region.

The FARC's kidnapping patterns also changed after the *paras* become a significant rival. Whereas before the group targeted high-level Colombian officials, diplomats, and industrial specialists such as oil workers, it has become increasingly indiscriminate about whom it takes, as evidenced by the story at the beginning of this chapter.[169] The FARC has established a pattern of kidnapping civilians merely suspected of supporting the *paras*. According to Human Rights Watch, many of these abductions are not carried out purely for financial reasons, as evidenced by the fact that they are usually not revealed to the public and that there is usually not a ransom demand.[170]

Explaining the FARC's Transformation

What is behind the dramatic transformation in the FARC's treatment of noncombatants? Some observers suggest that the FARC's turn in behavior is due to the illicit industry in which it became involved. With the arrival of increased coca cultivation in the 1990s, much of it taxed by the insurgents, the department of Putumayo had become an important strategic and financial bulwark for the FARC.[171] This development suggests that the change in FARC practices was the result of the *type of industry* it invested in, which would support the resource-incentive thesis discussed in chapter 2. Indeed one local civilian told me that the insurgents became profit oriented, and individuals who joined during later years did so merely for money. Thus, the incentives to join the FARC today might mean that individual insurgents fight for material reasons rather than ideological ones. However, this account falls short in explaining why the FARC initially retained its contractual relationship with the people when it first became involved in the drug industry. Nor does it explain why other insurgent groups such as the SPLA, when faced with a windfall of resources from the international community after 1994, decreased its violent behavior toward local populations.

One feature that appears to support the resource-incentive thesis is that when the paramilitaries began offering more money to their soldiers, many of the individuals who had joined the FARC apparently for economic incentives defected to the *paras*.[172] According to the resource-incentive thesis, the FARC's coercive behavior reflected an effort to attract these opportunists, who, the hypothesis would have it, shaped the FARC's strategies.

Information from my research in the field and analysis of documents and other studies characterize the FARC as the most hierarchically organized group among the cases in this study. It would be unlikely that the entire group would change its tactics as a result of the economic aspirations of a few opportunists. Furthermore, these individuals left the FARC as soon as they could and joined the ranks of the AUC since the AUC offered so much more. Thus, we would expect to have seen a decline in the FARC's coercive behavior after these opportunists had left to join the AUC. Yet just the opposite happened.

Some writers claim that the FARC's behavior stems from its increasing desperation. Some researchers in Colombia maintain that "the increasing number of civilian injuries from bombs and mines reveals a progressively more indiscriminate, terrorizing FARC," behavior that reveals that the FARC is desperate.[173] Others claim it is a lack of communication with locals that caused this change in the FARC's behavior. The people have less communication with the FARC now, and so the people are not aware of their intentions. People do not want to be seen communicating with the insurgents for fear of retribution from the *paras,* and vice versa.[174] However, neither of these claims fully explains the insurgents' behavior toward noncombatants. The desperation hypothesis does not systematically explain the insurgent group's behavior, nor does it explain why the FARC is more desperate today than it was years ago when it had neither the manpower nor the resources to carry out its activities. The lack-of-communication hypothesis does not take into account the increase in technology in recent years and the improvements in communication that the insurgents have at their disposal, such as cell phones, satellite phones, and the Internet, technology that was not available at the FARC's inception and that if anything has increased the group's ability to communicate with local citizens. Furthermore, we would expect the FARC to have had more contact as time passed because they are in more regions of the country than they were at their inception.

The true answer lies in the fact that the FARC faced a major threat from the paramilitaries to its resource base and thus to its survival. The FARC's decision to adopt a more aggressive military strategy, particularly following the annihilation of the UP and its political ventures, forced on the FARC an immediate need for a higher level of resources than it had been receiving from taxing peasants. It thus had to find a means to overcome an effective counterinsurgency strategy on the part of the *paras* and therefore had to contend quite strongly for the support of local people. The violence enacted by the *paras* was effective at preventing supporters from acting on the basis of their loyalties and forced the FARC to find other ways of asserting political primacy in these areas. Hence, the FARC entered into the drug industry and—for a time—was able to maintain its contractual relationship with local civilian populations. The FARC continued to look after civilians, protecting them and their crops from drug traffickers and making sure they set aside agricultural lots for subsistence farming.

As stated earlier, the paramilitaries invoked fear in people who supported the FARC. As a consequence, the FARC sought resources through other channels. So the FARC did not change its behavior because of its participation in illicit activities—namely, the trafficking of narcotics—but rather the group was forced to compete with other armed groups in the area for resources vital to its existence. The FARC could not take advantage of a relative absence of state authority to set up a parallel political structure. The addition of the paramilitaries to the dynamic was the causal mechanism for the FARC's switch from contractual to coercive behavior.

Why, then, with the onset of a substantial rivalry for resources, did the FARC become highly coercive toward noncombatants? First, with rivals such as the paramilitaries, the FARC's thinking shifted to the short term; not only was it trying to achieve its military objectives, but with the *paras'* presence the issue of its very survival assumed new and highly uncertain levels, which moved survival to the forefront of its concerns. As I mentioned, it has been argued that this kind of desperation led to the FARC's violent behavior. The desperation theory dictates that a group will rationally decide to act violently if the alternatives are worse.[175] In the view of this theory, then, insurgent groups that are failing have little to lose, so they will behave violently even if the odds of success are low, because the prospects for failure are guaranteed with the status quo.[176] A desperate group will compare the certainty of failure with the slim chance that it will win or at least improve its situation through violence. Thus, insurgent groups will choose to initiate coercion against civilians if they have little chance of winning.

However, the desperation thesis is based on speculative assumptions about how insurgent groups see the world. In the case of the FARC, as mentioned in preceding pages, the group was actually growing in strength and had demonstrated so in several battles against the Colombian military. Because of that growth, the FARC needed to augment its resources on a much higher scale as quickly as possible. Peasants were no longer in a position to supply the group willingly (or at least without excessive coercion or fear of retribution from outsiders), and the fastest and most obvious way to acquire the needed resources—particularly if a group is only considering the short term—was to extract them by force. This explains why several civilians I interviewed described the FARC's more recent behavior as "indiscriminate." As one individual told me, the FARC was coercive when it lost the upper hand.[177]

Events that occurred in several villages in 2000 are an excellent example of the group's change in behavior. I interviewed approximately twenty individuals in villages in an area called Montes de Maria in October 2006. These farmers and their families were victims of numerous atrocities at the hands of both the *paras* and the FARC. At the time of the interview, people were slowly returning to the village because the violence in the area had decreased. Yet only the men—the heads of six families—had returned to farm the land full-time. The women and children remained in the nearest city, fearing the return of both the insurgents and the paramilitaries; the land mines laid down by both groups of armed actors were an additional reason to stay away from the village.[178] I asked one man, a farmer who had returned to the area with some of the other men, to talk about the FARC in earlier years and the group today. He said that the FARC had come into Montes de Maria in 1995. Then, the insurgents were disciplined and actually helped the villagers. They had a discourse that was characteristically helpful. After a time, he continued, the FARC stopped investigating human-rights abuses; it no longer bothered to find out who was on what side of the war; it just killed without asking questions. The change, he stated, was due to the presence of the paramilitaries.[179]

The presence of the *paras* made it necessary for the FARC to defend itself and its resources. The FARC, in the mid-1990s in Montes de Maria, was disciplined and investigated human-rights abuses. Things changed, however, when the paramilitaries arrived. The FARC and the *paras* fight, and the locals are caught in the middle.[180] A local priest stated that when the paramilitaries moved into the northern departments, one could distinguish between the different armed actors because they had different modes of operation. Now the various groups look more and more similar.[181]

The case of the FARC, however, points to a nuance in this theory of coercive behavior and the existence of rivals. If the presence of rivals is what instigates coercive behavior toward noncombatants, why did the FARC not become coercive with the presence of other groups such as the ELN and the M-19 in the 1960s and 1970s?

On first glance, this discrepancy appears to be strong evidence against my theory. But a closer look at the case study makes the reasons for this behavior become clearer. It appears that in this case, the differences and similarities between these various groups did not initiate active rivalry. The ELN, the M-19, and the FARC fought the same enemy—the Colombian state—and did not clash ideologically. Also, these three groups did not originate in the same regions of the country. The M-19 based itself in urban areas, whereas the ELN came from the northeast. The FARC first developed a base in Tolima. Thus, the FARC did not compete to control the political allegiances and resources of the same individuals or communities, and coercive behavior toward civilians was rare simply because there was no need for it.

It also appears that the three insurgent groups had an unwritten agreement to maintain boundaries, a fact that was very important in limiting intrainsurgent fighting and factional splits. In Aruaca, a region in the north of the country, local citizens claimed to have seen ELN cadres moving in and out of villages. As one local resident stated, the villagers were not bothered by the insurgents, and the group even organized water cooperatives.[182] In the 1990s, the FARC moved in, and though there were some minor conflicts, nothing happened that severely affected the local citizens. There appears, then, to have been at a minimum coordination and at a maximum cooperation between these groups preceding the 1990s, which begs the question, why would insurgent groups cooperate with one another? Although one can speculate that the "common enemy" notion helps explain cooperation, one could also argue that it is a shared ideology or similar organizational structures that contribute to cooperation among armed groups. This question necessitates further study.

From 1999 to 2000, the paramilitaries expanded into the region, and violence against civilians increased. Today, the FARC and the ELN engage in armed conflict with each other, which one local civilian claims had not been common.[183] In the past, if there was a problem between the groups, the insurgents worked it out and did not involve local residents.[184] It also is likely that this cooperation between groups contained intragroup factionalizing, as clearly delineated spheres would have decreased chances that adventurous commanders could call on rival groups to support them in their ambitions within a particular insurgency. Thus, one did not see the kinds of splintering associated with more coercive strategies toward local civilians, such as what appeared in the SPLA.

Although the main cause of the FARC's change in how it treated local civilians was the entry on the scene of the paramilitaries, the type of resources the FARC extracted also played a role. The drug industry is an illicit one; it is an environment with its own norms that is more prone to acts of violence than other types of resource extraction. So although it was not the group's involvement in the drug industry per se that affected its behavior, it did affect the type and strength of the other actors involved.

On the basis of the data I collected in the field and the analysis presented here, I separate the FARC's evolution into three periods, which are summarized in table 4.1. FARC1 begins with the group's formation in 1966. As evidenced by the empirical data, this was a time when the FARC had few rivals, in the sense that it alone extracted resources from the

TABLE 4.1
Measuring Rivalry, Illicit Resources, and Coercion throughout Three FARC Periods

Period	Presence of Rivals	Use of Illicit Resources	Coercive Behavior toward Civilians
FARC1: 1966–annihilation of UP	Low	Low	Low
FARC2: Late 1980s–formation of AUC	Low	High	Low
FARC3: Presence of AUC–today	High	High	High

peasants it represented. Although other movements such as the ELN and the M-19 operated in some of the same areas as the FARC at this time, particularly in the 1970s and 1980s, evidence points to low levels of coercion as a result of their interactions. Also at this time, the ELN and the M-19 obtained resources mainly from the local communities from which the FARC also drew support. Although the FARC was indeed an armed group, it did also address the politics of its goals, particularly while partnered with the PCC. FARC1 ended with the annihilation of the political party, the UP.

FARC2 began with the expansion of the FARC's military operations, which necessitated a large amount of resources. Thus, the FARC took advantage of the financial windfall that drug trafficking brought to many of the areas the group controlled. Even though use of illicit resources satisfied the FARC's needs, it maintained a contractual relationship with civilians because the *paras* were not yet a threat; the FARC's resource pool was not yet severely threatened. The large landowners and drug traffickers, however, were quickly becoming frustrated with the FARC's practices, and their hostility constituted a minor threat to its control over resources, one that, as this chapter relates, produced a major rival in the form of the *paras*.

One may speculate that there is a relationship between the type of resources and the onset of rivals. The illicit nature of drug trafficking is more likely than other types of resource extraction to create competition, due in part to the large amounts of money to be made. The competition created by the FARC, once it joined the trafficking industry, spurred a response from cartel owners and other Colombian elites that eventually took the form of the AUC. It was in turn *this* rivalry that pushed the FARC to adopt more coercive behavior. The FARC could no longer retain its contractual relationship with local civilians because access to its resources was being threatened. As a result, the FARC's time horizon shifted to the short term. In such circumstances, when an insurgent group has short-term time horizons and is under attack from rival groups, the most efficient and quickest way to obtain resources is by force. FARC2 was relatively short, and though marked by the absence of active rivalry, it ended with the onset of paramilitary forces.

The third period was (and has been) the most coercive point in the group's history. The paramilitaries, with support from the Colombian government, the drug cartels, and large landowners, continued increasing the number of active forces they had fielded and considerably augmented the number and technology of the arms at their disposal. This development created a rivalry between the FARC and the *paras* in which local resources were the prize and coercion was the means. Thus, the paramilitaries constituted a severe threat to the FARC's resource pool, whereas the other insurgent groups such as the ELN posed only minor threats. The money, arms, computers, cell phones, and other resources that the FARC obtained from its involvement in the drug industry brought it much support in its competition with the *paras*.

One could argue that in the case of the FARC, the real rival is not necessarily clear. The paramilitary groups were, in fact, connected to the Colombian government in various ways, as discussed in the preceding pages. Indeed, an argument could be made that the *paras* are in fact the way that the state in Colombia competes. Yet one could also argue that the *paras* were not necessarily an extension of the state: they were not under the thumb of the Colombian military, and to argue that they were would deprive these groups of the autonomy they had (and may still have). The paramilitaries committed atrocities (along with the FARC), and when these atrocities happened to work in the Colombian government's favor— when, for example, they were perpetrated against villages that supported the FARC—the state was content to look the other way. Along these same lines, it is also important to remember that rivals must compete over *something*. The paramilitaries were active rivals to the FARC because they were threatening their resources that came from the local communities and the drug-trafficking industry. To claim that the state was the real rival to the FARC would be akin to saying the state was involved in the narcotics industry, which in turn would place not only the Colombian government in a new and dishonorable light but also its supporters, namely, the U.S. government.

The Future of the FARC

Several events highlight the latest era of the FARC's history, including the end of the peace negotiations and the subsequent relinquishing of the *zona de despeje* by the administration of President Pastrana, which marked a new phase in the life of the FARC. In addition, attacks against civilians and the kidnapping of foreigners have decreased in recent years, largely attributable to President Alvaro Uribe's renewed military assault on the insurgents.[185]

Peace negotiations between the FARC and the government of Colombia under Pastrana came to an end when the FARC hijacked and kidnapped a Colombian senator from an aircraft in February 2002. This hijacking also spelled the end of the Pastrana administration. During Uribe's subsequent inauguration later that same year, the FARC launched a mortar attack on the Presidential Palace where President Uribe was being inaugurated. Following several kidnappings, including the abduction of American contractors, Uribe launched a large military operation into FARC-controlled territory. The operations were largely successful, as the FARC was forced to retreat and lost control of territory it had controlled for decades.

Part of Uribe's assault on the FARC included the mandate to capture key leaders of the insurgent group. In 2007, the Colombian government announced that two high-level commanders, Tomas Medina Caracas and Gustavo Rueda Diaz, had been killed. Medina Caracas had been considered by Colombian authorities to be the man in charge of the illegal drug trade for the FARC and the head of the Sixteenth Front of the group's Eastern Bloc.[186] Rueda Diaz had been commander of the FARC's Caribbean Bloc.[187]

Adding a twist to the FARC's history, the controversial president of Venezuela, Hugo Chavez, became involved in peace negotiations between the group and the government of Colombia in 2008. This development is interesting not because of the involvement of Chavez per se but because it has been widely acknowledged for some time that in the past Venezuela harbored some of the FARC's leadership. Venezuela and Ecuador were implicated in supporting the FARC in 2008 when, during an assault on the group, the Colombian military uncovered a laptop belonging to the insurgents.[188] These assaults, along with the release of several prisoners, most notably Ingrid Betancourt, a former Colombian presidential candidate, made 2008 a critical year in the weakening of the insurgent group.

Although the FARC has experienced high levels of desertions of late, the group continues to carry out attacks on the Colombian armed forces and police, as well as on civilians.[189] FARC rebels reportedly attacked a police station early in 2009, leaving several children and one woman dead.[190] In February 2009, according to Human Rights Watch, the FARC tortured and killed seventeen Awa Indians who the insurgents believed were assisting the government. This report was backed by several NGOs operating in Colombia.[191]

The assaults on the FARC's leadership and the death of the group's leader, Manuel Marulanda, in March 2008 have sparked speculation that the insurgent group is indeed weakening. If anything, the deaths and apprehensions of many of the group's top-level command have meant the loss of much of the FARC's original ideology. With its original objectives brushed to the side, the FARC may become more susceptible to its business objectives. That is, over time, the FARC could look less like an insurgency and more like an organized criminal group.

Like the case of the SPLA discussed in the preceding chapter, the FARC case supports the theory of active rivalry by demonstrating how and why an insurgent group changes its treatment of noncombatants from contractual to coercive. The analysis here reveals several key points. First, it highlights how the type of resource that insurgent groups need or want can vary over time. Specifically, when the FARC developed in the 1960s and 1970s, the resources it received were largely community based. When the FARC found its political avenues cut off, it expanded its military sector and found itself in need of additional resources. Thus, it began benefiting from the coca-growing and trafficking industry. This course of events further emphasizes the secondary role resources play in shaping insurgent strategies over time.

The FARC case, like the PKK case discussed in the next chapter, also demonstrates that some insurgent groups begin with a predisposition to pursue political and ideological goals but can be distracted away from that path. Moreover, the changing patterns of behavior in the FARC (as in the PKK) suggest that illicit-resource trafficking is not necessarily an obstacle to the development of contractual behavior. As shown in the following chapter, the PKK also chose to behave contractually and have more friendly relations with local civilians while exploiting illicit resources, participating in illicit economies such as drug and human trafficking. But the FARC was not able to maintain its contractual relationship with local residents while at the same time managing the threat from paramilitary forces. Thus, it was the presence of rivals that ended the FARC's contractual relationship with the peasant population.

Finally, the FARC case displays what at first appears to be an anomaly—the existence of several groups displaying contractual behavior while operating simultaneously in many of the same places. Specifically, the ELN, the M-19, and the FARC began during a similar period of time and operated throughout the country. Later, at times, these groups came into contact with one another, though they continued for the most part to maintain contractual relationships with local communities. This evidence suggests that some insurgent groups can, at a minimum, operate in the same geographical regions with other groups without exhibiting coercion toward local populations. At a maximum, these groups can actually cooperate with one another. The presence or absence of rivals—groups drawing from the same pool of resources—remains the determining factor of insurgent treatment of civilians. As the following chapter on the PKK demonstrates, rivals do not have to be other nonstate armed groups, and resources come in multiple forms.

5

Freedom Fighters or Terrorists?

The Ongoing Transformations of the PKK

The crisis consists precisely in the fact that the old is dying and the new cannot be born; in this interregnum a great variety of morbid symptoms appear.

—Antonio Gramsci, *Selections from the Prison Notebooks*

Dilan is a female member of the PKK. She is short and stout but a bundle of energy and movement. She tells me she is from Diyarbakir in southeastern Turkey and that she joined the Kurdish insurgents in 1995. She was trained in Greece and Syria and in 1997 was sent to northern Iraq—what she calls "south Kurdistan."

I ask her why she joined the PKK. She says she already had family members "in the mountains," indicating the mountains of northern Iraq and southern Turkey where the PKK hides. In high school, she was detained by the Turkish police and tortured. She lifts up part of her shirt to show me the scars. Dilan continues, saying she had sympathized with the PKK, in part because members of her family had joined the organization. She tells me she had a brother and sister who died while serving in the insurgent group and has two additional sisters who are still in the mountains.

Dilan is at ease discussing such things with me and makes every effort to explain the insurgents' position on the war. Absent is the violent nature that is rumored to characterize the PKK. Rather, I watch as PKK soldiers break bread and tend to communal duties in the camp.[1]

The convivial image of local cadres just described is at odds with the fractional and often violent images of the PKK portrayed in the media. Today, the PKK is perceived to be returning to its violent beginnings, when it attacked the very civilians it claimed to represent. The divergence between on-site situations as I experienced them and the characterization of the PKK's leadership under Abdullah Öcalan as violent terrorists illustrates the state of ambiguity that the PKK finds itself in today.[2] This uncertainty as to the PKK's future and the lack of unity with other pro-Kurdish groups in Turkey contribute toward its increasingly violent, coercive behavior. Tracing the PKK's origins and evolution sheds light on how this transformation occurred.

The PKK's formative years of the mid-1970s played out much like those of the SPLA, with soldiers frequently engaging in high levels of coercion as well as numerous recorded human-rights abuses amid serious factional rivalries. However, unlike the SPLA, the PKK has undergone more than one major change in its behavior toward civilians, and these changes continue. The transformations, from ultraviolent nationalist movement to democratic representative of Turkey's Kurdish population to a fractious organization, distinguish this group from the others I have discussed in this study. More so than in the cases of the SPLA and the FARC, the state involved in the PKK case, Turkey, has undergone a political transformation with regard to its use of coercion in its relationships with local communities. The PKK's behavior toward local communities has mirrored the changes in the state's treatment of noncombatants. This chapter highlights this relationship between state uses of coercion and insurgent-group behavior toward local communities. It also shows the unintended effects that reforming state policies can have on local communities; in particular, this study explains how the increasingly democratic nature of Turkish politics has provided incentives for PKK agents to respond by pursuing a more coercive policy.

The PKK case demonstrates that the state can be a direct active rival for resources. As we have already seen with the SPLA and the FARC, the explanation for the PKK's changes rests in the presence or absence of significant rivals—states, factions, and rival insurgencies—for resources. In the same vein, the PKK case shows how popular support can be an important resource for insurgent groups.

This chapter focuses first on the evolution of the PKK, beginning with a description of the environment from which the insurgent group sprang and highlighting the changes that the insurgents exhibited toward Turkish Kurds. Following that introduction is an examination of several indicators that point to a rupture in the unified veneer of the PKK; in recent years, these indicators point to the possibility that the leadership of the

PKK is factionalizing. These indicators include the fact that the brother of the PKK's leader left the insurgent group. This defection occurred at the same time that the PKK cadres were increasing their coercive behavior toward Kurdish civilians in Turkey, a policy the group tried to abandon during the 1990s. After a discussion of the PKK's finances and the level of resources the PKK has needed over its thirty-year existence, the chapter concludes with an analysis of the influence that the state can have on how insurgents treat civilians.

The "Mountain Turks"

As is the case with the SPLA and the FARC, social, economic, and political divisions within core bases of support have shaped the dynamics of the PKK. The group claims to represent ethnic Kurds in Turkey, most of whom occupy an area known to them as northern Kurdistan, which is officially southeastern Turkey. The estimated twenty million Kurds in the Middle East are among the world's largest ethnic minority group without a state. Their habitat spans at least four countries: Turkey, Iraq, Iran, and Syria (see map 5.1). This dispersion reflects the diversity of the Kurdish population: Kurds speak different languages and practice different religions. For example, Kurds in Turkey speak a dialect of Kurdish called Kurmanci, while those in northern Iraq speak Sorani. There also exist several Kurdish subdialects, including Gorani, Zazaki, Feyli, Kermanshahi, and Laki. Despite the fact that some scholars characterize the difference between Sorani and Kurmanci as similar to the difference between English and German, others argue that their subdialect status under one language represents the unity of the Kurds.[3] However, in my fieldwork I found that the two dialects enhanced the differences between Kurds more than it united them, which illustrates one of the many ways in which Kurdish populations today are more distinct than they are cohesive.

As a group, Kurds in Turkey are poorer and live in an environment of insecurity compared to other citizens of the country.[4] Over 65 percent of Turkey's Kurdish population lives in the predominantly agrarian eastern region, one of the poorest areas of the country.[5] Social and economic differences between this part of Turkey and the western areas dominated by ethnic Turks are glaring. During the 1990s, the western region's per-capita gross national product was US$2,000, compared to the eastern region's US$700. The western portion of the country's infant mortality rate was 43 per 1,000 live births, the eastern region's was 60; the west's illiteracy

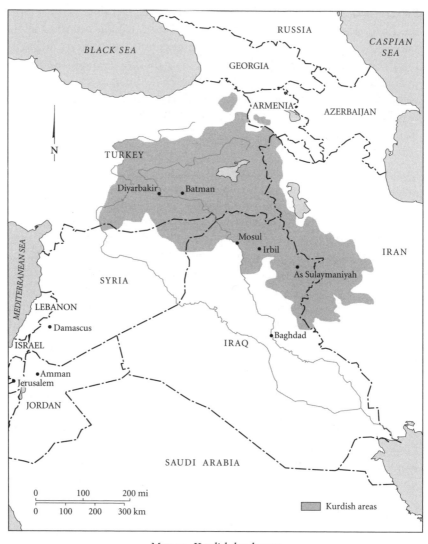

Map 5.1. Kurdish lands 1992
(Perry-Castaneda Library Map Collection, University of Texas Libraries)

rate was 14 percent, the east's was 26 percent; the western region's estimated number of health professionals per 1,000 people was 3.2, whereas in the east it was 2.[6] This environment is characterized by insecure access to land, income, education, health, possessions, and state resources.[7]

Kurds in Turkey also struggle over cultural autonomy: the use of their own language, schooling, and cultural discourse, which is in part related to the "Europeanization" and secularization of Turkey. For more than two decades, the Turkish government operated under a state of emergency in the eastern region; an estimated thirty-five thousand people were rounded up and killed between the early 1980s and the late 1990s; schools were closed in three thousand villages, leaving 1.5 million children without primary education; thousands of villages were evacuated, and millions of people were forced to leave the region.[8]

Unlike the SPLA and the FARC, the PKK is largely an ethnonationalist insurgent group. One might assume that such a group would be most unified and most willing to seek the support of local Kurdish populations. However, the PKK's claim to represent a specific segment of Turkey's population does not exempt it from the brutality that often characterizes other insurgent groups' relations with civilians. The PKK has been called "the most violent, radical, and successful Kurdish movement to emerge in Turkey in years."[9] Why would a group that at once needs the support and resources of its fellow ethnic minority members and the sympathies of the international community opt for a strategy of illicit terror toward these very civilians? Furthermore, why did the Turkish Kurds see a decrease in the level of PKK violence, only to undergo increased coercion once again?

The Development of Kurdish Nationalism

The Kurds—though a large ethnic bloc in the Middle East—developed nationalist tendencies much later than groups such as the Arabs, the Persians, and the Turks. Their delayed nationalist movement is the result of several factors. First, because the Kurds inhabit a mountainous region, they have been scattered and relatively isolated from one another. They also lacked a historically strong central governing structure such as those that developed in the plains of the Tigris and the Euphrates or in the Nile valley. Geography, then, and a nomadic way of life encouraged and strengthened the divergence of several different Kurdish dialects and cultures.[10]

Political divisions have also constrained the opportunity for the Kurds to develop a concentrated nationalist movement. The Ottoman and Persian Empires divided Kurdish populations for the past five hundred years, and then Turkey, Iran, Iraq, and Syria separated Kurds from political centralization for the past seventy years. Furthermore, Kurds lived in isolated regions of larger empires. The relative alienation from imperial centers slowed the Kurds' development as a strong, united people.[11]

The way that some political units legally grouped its citizens also contributed to the slow growth of Kurdish nationalism. Under the Ottoman Empire, the Kurds and other Muslims were a part of a larger Sunni Muslim center within this multiethnic empire. Although the Ottomans were cognizant of its minorities, it defined them in religious rather than ethnic terms. The Muslim core was made up of Turks, Arabs, and Kurds, and while their languages and cultures differed significantly, their religion did not, and all were recognized equally as Muslims.[12]

The nineteenth century brought new elements that induced a change in the relationship between the Ottoman administration and the Kurds. There was increasing imperial intervention in Kurdish regions, including the taxing of Kurds for troop support and war between the Ottomans and Russia and Iran, which touched Kurdish areas. Imperial intervention not only brought revolt within the Kurdish communities themselves, where challenges to the privileged Kurdish overlords developed, it also ushered in increasing challenges and outright rebellion against Turkish rule throughout the Ottoman Empire in general. Unrest in Kurdish regions was not uncommon, though at the time they were not nationalist in character. Rather, these revolts led to the consolidation of shaykhs and *tariqat* (religious order) leaders.[13]

During the late nineteenth century, the Ottoman state began differentiating between Kurds and non-Kurds. Among the first instances of this differentiation in Kurdish areas by the state in Istanbul was the 1891 creation of Kurdish regiments. These battalions were designed to maintain order in the eastern provinces as part of the Ottoman state's campaign against the Armenians. This attempt by the state to draw a distinction between Kurds and non-Kurds strengthened tribal links among them. Further sparking Kurdish identity was the development of the first Kurdish national newspaper, *Kurdistan,* published in 1898 by Kurdish exiles in Cairo.[14]

Although the Ottoman Empire faced challenges from Kurdish nationalism in the late nineteenth century and early twentieth centuries, it was the Turks themselves who helped bring about the empire's eventual downfall. Reform-minded pluralists challenging the old edifice of empire united with Turkish nationalists and secularists in what culminated in the Young Turk revolution of 1908. This revolution was a turning point in the country's history, as it marked the beginning of the end for the Ottoman Empire and reversed the sultan's decision of 1878 that resulted in the suspension of the parliament.[15] This revolution also sparked several contradictory tendencies. First, secularism and constitutionalism replaced the emphasis on Islam, which ignited an atmosphere of liberalism and encouraged many Kurdish intellectuals to look to Ottoman liberal movements and constitutional reform as a way to achieve more national rights. Kurdish political and cultural groups blossomed in places such as Istanbul but also in rural areas in the southeast. Second, while constitutionalism worked in favor of the more modern elements of the Kurdish elite, it led to an antiregime reaction among the leaders of the religious orders. Some of the shaykhs revolted. The Young Turk regime thus turned to pan-Turkism to assuage the domestic and international pressures and consolidate power. When the Ottoman Empire entered World War I, the Kurds in the end fought alongside its armies.[16]

The Kurdish issue is not merely an ethnic or economic one. Nor is it an issue of "separatist terror," as it is characterized by the Turkish state.[17] Turkey's "Kurdish question" has a long history.[18] The Allied Powers of World War I pushed the issue of Turkey's Kurds into the international arena in 1920, when the Treaty of Sevres was signed. The treaty's section 3, articles 62–64, called for the creation of an autonomous Kurdish region in southeastern Turkey that would eventually obtain independence. However, this treaty was superseded by another signed in 1923 when Allied Powers and Kemalist[19] Ankara signed the Treaty of Lausanne, rendering Sevres null and void. This move came in the wake of the Turkish counteroffensive against Greek invaders in Turkey's western region, reflecting the international community's recognition that the nationalist Turkish forces had the sovereign right to create their own national policy. Lausanne confirmed Turkey's annexation of what might have become Kurdistan. Although the treaty contained a clause that addressed the protection of minorities, this clause extended only to non-Muslim minorities; it made no mention of ethnic Kurds within Turkey's borders.[20]

In the wake of independence in 1923 and under the country's first president, Mustafa Kemal Atatürk, Turkey instituted a social-organization program highlighting Turkish nationalism (*milliyetçilik*), including a focus on the ethnic and cultural roots of the country's Muslim majority.

Atatürk developed a new state ideology that became known as *Kemalism,* a strict concept of the nation-state in conjunction with an extreme form of nationalism and rigid Turkish centralism. Underlying this concept of the Turkish nation, following the fall of the Ottoman Empire at the hands of the Allies during World War I, was an attempt to create a culturally homogeneous and unified state.[21] Thus, Turkish nationalism took shape in the face of a deeply entrenched fear of minorities, a characteristic not uncommon in newly formed ethnically heterogeneous states.[22] Under the principle of nationalism, the Turkish government strongly discouraged open demonstrations of Kurdish identity or of any other minority.[23] In 1924, for example, the government banned all schools, organizations, and publications that were Kurdish, along with religious fraternities. The first Turkish Assembly, which included seventy-two representatives from Kurdish areas, was dissolved as well.

The development of a civic sense of Kurdish nationalism was preempted by the 1925 Kurdish-led Shaykh Said Rebellion and the lengths to which Turkey went to repress it. Uprisings during the 1920s and 1930s led the government to restrict Kurdish rights further, and the notion of protecting the republic's territorial integrity through ethnic cohesion became preeminent.[24] One result was the government's ban on the use of the Kurdish language in 1924. To demonstrate how these policies were implemented, an official in the Socialist Party of Turkish Kurdistan (SPTK) related the following story concerning its attempt to publish a Kurdish-Turkish journal, *Roja Welat,* during the mid-1970s: "When our friends applied for permission they were told by the police, 'you cannot publish a Kurdish paper. If you do, we will cut your heads off. . . . You can publish in English, French, or even in Bengali or Vietnamese if you like. But not in Kurdish.'"[25] Citizens were forbidden to listen to Kurdish radio and TV programs broadcast from outside Turkey, sing in Kurdish, and sell Kurdish cassettes and records. Those who registered their child's name with the government had to use Turkish names.[26] In the ultimate denial of a separate identity, the Turkish government began referring to Kurds as "mountain Turks."[27]

When Atatürk died in 1938, the rule prohibiting official references to Kurds as a distinct community remained in force. Assimilation of linguistic minorities became official government policy.[28] Since that time, the Kurdish regions of Turkey—primarily the southeastern parts of Anatolia (see map 5.2)—have been under nearly continuous military or semimilitary control.[29]

Map 5.2. Turkey 2002 (Perry-Castañeda Library Map Collection, University of Texas Libraries)

The nature of Turkey's political system, especially in regard to Kurdish demands, encouraged the development of a Kurdish movement that was highly radical. During the 1960s and 1970s, Kurdish activists looked to radical movements elsewhere in Turkey in an effort to develop a common cause. Kurdish activism took several forms, some more radical than others. Many of their groups operated outside the state as well as within it, which explains the PKK's early links to Syria and to Kurdish cells in Europe.[30] During the summer of 1967, massive student demonstrations took place in nineteen Kurdish cities and towns, including one event with twenty-five thousand protesters in the southeastern city of Diyarbakir.

One set of activists formed an ethnic Kurdish organization called the Kurdistan Democratic Party of Turkey (KDPT). Part of the KDPT's political platform called for proportional representation of Kurds in Turkey's parliament, but it also included a more controversial element: demarcating "Kurdistan," with Kurdish as the official language and an exclusive government bureaucracy.[31] For the Turkish state, this move verged on secession. Kurdish activism also appeared in the form of Revolutionary Culture Centers of the East, organizations that taught Kurdish culture under the tutelage of Kurdish intellectuals in Ankara and Istanbul.

Sitting on a hill in the PKK camp in northern Iraq, I talk with one insurgent as we share a watermelon. Her nom de guerre is Media. She tells me about the origins of the insurgent group, what originally motivated the group, and why people joined.

The movement began with Abdullah Öcalan and other university students in Ankara, she explains. They realized there was a need for change within Kurdish society in relation to Turkey. Öcalan saw that other Kurdish organizations were mimicking the Turkish system. "They were not thinking independently," she says.

In the university, Öcalan and others organized students and studied other nationalist struggles. They realized that they had to find a structure that was most fitting for the Kurdish movement to organize around. They then spread the word around Turkey to other Kurds. Many people, she says, did not even know they were Kurdish.

At first, the movement that became the PKK was organized hierarchically, Media explains. This specific structure within the organization made all the decisions because, she explains, the thinking of the Kurdish people had not fully developed. People had been told for years that they were lazy and dirty, and so they looked to Öcalan and the other university students to tell them how to organize and what to do.[32]

The Formation of the PKK

The Kurds' attention to their own culture was a direct response to the policy of assimilation that the Turkish state was following. During the early 1960s, Kurdish children were sent to boarding schools in large villages where speaking Kurdish was prohibited.[33] Turkey's distress at increasing Kurdish nationalism grew when, in March 1970, the Kurdish Democratic Party (KDP) in Iraq came to an agreement of autonomy with the central Iraqi government in Baghdad. Kurdish repression in Turkey increased as the government outlawed Turkish leftist groups that focused more on Kurdish economic marginalization, including the Socialist Party of Kurdistan and a group known as Rizgari (Liberation).

A radical offshoot that sprang out of this proliferation of activist groups was the PKK. Founded by a group of university students in 1974 as the Ankara Democratic Patriotic Association of Higher Education, this group mixed nationalism with Marxist-Leninist ideology and called for a united Kurdistan. It saw itself as the "vanguard of the global socialist movement."[34] The PKK's main objective was to create a greater Kurdistan that combined all Kurds in all states into one nation by establishing a northern Kurdish state in southeastern Turkey. In 1977, several of the group's leaders met in Diyarbakir and produced a draft of the PKK program.[35] This program recognized two main objectives of the Kurdish revolution: to establish an independent Kurdish state and to eliminate the "feudal and comprador exploitation, tribalism, religious sectarianism and the slave-like dependence of women," which manifested itself in conflicts that pitted the PKK against armed militias of feudal landlords in the southeast.[36]

The PKK differed from other groups that developed during this period of radicalism. For example, it placed a great deal of emphasis on armed struggle and thus did not cooperate with other Kurdish groups, most of which were dedicated to nonviolent action.[37] The PKK acted on the premise that "all those not with us are against us." Hence, the PKK opposed all other Kurdish organizations and activists and railed against what it believed to be their minimalist goals.[38] The effect of such rivalry was further factionalizing among the Kurdish population and subsequent group rivalry. For example, in 1977, Haki Karaer—a founding member of the PKK—was killed in Gazientep by a PKK faction called Isterkasor (Red Star). The impact was such that the Gazientep branch broke away from the PKK and founded a separate group called Teko-sin. Further conflicts arose against other Kurdish groups such as the Devrimci Halkin Birligi (Revolutionary Unity of the People), the Kalkin Kurtulusu (Liberation of the People), and the Revolutionary Democratic Cultural Association (DDKD).[39] The factionalizing of Kurdish groups solidified the antagonism between the PKK and other Kurdish organizations.

Abdullah Öcalan quickly became a central figure in the group. The PKK depended on his leadership in many ways, and the group's ruthlessness reflected his attitude. The organization became known popularly as "Apocus," or "Followers of Apo," Öcalan's nickname—a word that also means "uncle" or, in Kurdish, "holy figure." Öcalan was a charismatic figure, "fast-talking and quick-thinking," and often given to exaggeration.[40] At one point he claimed to be the leader of twenty million Kurds in Turkey, though at the time many Kurds were opposed to his extremist views and preferred to place their support with more democratic Kurdish parties.[41] Like the SPLA's leader, John Garang, Öcalan was part of the urban intellectual elite. He was a student in Ankara, where the group that became the PKK took shape. This origin contributed to his inability to identify with most agrarian Kurds from other parts of the world.

Thus, the PKK formed in a similar manner as many radical groups in the 1960s and 1970s. Its leadership emerged out of small groups of university students and elite intellectuals, the self-appointed representatives of a broad population, though its members failed to include individuals from agrarian groups. This lack of inclusiveness was a problem that beset many insurgencies that arose during this era, and it presented a distinct challenge: how can a narrowly constructed leadership gain the allegiance and material support of a wider population? The SPLA found itself in the same dilemma, which led the group through significant discord and splintering and increased its coercive behavior. The FARC, on the other hand, initially was united with Colombian *campesinos,* and thus its logical policy was to enhance its contractual relations with local citizens from the start.

I ask Dilan to tell me about the structure of the PKK. The PKK, she says, is a Marxist-Leninist organization with a central command structure. The military structure, she says, is located in the mountains. This arm of the organization receives information from the leadership command above and tries to implement it from below. There was a hard and fast hierarchy in the military arm until 1997, she explains.[42]

The Evolution of the Political and Military Arms of the PKK

Following the Turkish military coup of 1980, the PKK retreated to Syria, where it founded a military wing for its organization, called the Kurdistan Popular Liberation Army (ARGK).[43] The armed insurgent units operated in small bands, using bases in Syria and northern Iraq to stage attacks inside Turkey. Yet the move to Syria not only encouraged military action but also spurred a political reaction within the PKK. Shortly after the move to Syria, the PKK held its first congress at the Lebanese-Syrian border. Meanwhile, the PKK expanded its contacts into Western Europe by forming links with Kurdish groups in exile there.[44]

The PKK held a second congress in 1982. As one outcome of this meeting, the PKK clarified its political strategy. It adopted a political program that identified three stages of the struggle, in explicitly Maoist fashion: (1) strategic defense, (2) balance of forces, and (3) strategic attack period. The first phase of the program involved armed propaganda activities, including attacks against state collaborators and the buildup to precede an armed movement. The second phase consisted of creating "liberated" zones, where the PKK based itself and communicated with the Turkish radical left in an effort to prepare armed forces for large-scale guerrilla war. The final stage of the political program called for a full-scale offensive and the abandonment of active defense, which in the end would lead to a full-scale popular uprising in southeastern Turkey.[45]

Despite the apparent consensus within the PKK regarding its politics, the congress and Öcalan, in particular, further alienated the PKK from other Kurdish groups. For example, he alienated several of the original members of the Central Committee, and one of his opponents was imprisoned, tortured, and coerced into signing an admission of immoral conduct and eventually executed by the insurgent group.[46] By purging the PKK of dissenters, Öcalan could consolidate power and embed his position of leadership within the organization.

Öcalan wanted more than just to make a name for himself and his organization among Kurdish circles inside Turkey. He also sought to increase his dominance of the PKK by involving Kurds outside Turkey. During the 1980s and under the direction of Öcalan, the PKK allied with

Massoud Barzani's Kurdish Democratic Party (KDP), which was operating in northern Iraq. The KDP, founded in 1946 by Mulla Mustafa Barzani, had over ten thousand *peshmergas,* or fighters. The alliance with Barzani, then, was advantageous for the PKK as it secured more soldiers to fight if needed. Under the agreement between the PKK and the KDP, the two groups committed to fight "imperialism" and to cooperate with various other revolutionary forces in the area in order to develop new alliances and strengthen forces.[47]

However, this alliance did not dissuade Öcalan from questioning the strength and support of members in his own group. He carried out several purges during this period in the PKK's history. Several of the individuals involved in these eliminations were tortured, forced to confess to being traitors, and eventually executed.[48] The PKK's violent tactics against Kurdish civilians, as well as against members of the KDP itself, led the KDP to sever its alliance with the PKK in 1987. For example, in addition to Kurdish attacks targeting village guards, the PKK has also targeted their families. Öcalan has stated that "the violence alternative may be difficult and painful, but it provides results."[49] In a statement dated May 1987, the KDP denounced the PKK, referring to its tactics as "terrorist operations" in the country and abroad. The KDP proclaimed that the mentality behind the PKK's actions to liquidate individuals was against humanity and democracy and out of line with the national liberation of Kurdistan.[50] Öcalan's response was to highlight the need for authority and control in the group, and he declared that there would be no concessions, citing the Communist Party of the Soviet Union as an example of centralization. "We believe that today in Kurdistan, the movement should be based on discipline . . . and central control."[51] The PKK's policy created further rivals for the PKK while at the same time cutting off resource options by alienating local residents.

The PKK responded to the pressure of popular interests by creating a Kurdish Parliament in Exile (KPE). Formed in 1995 in The Hague, the KPE claimed to be the authoritative representative of Kurds. This body became the first step in the creation of a national parliament. Its goal was to return from exile to Kurdistan and set up a Kurdish national parliament.[52] Although the KPE denied acting as an instrument of the PKK, most of the KPE members were sympathetic to the PKK and belonged to its armed wing. In fact, the PKK's political wing, the National Liberation Front of Kurdistan (ERNK), was reported also to be an important element of the KPE.[53] The KPE, along with the ERNK and the congresses it held, were arguably ineffective. Like the structures developed by the SPLA during its first few years of reform, the institutions the PKK developed were largely mouthpieces for its leadership. The PKK remained an authoritarian organization under the control of Öcalan. However, unlike the SPLA, the PKK did not have Western donors pressing it to adopt democratic reform, using money and resources as incentives. Whereas the SPLA evolved into a repository for development monies from countries such as the United States, the PKK lacked such large-donor support. In addition, Turkey, as an ally of the United States and one of the few democratic countries in the region, has had a special position in the Middle East, acting as a "democratic blockade" in the region. When the United States proclaimed the PKK a terrorist group, the insurgents were blackballed from official Western support. Thus, the PKK operated with limited means largely outside its homeland while facing significant internal and external rivals. The logical result of such a challenging environment was a high level of violence against civilians.[54]

Violence

Most of the academic studies of the PKK's earliest years refer to nontargeted coercion against local populations where the group operated. During the late 1980s and early 1990s, when Turkish Prime Minister Süleyman Demirel declared that the state was ready to begin a dialogue on the Kurdish issue and that Turkey recognized its "Kurdish reality," one source writes that the PKK feared being marginalized if a political process were to take place without its involvement. In response, the group launched a number of operations "to remind others that nothing could be accomplished without PKK participation."[55]

One of the PKK's strategies was to target village guards. The Turkish government established a village-guard force of some fifty thousand to fight the PKK after the group launched its armed campaign in the early 1980s.[56] The PKK often killed village guards and their families en masse, justifying such behavior as part of the class struggle that many radicals believed was embedded within the conflict.[57]

Arguably, the violence the PKK carried out against its own people was based on societal divisions. As one observer said, "Much of the PKK's violence was directed against the haves in the name of the have-nots."[58] Thus, for some Kurds, the PKK was a soldier for the disenfranchised.[59] But these societal divisions differed factually from what the PKK preferred them to be. Instead, some erstwhile supporters saw the PKK as an oppressive elite force, a reflection of the PKK's origins among university intellectuals. This feature of the conflict was a fairly common response among the people I interviewed in the field. In one such session in northern Iraq, a female PKK fighter who called herself "Sirin" told me that civilians who criticized the movement perceived PKK members as part of the elite. Sirin, who joined the movement in 1997, then substantiated this sentiment when she said that those who criticized the PKK were largely uneducated villagers.[60] Sirin's comments once again highlight the importance of the PKK's origins as a student organization and its dissociation from the rural population, much like the SPLA.

Whether or not the PKK defined its struggle in terms of class or secession, its real target was the Turkish state. This initial focus, defined as "revolutionary revenge," affected all levels of Kurdish society inside Turkey. The PKK therefore targeted civilians who accepted protection or benefits from the Turkish state as well as Kurds who worked with Turkish institutions.[61] In the group's own words, revolutionary revenge "defines almost everyone not supporting the PKK as a target for revenge."[62] Sahin Donmez, who later left the PKK and became an informer for the government of Turkey, explained that "the best method to spread Marxist-Leninist ideology was 'armed propaganda.'"[63] It is clear that the PKK—or its leaders—viewed violence as a prerequisite to achieving Kurdish aims. In an example of this perspective within the PKK, the group claimed that

> action [was] preferred over political reflection. . . . Violence . . . will in Kurdistan not only be the midwife assisting in the delivery [of a new society] but will create everything anew. Revolutionary violence has to play this role in Kurdistan, and it will, we say, assume the form of revolutionary revenge.[64]

Although gendarmerie posts and military convoys were often targets of this violence, the PKK became notorious for its treatment of civilians. Rape was not uncommon. During an attack in the city of Mardin, sixteen children and eight women were killed. This event was described as "the worst massacre ever committed by the Kurdish insurgents fighting an undeclared war against the Turkish Republic."[65] The PKK also kidnapped and killed Turkish teachers in the southeastern part of Turkey and burned hundreds of rural schools in order to show that the PKK could effectively challenge mainstream Turkish institutions. These acts against the education system also served to widen the cleavage between Kurds and Turks and in some cases won the support of the local Kurdish populations. This strategy assumed that "support" from the local population required that they be left with no other alternative.

The PKK's leaders realized that the real key to success lay in dominating the lives of local residents and controlling access to resources in its areas of operation. If the PKK could chase out the state, it would replace the state vis-à-vis the civilian population—providing them with protection and services—even while still using highly coercive means to force local people to side with them instead of Turkish institutions. In this respect, the PKK strategy looked much more like a racketeer's effort to sell protection. "State building" (or replacing the state with an insurgency that wants to create a new state) thus came to resemble the "state building as organized crime" famously described in Tilly's work, though in this instance the state builder had to convince local residents to reject what might have been a viable and less toxic alternative.[66]

Insurgent groups engage in tactics wherein they prod the state into retaliating against communities that officials perceive to be supporting insurgents. Such a move provides a propaganda victory for insurgents, who can point to such incidents as justifying their claim that the state is a threat to the people and that local citizens need insurgents to provide protection against state violence (which the insurgents' presence ultimately brings). This strategy thus uses the insurgents' coercion to leverage the reactive behavior of the much more powerful state.

This chain of events is precisely what occurred as Turkish security forces increased their repressive measures against Kurds within Turkish borders. The strategy employed by the Kurdish groups, like that of the FARC in its earliest years, was referred to as *foco*. The *foco* theory of revolution was advocated by Che Guevara and Régis Debray. According to this line of thought, rather than awaiting the conditions for revolution, popular forces could create them. The countryside, they argued, was the proper place for revolutionary activity.[67]

The aggressive strategy that the PKK used during its formative years is not unique to this particular insurgent group. For example, this type of tactic has been used in insurgent campaigns against the U.S. military in Iraq. Insurgents in Iraq benefit from heavy-handed action of soldiers against local civilians.[68] Using women and children as the objects of attacks helps to convince Iraqi citizens that U.S. and Iraqi forces cannot protect them. On a global scale, groups such as Al Qaeda can claim that U.S.

treatment of Iraqi civilians simply reveals the true nature of U.S. power, that the United States is anti-Muslim and therefore will not protect civilians or promote democracy. The important point here is that insurgents use coercion against civilians not only to intimidate locals into supporting the insurgent cause but also to create an environment that forces a powerful state to use its superior resources to implement its own coercive tactics.

Yet many Turkish Kurds began to resent the PKK's violent tactics, viewing them as "brutal, reckless, and irresponsible."[69] As an insurgent group, the PKK depended in part on the support of local populations for food and shelter.[70] However, the PKK often resorted to demanding food, shelter, and other resources from civilians in remote villages, where its coercive practices did not easily inspire automatic generosity by local Kurds. Refusal was met with the execution of the head man of the village or the murder of the families of these local leaders. At other times, peasants were taken prisoner, and young men were forced to join the PKK to boost the size of its armed forces.[71]

Despite the overwhelming number of reports of violence and brutality committed by the PKK, Turkish sources highlight that there were some instances when insurgents treated some Kurdish settlements with kindness. For example, because there were few doctors in isolated villages, the PKK might bring in a doctor to look after the villagers, at times providing them with free medicine.[72] However, such reports of noncoercive PKK behavior—at least during the 1980s—are few. Conscious, then, of the need for allies, the PKK called for *havakiri* (action unity) for all Turkey's Kurds. Pro-Kurdish groups such as Rizgari, however, rejected the offer on the basis of the overtly violent tactics that the PKK had used against civilians. Rizgari banded together with several other Kurdish organizations to create an alliance against the PKK.

Not surprisingly, the PKK's coercive strategy created divisions within the organization itself. Several individuals within the PKK denounced its attacks on civilians and subsequently defected.[73] Huseyim Yildirim, a Kurdish lawyer living in Sweden and the spokesman for the PKK in Europe for several years, wanted to create a less violent rival group to the PKK, one that did not target civilians.[74] Yildirim argued at one point that "after the party [was] relieved from Apo, the armed struggle [would] start again. But this time women and children [would] not be selected as targets."[75] Although splinter groups have broken from the PKK, Kurds claim that the PKK is still led by Öcalan, despite his imprisonment.[76] A young Kurd in Diyarbakir, a student active in the PKK cause, was adamant about this point, as were all the PKK fighters I interviewed in their camp in northern Iraq.

In 1997, Dilan tells me, the PKK began to change. When I ask her to describe the change, she says the group developed a better understanding of the world and the need for democracy within the organization. "We had an awareness of the outside," she says, and the inner dynamics of the PKK began to transform.

War, she says, made Kurdish people sensitive to issues such as human rights, and the PKK was sensitive to this concern as well. This change, she explains, had not been a surprise. Öcalan had stressed change in the organization following 1995. When I ask her why it was not carried out then, she says that "the reality of the region" made it difficult. But Öcalan, she says, was a key part of the change in the PKK. He began noticing the paradox in society. When I ask her to explain this last statement, she tells me that the Kurdish people were fighting oppression, but at the same time the situation of Kurdish women as secondary citizens in society was not addressed.

In response to the subjugation of Kurdish women, the PKK supported the formation of the Party of Free Women (PGA) in 2000. The philosophy of the group, Dilan explains, is to fight against male-dominated understandings of the world. "They want equality and freedom," she says.[77]

Change

The early years of the PKK coincided with intense Turkish repression and martial law following the military coup of 1980. The armed focus of the Kurdish struggle during the early 1980s (with the launch of PKK attacks from Syria and Iraq) provoked Turkish security forces to increase repressive measures against the Kurdish population in general. "It provided the army with an excuse to obtain the means for its modernization and, especially, to carry out the nationalist plan of 'dispersion and assimilation of the Kurds' through depopulation and devastation of Kurdistan."[78] This began a new period in the PKK's development, shaping its treatment of civilians and its unity and providing Turkey's Kurds with a new identity.

Unification under the PKK

Despite the overwhelmingly violent beginnings of the PKK, its foundation helped create an identity within Kurdish society.[79] The PKK's popularity among young Kurds grew despite the violence it provoked. At its
inception, the PKK consisted of no more than fifty poorly armed youth,
but it "rapidly attracted hundreds and then thousands of young Kurds,
who were convinced that the Turkish state would acknowledge the Kurdish national phenomenon only if forced to do so with weapons."[80] This
attitude demonstrates that some sectors of society, especially based on
age, do not reject the use of violence. Youth are important in this regard
because many are not yet concerned with supporting a family. As we have
seen, the PKK began as a student-led organization and quickly attracted
additional young Kurdish activists. Hypothetically, under other origins,
the internal composition of the insurgent group could have been different. A non-student-based PKK could have given rise to a leadership with
field experience, one that was not part of the original elite, educated core.
Such a different origin also might have shaped how the group appealed
for popular support, perhaps opting for a contractual rather than a coercive approach. The previous chapter demonstrates that Colombian insurgents had such origins and thus were able to respond directly to the needs
of local peasant farmers in Colombia, garnering support among the local
civilians in the process.

The unification under the PKK that occurred during the 1990s reflected popular revulsion against the state's repressive measures. Though
large numbers of Kurdish activists initially were content to compete for
political power within existing state institutions, the political and armed
activity of the Kurds, both violent and nonviolent, during the 1980s and
early 1990s posed a severe threat to Turkish nationalism. As a result, the
Turkish armed forces intensified their targeting and repression of Kurdish
organizations, including those that chose to follow a nonviolent approach
to resolving the Kurdish issue. Turkish armed forces decimated Kurdish
parties, forcing many of them to disband. "The repression of the 1980s,
both in numbers of persons seized and imprisoned and in the extent of
systematic torture, was far worse than before. . . . The regime thus cleared
the way for the PKK."[81] The state's arrest of several Kurdish parliamentarians in 1994, including activist Layla Zana, further heightened the sense
of injustice regarding the way the Turkish government treated minorities. This renewed repression also helped bring rival groups and potential

supporters into the PKK's camp. Zana was imprisoned for speaking Kurdish in the parliament after taking the parliamentary oath and for her political actions, which were considered subversive to Turkish unity.[82]

Kurds created their own political history, too, notwithstanding violence from both the PKK and Turkish state. During the early 1990s, numerous, more middle-of-the-road Kurdish political and social organizations emerged in public political discourse without attempting to hide from the government or the PKK by remaining underground. The October 1991 elections were the first time that a genuine Kurdish bloc participated. Several deputies elected on the Social Democratic ticket broke away from the party and joined the Halkin Emek Partisi (HEP), or People's Labor Party, an organization that formed in 1990. HEP consisted of a mix of radical and traditional activists and, as a group, was outspoken in its support of Kurdish political and cultural rights.[83] Although several HEP members had ties to the PKK, others sided with more-accommodating social democrats and nationalists.[84] Despite this ostensible balance in the politics of its members, the HEP created concern among Turkish officials, who feared that it was acting as a spokesman for the insurgents.[85] The HEP's founders were indicted for inciting separatist propaganda, and in July 1993 the Turkish courts outlawed the party.[86] It formally disbanded in 1994.[87]

In anticipation of repression, several HEP deputies resigned to form another Kurdish political party. This organization, called the Party of Democracy (DEP), had explicit ties to the PKK. The Turkish government dealt with the DEP by lifting the immunity from prosecution of those members elected to parliament and arresting and charging them with crimes against the state.[88] The DEP reemerged soon after as another political organization, called the People's Democracy Party (HADEP), which achieved political gains when it participated in the 1995 and 1999 national elections. Such political participation signified that a distinct Kurdish political "house" had been established within Turkey's political system.[89] Yet like the DEP, HADEP was banned by the state for allegedly assisting the PKK. In its place, the Democratic People's Party (DEHAP) appeared.

Once the political avenues of these Kurdish organizations had been blocked, many of them disbanded and gave their support to the PKK. Thus, several of the PKK's original rivals folded themselves into its wings, which paved the way for the development of a contractual relationship between insurgents and a wide popular base of Turkish Kurds. Initially, the PKK had fought armed militias serving large landlords in Kurdish areas of Turkey as well as splinter groups and Kurdish political parties.[90] However, as the state's coercion toward ethnic Kurds increased, the number of significant rivals among the Kurdish parties dwindled. This situation appeared to legitimate Öcalan's strategy of tight central control, making it seem as though the PKK's use of violence was proportional and appropriate as battle lines now divided Kurds from the Turkish state. This was a crucial turning point for the PKK and for the Kurdish people in Turkey.

A New Structure and "Openness"

The loss of significant rivals during the 1990s dovetailed with statements from Öcalan regarding a change in the PKK's original tactics in treating civilians. During the 1990s, while the PKK's rivals dissipated, he appeared to be moving away from the PKK's focus on ideology, which dominated early rhetoric, toward realism and balance.[91] According to the insurgent leader, the PKK now realized that the killing of innocent civilians was self-defeating.[92] During times of war, one insurgent soldier explained, there is a need for a hierarchy to be successful in fighting. When the war ended, she said, referring to cease-fires in 1993 and 1995, "we could see the harm of a hierarchy."[93] In an interview with a reporter from the independent Turkish newspaper *Milliyet*, Öcalan downplayed the PKK's earlier tactics, claiming that the civilian massacres for which the PKK was responsible had been an "organizational mistake."[94] The attack at the Sirnak Coal Mine in May 1989 is a clear example of how the PKK's relations with noncombatant Kurds had begun to change. Before the Turkish military had taken control of the region, the government allowed local communities to take coal from the mine at night. Once the military moved in, however, such nighttime activities were punished with beatings and the destruction of animals used to haul away fuel. The PKK struck when several villagers were at the mine. After delivering a propaganda speech, the insurgents destroyed several of the coal company's automobiles. None of the members of the local population was harmed.[95]

Further changes within the PKK manifested themselves in internal reforms.[96] Several PKK soldiers I interviewed said the group became increasingly open to internal criticism during the 1990s. Members of the formal leadership taught others to learn about the organization of the group. Vertical mobility into the higher ranks of the PKK became increasingly inclusive, with ordinary Kurds able to move up the ranks and join the leadership.[97] The aim was to make Kurds active in the decision-making. There were changes to the "structure" or "openness" in the organization.

FIGURE 5.1.
Estimated Civilian Fatalities Perpetrated by the PKK

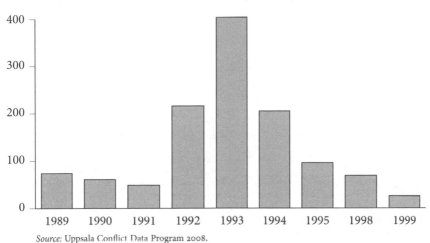

Source: Uppsala Conflict Data Program 2008.

The insurgent Media remarked that the PKK had made mistakes in the past. For example, the PKK did not educate people about health or culture—only about politics.[98] Many people in the past had lived according to what the PKK defined as feudal society. Women, for example, did not have the same status as men. According to Sirin, the PKK facilitated the development of a women's army, which was founded in 1994.[99] According to a PKK report, women have two roles in the organization. Some take part in military activities, while others work for the group's front organizations—organizations that help support the PKK's efforts.[100] "Everyone should have his or her own voice in the party," Media said. She went on to say that changes in the insurgent group were in part a response to the attention the PKK was receiving from outsiders.[101] Dilan told me that the PKK attained an awareness of the international environment and began looking at the world with a broader understanding.[102] Another woman, who called herself "Newroz" (which in Kurdish means "New Day"), said that the group was a place where females could "exist independently."[103] Newroz joined the group in 1991 and now serves as a congresswoman with the Kurdistan People's Congress (discussed later in this chapter).[104]

The PKK reached the zenith of its unity and popularity during the late 1990s, a time when it faced few significant rivals. Figure 5.1 illustrates the trend of one-sided violence perpetrated by the PKK against civilians in Turkey (Kurdish and Turkish) between 1989 and 1999. The statistics reflect the analysis presented here, namely, that the PKK's coercion peaked during the mid-1990s and tapered off by 1999.

Financing the PKK

The PKK has enjoyed a mixture of resources from local and international communities. As described earlier, coercion characterized the PKK's earliest method of collection: many of its resources in the 1980s came from looting local villages, and other sources of finance came from the overseas drug trade and money laundering. After the PKK adopted a more contractual approach in the 1990s, its fiscal support blended legitimate resources from local communities with the proceeds of illicit commerce.

Legitimate Sources

During the early 1990s, the PKK's political wing operating in Europe was basically a legitimate operation. Its public social, cultural, and political organizations existed in tandem with a parallel underground structure.[105] Within Western Europe, where much of the Turkish Kurdish diaspora settled, the PKK set up an organizational structure headed by a European Central Committee with headquarters in Cologne and Brussels, as well as national organizations in Germany, Belgium, France, the Netherlands, Britain, Switzerland, Italy, and the Scandinavian countries.[106] This structure facilitated the collection of funds through sales of publications, solicited contributions, and cultural events, which all went to support PKK activities.[107] The European arm was particularly active in raising money within immigrant communities in Germany. There, it amassed resources from the community through the collection of voluntary donations and "taxes" on individual salaries and business earnings.[108] Additionally, the PKK raised revenue from legitimate businesses that the PKK itself owned.[109]

The PKK also received nonmaterial support from countries in the region, such as safe-haven protection.[110] Syria, Greece, Iran, Russia, and Denmark all provided support in some form.[111] Denmark reportedly allowed Kurdish satellite-television stations such as ROJ-TV to operate in Denmark and broadcast into Turkey, in violation of Turkish broadcasting law. This station continues to operate. These media outlets were often linked to the PKK.[112] Furthermore, it has been argued that the Netherlands and Belgium supported the PKK by allowing PKK training camps to function in their respective territories. In November 1998, the Hanover police claimed that three children were trained by the PKK for insurgent warfare in camps in the Netherlands and Belgium.[113] Other support came in more reputable forms. The PKK also had ties, for example, with influential persons such as Danielle Mitterrand, the wife of the former French president.[114] Such direct ties to foreign dignitaries tended to augment the PKK's legitimacy.

However, many of the PKK's attempts at legal fund-raising outside Turkey were unsuccessful. Small-business owners in the diaspora had limited resources, and there was no large-scale ethnic Kurdish international business network on the scale of the Greek, Lebanese, or Chinese businesses that have historically provided resources for other insurgent groups.[115] Except for some isolated individuals, little progress was made in forming Kurdish corporations and large companies.[116] Thus, legitimate or legal sources of funding were limited.

Illicit Sources

Considerable financial support for the PKK has come from funds collected through money laundering, drug trafficking, arms smuggling, human trafficking, and extortion.[117] The U.S. Drug Enforcement Administration (DEA) reported that the PKK was (and possibly continues to be) involved in taxing drug shipments and protecting drug traffickers throughout southeastern Turkey.[118] Furthermore, organized crime is present among the Kurdish diaspora, facilitating extortion, drug-smuggling, and money-laundering activities to gather funds for the insurgents' procurement of weapons and ammunition. One report described the PKK as controlling the European drug cartel, smuggling narcotics from Southeast Asia and the Middle East into Europe.[119] These activities provided the PKK with extensive networks and ties to illicit resources.

After the 1980 coup in Turkey, many Turkish citizens, including members of the PKK, began immigrating to Europe, which gradually created a supply of human capital for the PKK to use on the continent. Historically, Turkey has been a key transshipment point for drug trafficking because its desirable geographic location connects Europe with Asia. In 1994, European narcotics specialists estimate that 60–70 percent of Europe's heroin passed through Istanbul. In addition, Tuncay Yilmaz, leader of the antinarcotics unit of the Turkish National Police in Ankara, maintains that the

PKK plays a dominant role in the country's narcotics-smuggling industry. Most of the heroin coming from Afghanistan, Iran, and Pakistan, for example, traverses Turkey on its way to Western Europe. Police in Italy, the Netherlands, Germany, and Scandinavia have investigated and uncovered the PKK's involvement in drug and arms smuggling in those nations since 1993.

Trends in police seizures of heroin and other drugs within Turkey illustrate the significance of the drug-trafficking problem. Heroin seizures in Turkey increased from 1,894 pounds in 1990 to 1.6 tons in 1994. Other areas of drug trafficking have been marked by similar gains. During 1993–1994, an average of 21 tons of hashish was seized annually, in addition to 2.7 tons of morphine. These figures are significant in light of the PKK's use of narcotics for supporting its campaign. These incidents tie the PKK to illegal drug trafficking and link it to drug trading as early as 1984 (the same year the PKK officially began attacks against Turkish forces). Not only is the PKK involved in transporting narcotics, but it has also extended its role into the production and marketing of drugs. The PKK has grown into a full-service business coordinating the production, use, and transportation of illegal drugs, particularly in Western Europe.[120] The amount of money generated from the PKK's involvement in such illegal activity amounts to hundreds of millions of U.S. dollars.[121]

Turkish officials are quick to connect drug smuggling to the PKK, though this theory is often disregarded by those who would prefer to rule out the possibility that the insurgent group is ideologically motivated rather than spurred on by profit. Some European intelligence officers blame Turkey for attempting to associate drug smuggling with the PKK to support a negative image of the group. Despite these hypotheses, however, evidence pointing to the connection between the PKK and illicit resources continues to surface. In February 2007, thirteen Turkish Kurds suspected of being PKK members were arrested on suspicion of money laundering in Paris.[122]

The Arrest of Öcalan and Its Aftermath

The PKK's popularity among Kurds and in the international community drew ire from the Turkish government. By the late 1990s, Turkish courts had issued seven arrest warrants for Öcalan, accused of forming an armed group to destroy the integrity of Turkey and of initiating terrorist activities that resulted in numerous deaths. After being expelled from longtime supporter Syria in 1998, Öcalan sought asylum unsuccessfully in several European countries. In February 1999, he traveled to Kenya, where the Greek ambassador agreed to house him. The next day, Kenyan officials escorted him to the Nairobi airport, where he was put on an aircraft back to Turkey and subsequently arrested by Turkish representatives.

In Turkey, Öcalan was incarcerated on the island of Imralı as the sole inmate of a high-security prison. The only communication he had (and continues to have) was through his lawyers. The Ankara State Security Court found Öcalan guilty of carrying out secessionist activities and sentenced him to death. This sentence was widely challenged by Kurdish and non-Kurdish communities alike, as well as by international organizations and several foreign governments.[123] PKK and political-party reactions to the sentence varied from demands for more violence against the Turkish state to an international campaign for Öcalan's release. In the meantime, the PKK declared it would continue its violence: "Without discrimination, every kind of violence is justified and legitimate. Every military or civilian institution, establishment, or personality that develops hostility against our people is a target for the Kurdish people."[124]

Elsewhere in Europe, Kurdish protesters demonstrated at the Greek and Kenyan embassies, in some instances taking diplomats hostage or setting themselves ablaze. In Geneva, thirty to forty protesters occupied portions of the main United Nations headquarters building, and in Zurich and Bern, demonstrators occupied Greek diplomatic buildings.[125] Switzerland warned that an execution could unleash a new wave of violence around the continent, and in Italy, the leader of the ruling coalition's largest party urged immediate action to be taken to save Öcalan. "We believe this death sentence delivered by the Turkish court against Öcalan is both absurd and very grave," said Walter Veltroni, chairman of Prime Minister Massimo D'Alema's Democrats of the Left party. Veltroni added that the sentence could seriously complicate Turkey's relationship with the rest of Europe. The British government also claimed it would lobby for the ruling to be overturned. It was thought that Turkey would commute the death sentence because it did not want to jeopardize its chances for membership in the European Union (EU).[126]

These protests took place in the context of several delays in Turkey's negotiations with the European Union over its eventual accession. To become a member of the European Union, Turkey would have to perform according to a variety of institutional and political standards. One of the demands was that Turkey extend cultural and political rights to its ethnic and linguistic minorities. In response to international pressure, the Turkish courts commuted Öcalan's death sentence to life imprisonment in 2002.[127]

This international outcry appears to have given the PKK incentive to continue its internal democratization. A locally responsive and popular insurgent movement seeming to campaign for "minority rights" would reap considerable political goodwill, which could translate into material support, as occurred with the SPLA and the surge in foreign support it received when it called the international community's attention to the rights of southern Sudanese. However, Kurds received a startling message from Öcalan in prison. From his cell, Öcalan proclaimed that the PKK would no longer strive to establish a separate Kurdish state. He ordered all members of the PKK to desist from violence and to engage in dialogue with Ankara on Kurdish issues. Many observers believed that this proclamation was a way to persuade Turkey to allow the PKK into the political arena.

The sudden change of heart by the PKK leader underscored a dilemma for the group. A wave of demonstrations by Kurdish communities in Turkey and around the world took place. Not only was there a feeling of betrayal among many Kurdish communities; there was also a general atmosphere of confusion among the PKK and its supporters. A bombing campaign by radical Kurds throughout the country lent further fuel to disorganization and rupture within the PKK.

Following Öcalan's capture and sentencing in 1999, the PKK once again went through a period of transformation.[128] Years of disunity and confusion within the PKK ensued. Arguably, this disorganization continues today. In early 2000, at a meeting of the PKK congress, members declared their support for Öcalan's initiative and maintained that the insurgent group would use only political means to achieve its objective of greater rights for Kurds in Turkey. In line with this new initiative, at the PKK's eighth party congress in 2002, the PKK changed its name to the Kurdistan Freedom and Democracy Congress (KADEK) and announced its commitment to nonviolent support of Kurdish rights. This group only lasted until 2003, when it changed its name once again to the Kurdistan People's Congress, or Kongra-Gel, a body meant to coordinate civil society.[129] In a show of the movement's continuing state of disunity and confusion, Kongra-Gel claimed to promote peaceful intentions, while at the same time it continued attacks in "self-defense" and refused to disarm. Although Kongra-Gel denied its connection to the PKK, Kurds and non-

Kurds alike knew better. The constant relabeling, more importantly, points to the internal disorder of the organization. Just as greater legitimacy for the SPLA came with its contractual behavior, the loss of legitimacy in the PKK was accompanied by its coercive behavior.

There are several people I speak to within the PKK camp who are not as positive about the "changes" in the PKK as some others are. Some even tell me that the insurgent organization has not really transformed much. Many of these people, though, speak frankly with me, seemingly without fear that there will be retribution for their criticism. One such person, for example, admits to me that there have been a lot of positive developments in Kurdish society because of the group, including the attempted transformation of the once feudal, male-dominated society. Women's rights have come a long way, she says. However, her tone is tempered by concern. She says that the PKK dominates Kurdish life, to some extent negatively. Speaking of the women's center in the camp, she says that some women do not want to go to the center because of the PKK domination. Many people want to speak up about the overpowering presence of the insurgent organization, she continues, but they are afraid of going against the group. The PKK, she says, is not really changing. Furthermore, she comments, Öcalan and others in the leadership do not think Kongra-Gel is accomplishing enough.[130]

Öcalan's capture and sentencing and his subsequent orders from prison led to a loss of authority among some Kurds. The events of 1999 not only psychologically disarmed Kurds but also led to the dismantling of institutions developed by the PKK. Öcalan continued to lead the group strategically—rather than merely ideologically or philosophically—from prison, an act that further weakened his legitimacy for many Kurds, because his presence in a high-security prison impaired his ability to judge appropriate tactics on a daily basis. He communicated through his lawyers, and his decisions were therefore often highly impractical. That Öcalan continued to lead in this way demonstrates how much the PKK, its daily operation, and more importantly its survival had come to depend on him.[131]

Turkey and the European Union

The Turkish government needed to show progress in democratizing after the late 1990s in order to convince European governments to allow Turkey to join the European Union. Turkey's candidacy for EU membership jump-started a spate of state reforms, many targeting the Kurdish community. For example, the government lifted the ban on publishing Kurdish-language books and broadcasting in Kurdish.[132] These reforms spurred a decline in the PKK's legitimacy. That is to say, the state facilitated a decline in support for the PKK. The EU reform process weakened Öcalan's position in the insurgency as the Kurds' sole protector.[133] These developments demonstrate how the creation of new political spaces can threaten insurgent groups' survival and—at least in the short run—lead to insurgent violence against civilians.

It also became apparent that the Turkish government had used the capture of Öcalan and political liberalization to divide the PKK. The situation created a serious dilemma for PKK members still at liberty. There were few practical choices open to them. The remaining leaders could adapt to the expansion of political opportunities that were occurring throughout Turkey, but in doing so they would have to compete with other groups for political power and risk losing the PKK's position as the main representative of ethnic Kurds in the country. In another option, the PKK could revert to the earlier strategy of trying to provoke retaliation from Turkish security forces. The solution, a Kurdish activist suggested, would be for Turkey's Kurds to distance themselves from the PKK and Kongra-Gel and their "narrow left-wing beliefs" and instead "take the middle road."[134]

Tears in the Fabric

This section explores recent internal divisions and increasing disunity within the PKK, as well as an increase in rivals, both violent and nonviolent, outside the organization.

Splintering Within

Since Öcalan's arrest in 1999, several events highlight the existence and importance of internal divisions within the PKK and demonstrate that the PKK is not as unified as it once was.[135] This development leaves scholars and analysts wondering if the PKK is also returning to its original, more coercive behavior. In 2004, rumors circulated that a split in the PKK leadership occurred and culminated in the expulsion of three veteran soldiers, including Osman Öcalan, Abdullah's brother. The chairman of the PKK, Zubeyir Aydar, shrugged off the possibility of an internal power struggle, though others within the PKK claimed it was a grave concern.

"The party has reached a critical juncture," one source within the PKK claimed. Younger members wanted change. The resignations of some of the younger members were a victory for older leaders unwilling to give up power.[136]

In July 2004, Osman Öcalan left the PKK and formed the Partiya Welatpareza Demokratik (PWD; Democratic Peace Initiative), which maintained that it wanted to work in peaceful ways for Kurdish rights and the broadening of political participation for Kurds throughout Turkey.[137] Another group of former PKK members told *KurdishMedia.com* that it had no option but to leave the parent body. "After Mr. Osman Öcalan and the others left the organization, we [tried] to democratize the organization from within in keeping with international democratic norms. Unfortunately, our efforts and the patience we expanded were in vain." This source went on to explain that the PKK was not changing in conformity with its stated goals (i.e., that Kongra-Gel would be a democratic institution and work with other Kurdish organizations). Instead, left-wing individuals, he claimed, were taking control of the group.[138]

These disagreements within the PKK resulted in its division into three groups: The largest group included Kongra-Gel's president, Zubeyir Aydar. The second-largest group included Osman Öcalan. The third group continued to support Abdullah Öcalan. This factionalizing coincided with the discovery of the body of a former PKK member near a camp in northern Iraq. Iraqi police intercepted an order near the scene of the crime; it was from Abdullah Öcalan and directed a squad to "liquidate breakaway dissidents."[139]

Several other events contributed to the splintering of the PKK, not the least of which was the capture and conviction of Öcalan and his subsequent statements that aligned with Turkish policy. The U.S. intervention in Iraq also created unprecedented opportunities in northern Iraq, where the population is overwhelmingly Kurdish. These opportunities include the formation of a federal Kurdish state, which is both a landmark for Kurds in Iraq and a positive sign for Kurds in surrounding countries. Kurds outside Iraq saw a possible Kurdistan in Iraq as a common gain for the movement for Kurdish liberation and an encouraging step toward a universal solution of the Kurdish issue.[140]

However, real progress in the Turkish political arena and the appearance of a federal southern Kurdistan posed a threat to the jailed PKK leader. Sirac Bilgin, the former spokesperson for the PKK, explained in a letter to the Kurdish people that the divisions within the PKK were also responses to events in northern Iraq. In his 2004 letter, Bilgin, who had recently left the PKK over a disagreement with PKK leadership, said Öcalan and the PKK, as well as its affiliated institutions such as Kongra-Gel, would try to sabotage independence at the federal stage, claiming that such a structure in southern Kurdistan would lead to more and longer wars in the Middle East. Several of the recent PKK dissidents publicly criticized this stance because it went against the goal of an eventual Kurdish state.[141]

As Bilgin explained, the splinter group led by Osman Öcalan wanted to create a nonviolent political arena in which to address Kurdish issues. This move posed a threat to Abdullah Öcalan because, under such circumstances, he would lose the role he played in maintaining relations with the Turkish state. Abdullah Öcalan continued to lead the PKK from prison while simultaneously attempting to acquiesce to the positions of the Turkish government. As stated earlier, he declared that the PKK's original objective would be amended. Since this change suited the aims of the government of Turkey, during the period in which Öcalan found his position as figurehead for the Kurds threatened (for example by his brother's attempt to intervene in the activities of the PKK both in its bases in northern Iraq and in its activities in Europe), the Turkish government worked in many ways that helped the jailed leader. According to Bilgin, "the Turkish state provided every kind of opportunity in order to make Abdullah Öcalan's speeches to be communicated without any restrictions."[142] Öcalan was able to broadcast his position against Kurds who supported federalism in southern Kurdistan.

> If a federal Kurdish State is set up first in Iraq and then in Turkey, we will see Turkey being swallowed up by bloody fighting. Turkey will not accept this. . . . We will not be the slaves or the sacrificial lambs of nationalism. . . . Jalal Talabani [founder of the Patriotic Union of Kurdistan and president of Iraq] has mobilized these [fake Kurdish nationalists] against Turkey. He has a plan; after a Kurdish federation in Iraq is established, he will come to Turkey to set up a new Kurdish federation there. . . . I have been struggling against [Kurdish] nationalism since 1992. The Turkish state has recently started to understand this.[143]

This statement from Öcalan to Turkey's Kurds revealed the environment of mutual reinforcement he and the Turkish government had established. Turkish officials discovered that the recent factionalizing of the PKK would cause them to lose control of Kurdish communities.

The person they could control was the one they had isolated in an island prison. Thus, Turkish officials helped Öcalan in order to rein in the political activities of other pro-Kurdish organizations that had arisen.

The question of why Öcalan denounced Kurdish independence remains. Why was he not in favor of Kurdish federalism in Iraq? Öcalan did not want to lose his grip on power in the PKK. From prison, Öcalan had few options, and he effectively demoralized PKK insurgents, rendering the PKK irrelevant to many Kurds in Turkey.[144] Like many leaders who find their position of power threatened, Öcalan attempted to manipulate security concerns to solidify his position within the PKK and garner popular support from Kurds. By speaking out against other Kurdish groups, he tried to entice people to unite with the PKK, in order to further legitimate his continued role as leader of the Kurdish insurgency.

As the PKK became increasingly irrelevant to local Kurds, who found that they could participate more effectively in political life, the group increased its coercion against Kurdish civilians. It is the fear of irrelevance that gives the PKK a strategic interest in promoting an environment of insecurity, and the PKK promotes this insecurity by using ethnicity as a tool. "Ethnic entrepreneurs then attempt to interpret events and the environment of insecurity to their constituents in ethnic terms, blaming the situation on 'Turkish suppression and disregard of Kurds.' Anti-Kurdish hardliners in Turkey feel that a climate of fear and denial of a 'Kurdish reality' will 'keep more people in line.'"[145] The PKK, it appears, operated on the belief that such a climate would ethnically politicize more Kurds and move them to align with the opposition. This environment of insecurity then promotes radicalization, engendering increased insecurity as Turkey responds with more repression.

This supposition supports one of the theories discussed in this study, that the nature and capabilities of the state are critical for shaping insurgent responses to local communities. If options for Kurds to operate from within the Turkish political system are continually suppressed, more of them are likely to pursue extrasystem strategies.[146] Indeed, this idea appears to be what the PKK had in mind in June 2004, when it ended its cease-fire. By the time the PKK announced another cease-fire in 2006, it was too late, and the call for an end to hostilities was rejected by Recep Tayyip Erdogan, Turkey's head of state.

These events illustrate the democratic strategies the PKK pursued vis-à-vis civilians when its leadership was confident that it had the support of the Kurdish community in Turkey—when it did not have significant rivals for such resources, which allowed the PKK to control the course of political developments.

Yet it seems that PKK violence against Kurdish civilians has not risen as dramatically as may be expected when insurgents face a loss of resources. The group's illicit resources may be a factor here, as the democratic opening within the PKK was occurring at the same time as the group was relying on overseas illicit commerce. Generally, such rent seeking provides incentives for insurgents to ignore local political demands. It also may be the reason why the insurgent group was not violent: its illicit sources of revenue had not been threatened.

New Groups, New Rivals?

The development of splinter groups has not been the only cause of the recent crisis within the PKK. The PKK faces rival hardliners in Turkey as well. In August 2004, several weeks after calling off a five-year unilateral cease-fire with the Turkish government, the Kurdistan Freedom Falcons (TAK) once again materialized in public notoriety, claiming responsibility for bombing two hotels in Istanbul.[147] The same group claimed responsibility for at least twenty attacks, including several in the main Kurdish city of Diyarbakir.[148] Nihat Ali Ozcan, a terrorism expert based in Ankara, maintained that TAK and other emerging armed Kurdish groups were products of a loose hierarchy within the PKK and were attempting to demonstrate that the organization continued to thrive. "They kept silent for almost a year to achieve legitimacy during Turkey's EU bid, but now they need these attacks to keep the troubled organization intact," he said.[149] In a similar vein, the Turkish government claims that TAK is a cover for PKK attacks on civilian targets.[150] The PKK, however, continually denies any affiliation with the group.

Another group dating back to the nascent days of the PKK resurfaced and joined the conflict's dynamic. The Turkish Revenge Brigade (TIT), a Turkish ultranationalist terrorist group, gained notoriety during the political clashes between left- and right-wing groups in Turkey and Kurdistan during the 1970s. TIT is believed to be responsible for over one thousand deaths during this period. Following the military coup of 1980, the group scattered, and most of its members were arrested during the first sweep by the new military command. The members were later released and integrated with the Turkish military intelligence agency, assisting with underground operations against Kurdish political and cultural figures during the Kurdish insurgency in the mid-1980s and throughout the 1990s. After maintaining a low profile, TIT is now believed to be one of many subsections of the gang collectively known as "Atabeyler." This gang's existence, which is allegedly acknowledged in the halls of government in Ankara, was unearthed by the Turkish political party known as Adalet ve Kalkınma Partisi (AKP), or Justice and Development Party, after an attack on the Turkish Council of State in May 2006, when a Turkish judge was killed and four other judges were wounded.[151]

A group that adds to the mass of pro-Kurdish-oriented organizations in Turkey is the DTP.[152] In October 2004, Leyla Zana and several former Kurdish parliament members announced the creation of a new political party. The DTP focuses on peacefully resolving the conflict between Kurds and Turkey, much like several Kurdish political parties attempted to do in the 1970s and early 1980s before they disbanded. "We former MPs . . . want to serve democracy and peace," Zana said.[153] The party claims to support Turkey's EU membership process while working for increased cultural and political rights for Kurds. As mentioned earlier, other Kurdish parties, including DEHAP, have joined this organization, a move the PKK may view as a threat to its resource base.[154]

Like the SPLA and the FARC cases, I divide the history of the PKK into three distinct periods: PKK1, from 1978 to the late 1980s; PKK2, from the early 1990s to 1999 and the arrest and sentencing of Öcalan; and PKK3, from the immediate aftermath of Öcalan's sentencing to the present (see table 5.1). PKK1 begins with the formal institutionalization of the PKK to the late 1980s, when the PKK had clearly changed its tactics. This era is characterized by vicious rivalry among Turkish Kurds. As some observers have noted, one of the weapons in the hands of the Turkish government during the PKK's nascent years was the rivalry between the PKK and other Kurdish groups. "The ruthlessness with which the PKK operated, their policy of revenge killings, not only against those who opposed them but also against those who merely failed to help, did much to alienate the local people."[155]

The second period, PKK2, began in the early 1990s. Because of increasing government repression of Turkish Kurds, Kurdish political parties disbanded, and many, as a final decision, aligned themselves with the PKK. Several Kurdish parliamentarians were jailed. These developments heightened interest in the Kurdish cause both inside and outside Turkey. During this time, the leaders declared that PKK tactics of the past were

TABLE 5.1
Measuring Rivalry, Illicit Resources, and Coercion throughout Three PKK Periods

Period	Presence of Rivals	Use of Illicit Resources	Coercive Behavior toward Civilians
PKK1: 1978–late 1980s	High	High	High
PKK2: early 1990s–1999	Low	High	Low
PKK3: 2000–present	Medium	High	Medium

misguided, and the PKK decreased its targeting of civilians and underwent a number of behavioral and institutional changes. One of the major contributors to this transformation was the dissipation of the group's rivals. As the state stepped up its repression of Kurdish groups, both violent and nonviolent, the PKK gained increasing support and became unified under Öcalan. Because the PKK had few serious rivals during this time, it also had more local support. These events follow Olson's state-building logic, in which groups ruling an area will extract resources more efficiently from local populations with increasingly contractual behavior—by providing goods and services in return for resources. However, the PKK also continued to obtain resources from illicit commerce, most likely because the profit made from such activities as money laundering and drug trafficking could not be discounted. This period ended with the capture and imprisonment of Öcalan.

The final period, PKK3, began in 2000. As described in the preceding pages, the hallmark of this period was the PKK's splintering. Several leaders broke away to start new groups and openly denounced Öcalan as he continued to lead the PKK from his prison cell. Further, internal conflict broke out concerning the status of Kurds in northern Iraq. The most significant developments affecting the presence of rivals in PKK3 are the reforms enacted by the Turkish government. As the country began making motions to join the European Union, the Turkish state enacted democratic reforms that focused on the Kurdish issue. Thus, the state, which had formerly been the sole oppressor of Turkish Kurds, began acting (to a very limited degree) as the protector of the Kurds. Turkey therefore became a rival to the PKK, pulling away popular support for the insurgent group. In confirmation of this understanding of events, several Kurdish civilians I interviewed in Diyarbakir noted that they (and leaders of civil society) are now trying to distance themselves from the PKK.[156]

The End of a Struggle or a New Beginning?

In many ways, the PKK's most recent years mirror those of the FARC: the group has experienced renewed direct assaults by the state it opposes and has adopted an air of uncertainty regarding its future as a cohesive entity.

In late 2007, the Turkish military, using U.S. intelligence, began an offensive against the PKK, targeting the group's bases in the Qandil Mountains of northern Iraq. The PKK uses these bases for cross-border attacks from Iraq into Turkey. Although the initial assault was limited, Turkey continued its air strikes against PKK camps in northern Iraq into late 2008 and early 2009.[157] Adding to the PKK's problems, Iraqi Kurdish forces are now working with Turkey to drive the PKK out of this region.[158]

Despite these blows to the PKK, the insurgents have not signaled any end to hostilities against Turkey. In fact, the group has supported the development of an Iranian military wing. In 2004, the PKK helped found an Iranian Kurdish group known as the Party for a Free Life in Kurdistan (PJAK). The PKK reportedly urged the growth of an armed sect of this group known as the East Kurdistan Defense Forces.[159] In February 2009, the U.S. Treasury Department classified this group as a terrorist organization, subsequently freezing all of PJAK's potential assets located in the United States. According to the Treasury Department, PKK leaders created PJAK as a splinter group and portrayed it as independent from the PKK. However, the ties between the groups are quite strong. The PKK formally institutionalized the Iranian group and selected five top PKK members to serve as PJAK leaders. PKK leaders also chose the members of PJAK's forty-person central committee.[160] Analysts see the U.S. action against PJAK's assets as a gesture of goodwill to the Iranian government, which has been fighting PJAK in Iranian territory and shelling the group's positions in northern Iraq. One assessment of the PKK's involvement in Iran is that the PKK is becoming more desperate and increasingly volatile.

Like the SPLA, the PKK experienced intense rivalry during its nascent years. In fact, there was rivalry both from outside the PKK and within it. During the second party congress, held in 1982 in Syria, differences of opinion surfaced for the first time. Some of the militants, who had established and worked for the survival of the PKK, left the organization. Some of these dissenters reportedly were murdered or arrested by the PKK leadership.[161] However, once Turkey stepped up its repression of Kurds (partially as a response to the revolutionary activity of which the PKK was a part), the number of significant rivals decreased, and the PKK's behavior toward Kurdish civilians became contractual. During the 1990s, throughout several cease-fires and despite continual state repression, the group remained contractual. Much like the FARC did in its early years, the PKK leadership began to splinter and hardliners emerged, and following 1999, the group began to show signs of returning to its original practice of mistreating civilians.

The PKK has exhibited coercive behavior toward Kurds while simultaneously promoting a Kurdish political agenda. During the early 1990s, it began providing public goods and statelike services such as policing, as well as a sense of identity, to fellow Turkish Kurds marginalized within the Turkish state.[162] Again, this behavior mirrors the first decade of the FARC's history. Yet following the capture of Öcalan, evidence suggests that internal disharmony arose. Internal power struggles sparked factionalizing in the PKK, increasing the chances that significant rivals would emerge. Meanwhile, cultural reforms by the Turkish state granted Kurds in Turkey freedoms previously prohibited. All these developments would suggest increasing coercion on the part of the PKK. However, the group's continued access to illicit resources means that it is still able to guarantee its survival and continue its political agenda. As a result, coercion against civilians has not increased in recent years as dramatically as one would expect. This circumstance highlights the notion that when insurgents rely on a diverse array of resources, there is less chance for them to become coercive toward civilians. I do not mean to imply that these groups are apolitical and concerned merely with acquiring resources. Resources do, however, play a key role in insurgent groups' survival; and as the active-rivalry theory suggests, when the lifeline to survival is threatened, the most efficient and effective way to acquire resources is through coercion. But if an insurgent group has control over different types of resources, it may be less likely to experience a threat to its survival when one type of resource is interrupted.

The Turkish state also played an important role in determining the behavior of the PKK. During the PKK's early history, it fought a coercive Turkish state. It used these conditions in a successful appeal to local Kurdish communities whom the state repressed. When a state is perceived as more coercive than an insurgent group, the insurgent group is likely to fill the gap in providing services to local communities, as occurred in the case of the SPLA. This filling of the gap is even more likely to occur when the state is corrupt and cannot control predations of its own agents or when it adopts a counterinsurgency strategy that punishes local communities for insurgent presence, as occurred in Kurdish communities. This environment makes it easier in a sense for insurgent groups to be providers of security, even if they are not extremely effective at doing so.

However, once a state begins to reform (moves toward the contractual end of the behavioral spectrum), insurgents will find their support from host communities declining and will resort to more coercive tactics in their treatment of noncombatants. Thus, in a reforming state, espousing democratic norms is more likely to usher in an increase in coercive behavior by insurgents against noncombatants. At first glance, this idea appears counterintuitive. Supporters of international norms of human rights and democracy, for example, contend that policies in these directions are good for a state's citizenry. Yet, as the PKK example reveals, state reform can actually *increase* the levels of coercion that local populations experience, even though such reforms are directed at these very populations. This phenomenon can be explained by the fact that the state acquires the new status of rival once it begins to reform. By reforming, the state attracts popular support away from insurgents in the form of a more open society.

It appears that Turkey's security forces and the PKK mutually, albeit unintentionally, reinforce each other, adding a further dimension to this insurgent group's story. "Without the PKK and its exactions, the army could not justify its control of the society, and without the terrible military repression in Kurdistan, the PKK would have a hard time surviving and recruiting among the Kurds."[163] Thus, it seems reasonable to hypothesize that the level of repression by the state will be proportionate to the people's support for insurgent groups. However, in Turkey this ratio of repression to support is mediated by the rise of Kurdish civil society and the inability of the PKK to maintain dominance over Turkish Kurdistan. That is, if civil society expands in Turkey, it will act as a threat to PKK, much as the SPLA experienced when southern Sudanese civil society began demanding democratic institutions. If faced with the decision to support either an illegal armed group (with limited resources and limited mobility) or a legitimate state that has access not only to domestic but also to international resources, local populations will choose the state. By taking away resources from the insurgent group, the state becomes another competitor. So, for example, Öcalan would be likely to oppose Turkey's EU membership because it would mean greater democracy in Turkey and further loss of PKK support as Turkish Kurds shift toward collaboration with the state. As a press release from the PWD explains, the process of Turkey's EU membership will strengthen democracy within Turkey,[164] which will result not only in sidelining state-supported Kemalism and its marginalization of minorities but also in alienating the PKK, because many Kurds who are tired of violence would view the PKK as an obstacle to Turkey's popular democratic reforms. When democracy becomes a policy of the state against which an insurgent group fights, insurgents are likely to be blamed for local mayhem. Thus, it may be that insurgents do not really transform their behavior but that local people change their perceptions of the insurgents. This hypothesis complements the idea that the nature and capabilities of the state are critical for shaping insurgent responses to local communities.

6

The Theoretical and Practical
Implications of Active Rivalry

"War is a great teacher," says a deputy brigade commander in the SPLA.

It is October 2001. We are standing on a dirt road at the border between Uganda and Sudan. He is traveling into southern Sudan to oversee the fragile process of removing land mines. The irony in the matter—which is not at all lost on the commander—is that the SPLA had laid down these land mines only years earlier. Now the insurgent group was being tasked by its central command to remove the mines. The change in the insurgent group's behavior between then and now is indeed perceptible.

The primary claim in this book is that insurgents treat local citizens violently when they face active rivalry. Therefore, the presence or absence of rivals determines the type of behavior that insurgents adopt. When an insurgent group faces low levels of competition (when the rivals are weak in comparison or when the groups are not competing for the same resource), violence against civilians tends toward the low (contractual) end of the spectrum. The existence of rivalry, not resources, is central to the insurgent-civilian dynamic. Rivals play a crucial role because competition threatens resources, and the lack of resources in turn threatens survival. Without rivalry, a group possesses control over the extraction and distribution of resources and thus has increased opportunities and expanding power and no need to resort to coercion. Whereas other studies have treated violence against local populations as a product of greed and recruit type, this book takes a different approach. I look at violence as an insurgent group's rational reaction to a threat to its survival. The three cases I have examined demonstrate the theory of active rivalry in varying ways.

The SPLA began in 1983 when a group of Sudanese army officers broke away and formed a group organized around fighting the government of

Sudan. The group was a military-focused organization, influenced by its Marxist backers in Mengistu-led Ethiopia. From its inception, the SPLA was plagued with infighting, largely a result of disputed leadership strategies and the fact that Garang's proclaimed objective was the formation of a new united Sudan, rather than self-determination. Thus, in addition to fighting military forces from the north and local government-sponsored militia, the SPLA faced several southern factions during its early development. The group was hardly a month old when several veterans of the south's first rebellion following Sudanese independence broke away from the group. These soldiers supported the idea of southern secession. Furthermore, the government of Sudan began funding militia groups in an attempt to clear out the Upper Nile region for oil exploration and to rid itself of the rebels in the south. Finally, a major split in the SPLA occurred in 1991 when several southerners protested Garang's "dictatorial" style. Thus, from early on, the SPLA had several rivals with which to contend and compete for resource extraction. It was therefore a highly coercive organization at the start, guilty of obstructing relief efforts, looting southern towns, and seizing food from rural civilians. Some SPLA commanders diverted humanitarian aid to sell. Other abuses included summary executions and disappearances, torture, and holding prisoners in harsh conditions, as well as using child soldiers.

When the Cold War came to an end, the SPLA found itself bereft of financial backers. The international community, backed by humanitarian agencies and human-rights groups that had reported on the devastating famine of 1988, began condemning the various abuses by both sides of the conflict. Foreign donors adopted a more visible presence, particularly in the south, where human devastation was most severe. This onset of international attention was followed by a decrease in the SPLA's rivals. Riek Machar's group, which had defected to the government in the early 1990s, severed its northern affiliation. Several of its commanders returned to the SPLA and were followed by smaller factions, while other groups dissolved altogether. Militias became less of a threat as international donors populated (and hence brought international focus to) many of the more vulnerable areas. To further decrease its rivalry, the SPLA established links to northern political parties via the NDA. Significant changes in the SPLA's behavior surfaced in 1994, when the group produced the Watershed, a document that spelled out policies for a civil administration and the development of structures that would foster democracy. The

Watershed agreement formally separated the military from the civilian administration.

The setbacks that the SPLA experienced during the early 1990s, in particular the increasing competition for resources and support following the split of 1991, forced the group to reexamine its strategy. Toward the end of the 1990s, Nuer commanders and soldiers returned to the rebel group. With the reintegration of rivals such as Machar and his group into the SPLA, the SPLA saw a decrease in significant rivals and was able to attain a nearly complete monopoly over the southern regions of Sudan.

In contrast to the SPLA, the FARC began as a mediating force in rural Colombian society, protecting various peasant communities in the southeastern region of the country. The organization came close to modeling itself as an alternative to the central government when the government agreed to create a demilitarized zone for the FARC, a geographically defined setting for the evolution of further peace talks between the group and the government. Such measures to bring the revolutionary left into mainstream political activity led to the development of the UP.

But the existence of rival groups was also significant in the FARC's transformation to more coercive tactics toward locals. Around the time the UP fell apart, drug cartels were pushed out of Peru and established operations in the frontier zones where the FARC maintained a significant influence. A break in many of the tentative alliances between the insurgents and the cartels occurred in 1987 when *paras* affiliated with the Medellín cartel, in complicity with the Colombian army, the police, and local landowners, attacked left-wing groups such as the FARC. Faced with increasingly powerful rivals such as the AUC and other right-wing paramilitary groups, the FARC adopted a more coercive strategy toward locals.

Unlike the SPLA and the FARC, the PKK has gone through multiple changes in its strategy and its treatment of civilians. In 1984 the PKK launched military operations against Turkey. Initially, the goals of the PKK included the creation of a Kurdish state. Following the deportation and arrest of Öcalan in 1999, the group underwent numerous tactical transformations. In a move toward a more realistic reflection of the political environment, some members attempted to shift the group's objective from a separate state to cultural and political autonomy. Interviews I conducted in Turkey and Iraq indicate that some PKK cadres do not accept these changes; it appears the organization is fracturing.

Theoretical Implications of the Active-Rivalry Theory

This book addresses several important theoretical themes. First, it examines what specifically drives insurgent violence. At a microlevel, this study shows that insurgent violence against civilians is a response to threats to these armed groups' survival. Violence against civilians is more likely when rivalry exists, as demonstrated by the case of the FARC, whose coercion against civilians increased after it faced paramilitary rivals. The fear of extinction can be a powerful motivator to commit violence. When insurgent groups are faced with active rivalry, they will resort to increased levels of coercion against civilians in order to retain a monopoly over resources. This control of resources is important because it aids in securing the group's survival. In Sudan, when the SPLA faced rivals from breakaway factions, its violence against the civilians of the south was high in comparison to later years. However, when assured of its monopoly over resources as a result of the decrease in active rivalry, SPLA violence abated. In a basic sense, dominance over extraction of resources equals power to penetrate and centrally coordinate the activities of local communities through an insurgent group's own infrastructure.

This book also highlights some of the flaws in many of today's conflict theories. The theories that focus on resources link resources to the level of coercion displayed by armed actors in contemporary wars. This argument, derived from the studies of World Bank officials and counterinsurgency strategists, implies that resources drive the behavior of groups: where there are large amounts of valuables available for the taking, soldiers have little incentive to treat local communities well. That is to say, insurgents shift time horizons (from short-term to long-term and vice versa) independent of the difficulty or ease of claiming resources. But I argue that insurgents in fact shift their horizons according to whether they have political space to maintain sole dominance over resources with relative ease. The new-wars view, informed by the historical state-building literature, suggests that contemporary conflicts are fought by individuals with little ideological justification who are often linked to global criminal networks.[1]

Although these theories may be useful in explaining some individuals' participation in using violence against civilians, they are less persuasive in the context of the cases under study here. The SPLA, for example, behaved coercively against southern Sudanese in the 1980s and early 1990s, despite the fact that it did not have an abundance of resources at its disposal, nor did it have many that would be considered illicit. In fact, it was during the SPLA's later years, when rivalry against it decreased and it had a plethora of resources coming into the organization from foreign sources, that its interactions with its host population became contractual. This evidence goes against the "abundant resources" and "greed" arguments, which claim that in times of excessive resources, violence against noncombatants is more likely. Rather, what explains the SPLA's behavior is the decrease in rivals it faced in the later years of the war.

Furthermore, the FARC in Colombia participated in the drug trade and simultaneously acted in a contractual manner toward the rural peasants it claimed to represent. The greed theory predicts that involvement in the drug trade by the FARC would attract recruits less invested in rural communities and more interested in short-term gains. Hence, violence would be the result. However, that was not the case. It was not until the paramilitaries posed a significant threat to the FARC's survival that it began behaving coercively toward noncombatants. The greed theory may be useful in, for example, predicting that if the FARC becomes more like a criminal organization, it would see an increase in recruitment. However, as an explanation for violence, the greed theory is unconvincing.

The theory of active rivalry is applicable to other cases, though it requires further empirical verification. The theory, for example, explains the change in behavior of the Basque insurgency in Spain known as Euskadi Ta Askatasuna (ETA). During the 1970s, ETA captured widespread national and international support in its fight against the Franco regime. However, by the 1990s, it had evolved from a cultural group advocating Basque tradition and identity to an armed insurgent organization responsible for hundreds of civilian deaths, both Spanish and Basque. Today, some observers would say that what was once a much-loved revolutionary movement is now a predatory organization that is feared and loathed by the majority of Basque citizens.[2] ETA's story parallels the PKK's in many ways. After the death of Franco, Spain democratized, and in 1978 three Basque provinces gained autonomy. Like the Turkish state, Spain became a rival to the Basque insurgency. Once civilians were granted freedoms that had been limited under the previous repressive regime, popular support for ETA declined. This broadening of civil liberties in Spain coincides with ETA's increased violence against civilians. By granting such liberties, the Spanish state became an active rival to ETA, drawing from it popular support and the local resources that came with such backing.

Rethinking Active Rivalry: Policy Implications

As this study shows, the theory of active rivalry is important for the future of conflict studies. For scholars, it provides a detailed depiction of insurgents by examining the logic behind their actions. In doing so, this account expands on the work of other scholars who see a shift away from studies that emphasize resource incentives. Most important, it addresses an important gap in the current literature on insurgent behavior: the explanation for change. Yet active-rivalry theory is also relevant to policymakers. This final section delves further into the policy relevance of active-rivalry theory.

The Importance of Strong Institutions

This books demonstrates how the degree of state presence or absence (and if presence, the nature of it) are important factors in shaping insurgents' behavior. Even within the new-wars and resource-wars literatures, there are varying degrees of explicit recognition that the weakness of state institutions matters. The nature of the state's ties to local communities is clearly important. States that marginalize communities while oppressing them spawn different kinds of insurgent groups than do states that marginalize communities while selectively co-opting people in those same communities. The latter type of state is likely to generate groups that have reason to be more violent in those communities because they have to force local people to make choices about whom they support and whom they betray to others.

This basic point has been made by several scholars. Fanon maintains that, at a certain point in the history of anticolonial struggles, government repression encouraged the colonized to participate in violent struggle.[3] Kitson also asserts this point in his memoir of the Mau Mau rebellion in Kenya, and Kriger emphasizes the importance of government coercion and repression in relation to the linkage between popular support and insurgent violence in her account of Zimbabwean guerrillas.[4] The literature also indicates that insurgents enact strategies that intensify government repression because doing so will hasten the mobilization of local populations. In this dynamic, the state is made to look like the least favorable option for local communities. The Brazilian insurgent leader Marighella presumed that attacks on government installations would provoke the central Brazilian regime to retaliate with repressive measures.[5] In a more contemporary context, Ford confirms the importance of the relationship between local populations and insurgent groups in trying to explain the apparent passivity among the Iraqi population in relation to the insurgency inflicting violence on U.S. and Iraqi troops, as well as on civilians.[6]

Although there is a large counterinsurgency literature on degrees of state "niceness," this study goes a step further and considers how state policy affects the behavior of insurgents. Interestingly, the state seems to be the only actor in this dynamic that can choose to compete for resources and ultimately for control. The state *can* enter the dynamic as a competitor, and it does so if it is reforming and has the potential to offer something better than what the insurgents are offering. For example, Turkey has chosen to enact several limited reforms aimed at granting Kurds a degree of cultural autonomy. Meanwhile, Colombia chooses not to enact reforms that would benefit the peasant farmer population. Furthermore, the government of Colombia has support for *not* liberalizing, as doing so would empower such left-wing groups as the FARC, which would have gone against the most recent Bush administration's War on Terror. Instead, as chapter 4 maintains, the United States supported Colombia's military buildup over the years, which in turn has been used in many ways against the peasant populations.

Unlike states, which have a choice to enter the arena of competition, insurgent groups are forced to do nothing *but* compete. If the state begins to reform, it will obtain both internal and external resources and will be able to obtain all the necessary power to defeat rivals. However, the PKK case in particular shows that state reform can cause an insurgent group to increase its violence against civilians in the short term, as the group tries to spark violence from the state.

Arguably, when an insurgent group has control over resource extraction, it can do whatever it wants, since there is no third party to stop it from employing violence to extract resources. But that supposition does not appear to be borne out by the facts. As North argues in his description of the contractual relationship between the serf and the lord during the European feudal era, the lord does have certain constraints placed on him with regard to the tactics used to extract labor from serfs. The scarcity of labor prior to the 1500s meant that lords were frequently in competition over serfs. As a result, the lord had an incentive to abide by the contractual agreements, which included protection from outside invaders. If lords did not do so, serfs would flee.[7] Likewise, insurgents find it more efficient to establish and abide by a social contract, much as a state would, because peasants can always leave the region in which the insurgents operate. Thus, an insurgent group that is just, in plain terms, nasty and chooses to coerce civilians it represents would in time force those civilians to leave the area. If those civilians were some of the only source of resources for this nasty insurgent group, the group itself would soon find itself on its way to extinction (unless of course it finds other resources).

The Impact of Weak Institutions in Current Conflicts

In a practical context, less state presence means that there is more likely to be insurgent activity. Though this observation appears obvious, the critical point is that the type of state presence (repressive or contractual) can determine the type of insurgency that develops. In particular, the type of state institution can shape the behavior of insurgents in relation to the civilian population. A strong state—one that is contractual and thus provides its citizens with public goods—is likely to find few people turning to an insurgency for security and opportunities. On the other hand, a repressive state or one that does not provide public goods such as security and economic opportunities for its citizenry will create an environment that is conducive to insurgent support.

The capacity of states is also important in determining the types of organizations that develop within them, because a weak state can offer opportunities for entry into specific types of structures.[8] For example, in weak states, criminal economies emerge with increased ease, as there are fewer mechanisms to regulate their growth. An uneven distribution of state capacity—particularly according to ethnic or tribal affiliations—creates the opportunity for criminal organizations to operate across borders that share ethnic or tribal affiliations.[9]

Furthermore, economic pressures during periods of reform or transition can provide incentives for people to enter into criminal economies. For example, in Afghanistan, the lack of security, a struggling economy, and weak institutions of governance are creating a fertile environment for the resurgence of the Taliban. Six years after the conclusion of Operation Enduring Freedom, the Taliban is now a powerful insurgent force organized like and employing terrorist tactics that threaten democracy in Afghanistan and the region.[10] The use of suicide attacks, improvised explosive devices, and the beheading of hostages are tactics that the Taliban increasingly adopts.[11] For example, suicide bombings, virtually unknown in Afghanistan before 2005, rose to 139 in 2006.[12] The Taliban now operates through autonomous cells, employing individuals with varying ideological commitment to the group's overarching goals. The continuance and resurgence of the Taliban as a decentralized organization hinders domestic reconstruction and the development of a stable democracy. The lack of strong state institutions has contributed to the Taliban's reentry into Afghanistan as a loosely aligned network made up of criminal entrepreneurs and insurgent operations.[13]

Democratization: The New Ideology

This book also has counterintuitive implications. It highlights how well-intentioned reform often carried out by states under the aegis of democratization can actually lead to increased insurgent violence against civilians. National governments and global norms that offer host populations access to new political channels can encourage insurgents to become more violent toward civilians. That is, as the governing regime and international organizations such as the United Nations recognize and grant various forms of group rights and encourage autonomy to communities where insurgents operate, those armed actors—feeling their support networks and resources threatened as civilians shift their support to the reforming state—are likely to increase their use of coercive measures against locals.

Largely, policymakers' assessments of liberal norms and values are optimistic.[14] That is, they support the idea that democracy naturally leads to the peaceful coexistence among peoples and states. Norms are rules that explain patterns of observable behavior and discourse; they represent the repetition of acts instituted in a visible space.[15] The norm of democratization suggests an emergent world order composed of democratic states and international and nongovernmental organizations that uphold and protect human rights. Democracy is a system of political governance in which decision-making power is subject to the controlling influence of citizens who are considered to be political equals. Such a system is inclusive, participatory, representative, accountable, transparent, and responsive to citizens' aspirations and expectations.[16] Democratization is therefore the set of rules by which previously authoritarian, nonrepresentative governments must abide in order to transform into democratic states.

States have attempted to spread democracy as a system of governance through economic policy and through the force of their militaries. The promotion of democracy has become a foreign-policy objective for numerous existing democracies and is now a driving force in international politics, especially with regard to relations of powerful countries to developing countries. The increase in the number of democratic regimes suggests that these developments are not entirely the result of internal state processes.[17] Democratization in Africa, for example, became a part of a larger worldwide movement to transform nondemocratic governments as a result of the economic and political liberalization occurring around the world during the 1980s, particularly after the collapse of communism as a state ideology. International donors and Western powers adopted the post–Cold War democratization project of the hegemons and exerted subtle and interventionist pressure on developing countries.[18] Furthermore, in Latin America, military dictatorships began to fall apart.[19] Between 1972 and 1993, the number of democratic governments more than doubled, rising from 44 to 107.[20]

Neoconservatives evaluate regimes on the basis of their values. This view appeared during the 1980s (though it did not begin then) when Reagan labeled the Soviet Union an "evil empire."[21] Deeply embedded in today's neoconservative model is a concern about the nature of regimes. The world witnessed how forceful such a justification could be when the Bush administration invaded Iraq in 2003. George W. Bush used normative statements to classify many nondemocratic regimes, which in turn served to justify the West's aggressive behavior toward states that previously enjoyed the protections from outside interference in their internal affairs that their sovereignty gave them. One of the arguments that the Bush administration provided for invading Iraq was that Saddam Hussein and his regime kept freedom from Iraqis. Bringing freedom to the Middle East via democracy served to rationalize Bush's foreign policy. But even a regime that is considered dissolute in the neoconservative perspective, such as Saddam Hussein's, is classified as a state according to the international system. "Evil empires," however, are more likely to be a target for democratic states. Implicit in these acts of forced democratization taking place globally is that to enjoy the political and economic benefits of the current international system, a state will have an easier time if it is a democracy. Of course, not all democratic states treat nondemocratic countries this way. For example, George H. W. Bush renewed China's most-favored-nation status in spite of that country's abuses of citizens during the Tiananmen Square massacre.

Despite findings on the relationship between good human-rights records and the acquisition of economic aid from the United States, countries perceived to be of vital importance to U.S. national security receive aid regardless of their status as nondemocratic states.[22] This fact demonstrates that weaker states and those that threaten U.S. strategic interests are most vulnerable to the pressure of democratization. In the context of insurgent groups, democracy should be a valuable resource for insurgents that provide their constituents with public goods and the ability to participate in their own governance. Providing democracy today (even as an insurgent group) is comparable to being "anticolonial" in the 1960s or "antiapartheid" in the 1980s.

Yet in examining democratization in the context of insurgent groups, we see that it can have opposing effects. At times, some insurgent groups can be positively affected by democratization, adopting its tenets in order to obtain resources from Western donors. Democratization can thus be integrated into a group's political strategy and can itself be used as a resource. At other times, democratization can have unintended consequences, as when reforming states that are being challenged by nonstate armed actors see an increase in the incidence of violence against minority communities that insurgents claim to represent.

Contemporary insurgent groups are guided by the influence of world powers, which dictate the development of norms of democracy and thereby the recognition of such principles as human rights. It is thus reasonable to link insurgent groups' behavior to the norm of democratization, including norms against ethnic cleansing, genocide, and other standards of international law. Acceptance of democratization and its accompanying requirement of respecting human rights is a precondition for participation in international political and economic arenas. At the same time, insurgent groups' adherence to international norms such as democratization is particularly fascinating because these actors (who lack the international and legal status of states) are neither required nor legally entitled to acknowledge the applicability of international norms to their struggles. By publicly committing to international standards of democratization, for example, insurgent groups incur costs, since this norm not only restrains the military options available to them, but it also exposes them to increased international scrutiny.

Democracy facilitated the SPLA's attainment and maintenance of a monopoly on control toward the beginning of the twenty-first century. Following the events in the United States on September 11, 2001, the southern-Sudanese cause moved even further up the ladder of international priorities in the name of global security. The United States placed Sudan on its annual list of states supporting terrorism when information became available that between 1991 and 1996 the Islamic regime had given refuge to Osama bin Laden and others marked as "terrorists." With U.S.-imposed economic sanctions against it, Sudan and its internal issues moved into the international spotlight.[23] The effect in southern Sudan was of some importance to the SPLA, as the post–September 11 environment placed it on the side fighting supporters of "terrorism." Two SPLA commanders in the liberated town of Rumbek confirmed this shift. They told me that the terrorist attacks of September 11 increased the West's empathy for the southern Sudanese.[24] Khartoum's established support from Islamic states and international organizations made the government of Sudan a natural (and at that time acceptable) enemy of the United States, one of the SPLA's largest supporters. After September 11, the SPLA adroitly used democracy to its benefit, acquiring further aid from Western countries and raising sympathetic awareness of its cause. Democratization provided the SPLA with the opportunity to acquire resources by changing its formerly violent behavior toward its constituents. Under this guise, the group received international donor monies and other forms of support. The international environment thus provided the SPLA with a framework from which to operate. At the same time, the SPLA's ability to exercise control over resources and donor agencies gave the group the impetus to reduce its strong-arm tactics against civilians.

However, democratization does not always have positive or violence-mitigating effects. In the case of the PKK, democratization had violent consequences. Turkey's candidacy for EU membership initiated reforms that targeted the Kurdish community. Thus, the state, which had formerly oppressed Turkish Kurds, became their protector. When a state begins to reform, insurgents find that their control over host communities begins to decline. The insurgents will then resort to more coercive tactics in their treatment of noncombatants. This phenomenon may appear counterintuitive, because supporters of international norms of democracy, for example, lead us to believe that policies in that direction are good for the citizenry. However, according to the active-rivalry theory, once a state begins to reform, it becomes a rival or competitor to the insurgent group. In reforming, the state begins to attract popular support away from the insurgent group because such support is accompanied by material goods.

Once a state begins to reform, its access to resources actually increases. Foreign democratic governments and institutions such as the International Monetary Fund and the World Bank are likely to reward such reforming behavior in order to ensure that the state remains moving in a contractual direction. Foreign governments will, for example, remove economic sanctions, increasing the availability of resources and the flow of development into the country. Turkey's membership in the European Union, for example, is contingent on reform in the area of human rights, particularly with regard to Kurdish and Armenian populations. Yet, as my analysis suggests, this process draws resources away from insurgent groups that are in opposition to the state and contributes to a group's decline in popular legitimacy.

Such state reforms spurred a decline in the PKK's legitimacy. That is to say, the state facilitated a decline in the PKK's support. "The EU reform process is weakening Öcalan's grip," said Hasim Hasimi, a former Kurdish lawmaker. "The EU has robbed him of his role as the Kurds' sole protector."[25] As the PKK became increasingly irrelevant to local Kurds, who found they could participate more effectively in political life, the PKK increased its coercion against Kurdish civilians. As noted in chapter 5, several Kurdish civilians I interviewed in Diyarbakir noted that many Kurds were trying to distance themselves from the PKK.[26]

As Turkey's politics became more open to the political demands of moderates in Kurdish communities, splinter groups of the PKK become more violent. Their evolution began to resemble the trajectories of insurgent groups in liberal democracies elsewhere, such as ETA. For example, the radical group known as TAK materialized again following a unilateral cease-fire with the Turkish government. This effect can be seen in other cases as well. The political opening in Ireland and Britain to the IRA's supporters brought a large measure of local groups' rights, but it also spawned rejectionist groups such as the Real IRA. The Red Brigades in Italy and the Baader Meinhoff Gang in West Germany in the 1970s also had to operate in a democratic setting. In those cases, the groups simply were not appealing to their target communities compared to the services states could offer. So, like the PKK in the 1980s and its fragments again in the 2000s, their strategies focused on provoking retaliation against communities of would-be supporters. In sum, it appears that democratic policies in these states weaken broad-based insurgencies. Less expected is the tendency for these broad-based insurgencies to spin off increasingly violent insurgent subgroups organized around remnants of supporters from the broader group.

Again, the nature and capabilities of the state help shape insurgent responses to local communities. If options for Kurds to operate from within the Turkish political system are continually denied, more of them are likely to pursue extrasystemic strategies.[27] However, a corrupt state that cannot control predations of its own agents or one that adopts a counter-insurgency strategy that punishes local communities for the presence of insurgents makes it easier for insurgents to acquire local civilian support, as these groups become a more attractive governing option to citizens, even if the insurgents are not extremely effective at it. Most important, insurgent groups facing repressive states are better able to appeal to outsiders with real or contrived reform programs that reduce coercion of local communities and are more likely to adopt international demands for democratic internal governance. However, these groups will do so only when they are confident that they can manipulate the implementation of such democratic reforms in ways that will increase their control over local communities.

Nevertheless, insurgents take the chance that outsiders will not view them as the dominant group. If their political control over host communities declines, insurgents risk being viewed as possessing diminished prospects for manipulating international actors. Thus, insurgents find themselves in a situation of *realpolitik* typical of states in centuries past: groups' poor performance is met with a lack of interest or aggression on the part of outsiders, but groups' effective control on the ground forces them to take account of local communities' interests.

Like any other resource-maximizing individual or organization, insurgents will adopt the strategy that best enables them to achieve their goal, as long as it does not threaten their survival. Therefore, these groups are more likely to take the interests of local communities into account in formulating their strategies when there is incentive to do so *and* if they will not lose their monopoly over resources. In practical terms, then, insurgents will become "better democratizers," although this shift is dependent on an underlying coercive element of insurgent strategy.[28] Insurgent groups can be manipulated to institute democratic reform, as demonstrated in the case of the SPLA and to a lesser extent that of the PKK. The key here is that insurgents will be democratizers as long as their survival is secure. In other words, though international and national environments influence the behavior of insurgent groups in relation to civilian populations, these variables are mediated by the insurgent groups and the politics on the ground. Indeed, insurgent groups do respond to the outside pressure of democratization, reaping the external and internal (local) benefits for doing so. However, insurgents are not under the

TABLE 6.1
Policy Lessons from the Active-Rivalry Theory

1. To deter violence against civilians in the long run, insurgents must have their access to resources taken away, or else they must be co-opted.
2. Democratization can lead to violence in the short run.
3. The type of state presence in a community will shape insurgent activity.
4. Insurgent groups can be manipulated to institute reform as long as their survival is guaranteed.

thumb of international forces or norms. For example, during the early 1990s, the European Union was involved in the peace process between the Colombian government and the FARC, with three rounds of peace talks taking place under EU sponsorship in Madrid, Bogotá, and finally Brussels. Yet, despite Europe's efforts to demonstrate to FARC leaders the material and political benefits of making a democratic shift, these rebels in the end chose not to sign on to a settlement.[29] Thus, forces fighting insurgents groups need to give them the kind of resources they need to create the conditions in which local reform can be implemented. However, these same opposing forces must be sure not to give the insurgents enough resources to overpower the government. This is a fine line, and one that is not standard across countries or regions. This point of analysis, of which this book just scratches the surface, is a topic that may very well become significant in governments' aid to breakaway groups in the future and thus deserves further attention.

Knowing that threats to survival drive violence allows policymakers and military strategists to fine-tune their objectives. If the goal is to decrease violence against civilian populations, then there are essentially two options: stomp the insurgency out by taking away its monopoly over resources or co-opt them. The first option, often referred to as a kinetic choice, is the simplest, but it is the messiest one because of the potential for violence and loss of civilian life. This option also brings with it the possibility of international condemnation. The second option (co-optation) involves a mixture of kinetic and nonkinetic strategies. It takes much longer and involves allowing the insurgency to retain a monopoly over resources and, in doing so, to get the insurgency to align with the opposing (or foreign) side. Table 6.1 summarizes the policy lessons of the active-rivalry theory.

Insurgent groups provide alternative forms of political authority. That has been demonstrated most acutely in Iraq and more recently in

Afghanistan, where the Taliban resurgence has proven to be quite strong. This study of insurgent behavior defines conditions under which contemporary insurgencies are likely to create linkages to local civilian populations. Insurgent groups that develop contractual relations with locals provide alternative political structures, which are becoming increasingly important in the antiterror environment. As governments place a higher value on the capacity of authorities to control resources, nonstate political structures that accomplish that goal may have more leverage.

Notes

NOTES TO CHAPTER 1

1. Among members of the movement, it is common to use the abbreviations SPLA and SPLM, the former representing the military arm of the rebel organization; however, these abbreviations are relatively interchangeable, and SPLA is used throughout this book in reference to the leadership of the movement.

2. Although much of the civilian devastation that occurred during the SPLA's early years were the "collateral" effects of battles between the insurgent group and the government of Sudan, many observers maintain that struggles against rival factions within the insurgent group claimed more civilian lives.

3. Daniel 2001.

4. Ibid.

5. This definition draws from O'Neill (1990), who defines *insurgency* as a struggle between a nonruling group and the ruling authorities in which the former consciously uses political resources and violence to sustain, destroy, or reformulate the basis of legitimacy for one or more aspects of politics. O'Neill distinguishes between *insurgency* and, for example, *terrorism*, which he defines as the threat or use of physical violence primarily against noncombatants, especially civilians, to create fear in order to achieve religious or ideological aims.

Although this book is not the place to expand greatly on this topic, it warrants remark that there exists a debate on a precise definition of *terrorism*. For earlier discussions on the meaning of the concept of terrorism, see Thornton 1964; Walter 1969; and M. Hutchinson 1978. For recent discussions on the topic, see Schmid and Jongman 2005; Hoffman 2006; and Chaliand and Blin 2007.

6. Some insurgent groups that engage in criminal activities such as arms trafficking and the drug industry over time become less focused on their political endeavors and more intent on the business of these illicit industries. For example, after a period of relative inactivity, in 2004 the IRA was accused of several bank robberies in Belfast. Analysts claim that the IRA has transformed itself from a once-insurgent group to a criminal organization. See Frankel 2005. This kind of transformation occurs among terrorist groups as well. Abu Sayyaf began as an Al Qaeda affiliate in the Philippines but now engages more in economically motivated kidnapping for ransom and in piracy than it does in terrorism. See

Shelley, Picarelli, Irby, et al. 2005, 36. Still, these groups continue to retain some sort of political agenda.

7. Tilly 1990. The prospect that insurgents can be contemporary state builders provides a springboard into analyzing and explaining their behavior toward non-combatants. Just as the study of contemporary rebels involves the analysis of the relations between them and local societies, the study of historical state building also examines the interplay of violent groups and local populations. The literature on past efforts among insurgents to build states (thus "freedom fighters" or "nationalist saviors" to some and "terrorists" and "bandits" to others) provides much more relevant theorizing about these social relationships that underlie definitions of ideology and about what is ultimately the target of this study: the variations in their behavior toward local populations.

Robert Bates notes that historically the strongest states grew out of the efforts of armed gangs to determine how to better organize their looting operations. These groups negotiated with local communities, encouraging them to continue producing resources to fund their armed organizations. Armed groups quickly discovered that it was to their benefit to heed the interests of local communities lest they drive their sources of material and economic support into bankruptcy (Bates 2001). Today, it is a common observation that some acts of violence do more political harm than good and that, hence, some armed actors limit atrocities (Snow 1996). Thus, contractual rebel groups may conclude that it is more advantageous to provide public goods and especially security to local communities that they can use as willing providers of resources, recruiting, and political support. This dynamic is demonstrated by Hezbollah in Lebanon. That group has created a state-within-a-state that protects its Shiite supporters, taxes them, provides social services, and fights foreign invaders such as the Israelis.

In a similar vein, Mancur Olson devised his well-known categories of bandits to explain how different armed groups have operated in relation to host communities. Armed groups enjoyed more success in the long run when they ensured that their local "victims" could continue to produce wealth, by permitting such basic social transactions as engaging in independent economic activity and allowing freedom of movement to foster economic development. In fact, Olson concluded that the most efficient armed groups were the most democratic ones. The more secure the "victims," the more they produced, increasing the amount of resources that the armed groups could extract, despite it being obtained through less coercive means (M. Olson 1993).

Olson built his interpretation on observations by Lucian Pye (1971), who observed variation among Chinese warlords during the 1920s. According to Olson's classification, there existed two types of rebels at the time: predatory "roving bandits," in the form of White Wolf, and "stationary bandits," in the form of Feng Yü-hsiang's National People's Army. Feng, the warlord leader of the Kuominchün, or NPA, in northern China, relied on personal relations and rewards to maintain control over a compact area and to move from being solely a military persona to a political one. This history indicates that, indeed, variation among rebel groups is not a new phenomenon but has existed throughout the world for years.

These observations suggest that, like states, rebels ought to confront overwhelming incentives to treat local communities well and listen to their interests, at least in the long term, even as other rebels in the same region and at the same time may choose other paths. This view of aggregate interests of armed groups is radically at odds with analyses such as Paul Collier's (2000a) that look at individual incentives. In the former view, there is no route to success that does not include discipline and some regard for community interests in return for support. In the latter view, such a dynamic would be impossible because the short-term interests of individual commanders or followers to grab what they can before someone else does would trump any other concerns.

History shows us that rebel groups can evolve in both directions. Tilly follows Weber in his claim that state making is the process of defeating internal rivals, a sort of conflict-within-a-conflict. The political actors responsible for this defeat then concentrate the administrative and coercive apparatus that form the institutional backbone of a strong state (Tilly 1990). This process varied among early state builders, and although it was not necessarily the most efficient form that arose, it *was* the organizational form that survived the selection process and developed out of early armed groups' adaptations to economic transformation and the politics of coalitional bargaining (Spruyt 1994).

One of the crucial elements in the evolution of the state (and by extension, a factor of success for rebel groups) is the social bargain between different actors. Much like the development of ties to local populations by Olson's stationary bandits, this bargain was one that centered on an agreement between actors with coercive power, on the one hand, and those with economic power, on the other (Spruyt 1994). Perry Anderson notes the importance of this social bargain between rulers and ruled. The construction and organization of the national state were a function of the relative weight and centralization of coercion. This idea is key to this book's argument, since rebel-community relations are based on coercion. In Anderson's analysis, absolutism was a functional requirement for states in Eastern Europe that wished to survive the geopolitical pressures from more competitive neighboring polities, particularly those in Western Europe. Although war provided monarchies with the political leverage to overcome resistance (Anderson 1979), society's principal armed groups nevertheless were forced to accommodate productive groups in society to get the resources and popular support they required to obtain their goals. As Anderson's different trajectories of state development demonstrate, these bargains were often forced (coercion), and the groups imposed severe penalties on those who refused them.

Despite the parallels between early state building and modern rebels, the historical literature leaves us without the resources to explain modern rebel behavior. In fact, scholars have used the historical analysis of state building to explain primarily the *lack* of consolidation in the developing world. In Europe, the competition for territory as a result of rising population growth and the consequent diplomatic pressures led to the formation of states (Herbst 2000). The "continuous aggressive competition for trade and territory among changing states of unequal size . . . made war a driving force in European history" (Tilly 1990, 54). In Europe, capital centers developed close connections with peripheral areas, which further enhanced state strength. Links to rural areas enhanced security, as border defenses protected the center from external competitors and at the same time fostered internal consolidation (Tilly 1990).

The particular avenue of European state building has been shared by few other regions of the world. For example, by 1975 Africa had the population density equivalent to Europe in 1500. Furthermore, unlike the relations that transpired between the capital centers and the rural regions in Europe, the colonial powers in many developing areas were not interested in fostering tight political ties to their periphery, except in a few sectors that were more easily controlled. The scarcity of land in Europe necessitated these more extensive ties for defensive purposes. The large expanses of land in places such as Africa, however, stifled any colonial drive to establish defensive borders and stunted the growth of large administrative state apparatuses with close ties to rural areas. Thus, during colonialism, much of the developing world lacked the internal consolidation that took place in Europe. Consequently, when these regions were decolonized, they did not have a strong central state. The period of decolonization further adds to the incongruence in using the historical state-building literature to analyze developing regions of the world. During that time, nationalists became heads of newly independent states that were molded according to the way colonial rulers conducted politics. That is, these new leaders based politics primarily in urban centers, with few links to peasant populations living in outlying communities (Herbst 2000).

Scholarship on areas further east than the early European states such as England and France provides partial insight into ways that some non-Western states developed and the motivations behind their particular state-building behavior. In the newly forming Ottoman state, for example, state building was not a result of the classical mix of capital and coercion. Rather, the Ottoman rulers chose to build states largely through public co-optation and bargaining with potentially violent nonstate actors. Their strategy was to incorporate the peasantry and rotate elites, keeping both groups dependent on the center. Bandits emerging from mercenary troops employed in the empire's wars were likewise more interested in accumulating resources from the state than they were in challenging it. Similarly, the Ottomans were willing and able to control and manipulate these bandits with bargaining and patronage politics, attesting to the empire's strength (K. Barkey 1994). This description provides insight into how some non–Western European states developed. However, it falls short in illuminating the motivations behind insurgent behavior. It does not explain how Ottoman state building, specifically the bargaining and co-optation of bandits, affected local communities, whether these communities had any influence over the decisions of bandits in this process, or whether bandits took their relations to local communities into account as they calculated how they would respond to Ottoman state entreaties. Relating state building that occurred within the Ottoman Empire to that of modern rebel groups is an imperfect comparison because the two do not share similar resources, strengths, or external environments.

In conjunction with this study, we see that early European state building converged on the model of the nation-state and the coercion-capital mixture that led to its development. Coercive-intensive states could mobilize massive armies through forceful means that necessitated the creation of large, bulky administrative structures. This led to the development of empires, which stunted the productive capabilities of the population. Capital-intensive forms were usually found near ports and relied on capitalists for purchased military power. These less bulky administrative structures took the form of city-states, as developed in Venice and the Dutch Republic. Essentially, these were businesses that became states, with little rural (national) depth. Capitalized-coercive state forms incorporated coercive techniques and capitalist resources. To extract the necessary resources for large-scale war, they built bureaucracies, tax-collecting apparatuses, and channels of communication. As this latter form was the most successful in battle (owing largely to its efficiency), these states fostered the dominance of the nation-state. The coercive-intensive and capital-intensive states could not compete and were defeated or adapted to meet the terms of war set by stronger states that fielded larger armies funded by capital (Tilly 1990). This description highlights how democratic states (in this study, contractual rebels) are more efficient revenue generators and warriors (M. Olson 1993). Yet this study finds that some rebels groups *diverge from* the coercive-capital combination. In southern Sudan, for example, the SPLA went from being highly coercive toward local societies to highly representative and statelike in its various functions. The FARC developed in the opposite direction, directly contradicting the rationale spelled out by scholars of early state building. In employing increasingly coercive tactics and involving itself in the international drug trade, Colombian rebels reject the development of more contractual strategies and closer ties to local communities. The historical state-building literature facilitates an understanding of *why* rebels are state builders and how they can be successful, but it does not offer adequate insight into why these nonstate actors often reject the classical state-building strategy.

8. Insurgent groups that are blamed for promoting state failure, for example, can turn out to be the basis for more efficient governance and commercial

organizations. They can also incorporate youth into markets and politics as these networks destroy old definitions of property rights and social obligations. Such groups have appeared in all of Africa's recent conflicts. In Somalia, for example, some insurgent groups were powerful enough to establish the yet-to-be-recognized Republic of Somaliland. This outcome stands in marked contrast to southern Somalia's sixteen-year conflict and its failure to construct a central government, despite sharing the experience of prewar dictatorship, similar resource endowments, and social structures.

Many people who participate in these activities envision governance in very different ways than do the international organizations and foreign workers who design and staff postconflict reconstruction efforts. Clear borders between public and private spheres and standard distinctions between business and government administration that prevail in early-twenty-first-century wealthy countries, for example, are not reflected in the organization of these armed groups or in the social networks on which they rely. Moreover, many of these nonstate groups struggle to manipulate the interests and resources of outsiders to channel these interventions to the service of their insurgent interests. Some groups reject the state as a model altogether. Groups such as "Taliban" in northern Nigeria have proposed instead to unite the Sahel of Africa into a caliphate similar to that established in the nineteenth century by Usman dan Fodio. Contention continues over the true aims of armed Islamist groups in Somalia: whether they envision membership in a larger Islamic commonwealth, the reconstruction of a state, or nationalist irredentism as their ultimate aim.

9. In a recent field interview in Nicaragua, I asked a former Sandinista commander about this broad definition of resources. She also characterized resources in a broad way. In particular, she said that popular support is a very important resource, as it brings material goods and personnel that an insurgent group would otherwise have to struggle to obtain (Tellez 2008).

10. The use of *political order* here is based on Max Weber's concept of legitimate domination, by which he means that the expectation of obedience to command rests on the basis of a belief that those who execute orders also share a community of interests with those whom they command (Weber 1946). Herein lie the reciprocal exchanges between communities and "legitimate insurgents" that define the nonviolent or contractual end of the spectrum of insurgent behavior with respect to host communities.

11. M. Olson 2000; Tilly 1985, 1990.

12. "Liberated zones" was first used to describe areas that the SPLA had conquered from the government of Sudan and controlled.

13. See, for example, Skocpol 1979, 1985; Herbst 2000; and Goodwin 1995. As I explain further in chapter 2, recent studies such as that by Kalyvas (2006) are exceptions and help to advance the study of conflict by examining its micropolitics.

14. See, for example, Enzensberger 1994; Holsti 1996; Kaldor 1999; and Beckett 2005.

15. M. Olson 1993.

16. Spears 2004.

17. Kalyvas 2006; Weinstein 2006; Humphreys and Weinstein 2006.

18. When I refer to "data" in this book, I refer to information I obtained through interviews that I conducted, as well as my analysis of primary documents and secondary sources such as historical texts.

19. One notable exception is the work of Gerard Chaliand. See, for example, Chaliand 1969.

20. See, for example, Bermeo 1986 and Kriger 1992. Whereas the study of social movements—of which many insurgencies are the outgrowth—relies extensively on participant descriptions, the study of insurgent violence has done so only sparingly. The rarity of this grassroots level of information reflects a research approach in which information is often gathered postconflict (when it is safer to enter these regions). But then participants may have moved or had time to shape their views to a certain political agenda, or there may be little data that has been recorded and is available.

21. Insurgents, like other contemporary violent nonstate actors such as terrorists, militias, transnational criminal organizations, paramilitaries, and youth gangs, are at a unique disadvantage in acquiring resources in comparison to states. Today, states (even weak ones) can gain access to economic resources through their relations and transactions with the international system. For example, states have access to funds through such formal channels as aid and military assistance, in addition to informal or illicit means such as smuggling and trafficking. Insurgents are limited to the latter means under most circumstances. Despite the fact that many insurgent groups provide alternative forms of governance, often to a group of people repressed or neglected by the state, insurgents and others are nevertheless regarded as inherently "illegitimate" vis-à-vis the classical state system. Phil Williams (2008) accurately notes that the U.S. military (and, may I add, other states) often inappropriately uses the term "ungoverned spaces." These areas, though they do not see the reach of the primary state of which they are a part, can often be alternatively governed by insurgents and other violent nonstate actors and do in fact possess political order.

22. Snyder and Jervis 1999.

23. M. Olson 1993.

24. Kalyvas 2006.

25. Weinstein 2006.

26. Weber 1946.

27. M. Olson 1993.

28. Richani 2002; Mario 2006.

1. Priest 2006b.

2. Safford and Palacios 2002.

3. Enzensberger 1994.

4. Holsti 1996; Snow 1996. These wars are also referred to as wars of the "third kind" (Rice 1988).

5. Kaldor 1999.

6. Ibid.

7. Beckett 2005.

8. Holsti 1996, 20.

9. See, for example, Reno 1998.

10. When I visited a PKK camp in northern Iraq in 2004, I often heard Marxist rhetoric spoken among combatants.

11. Hechter 2000.

12. Kandeh 1999.

13. The typologizing of conflict has been adopted by several fields of study, including economics. See Azam 2002; Collier 2000a, 2000b; Collier and Hoeffler 2001; and Grossman 1999. As one opponent of the new-wars thesis maintains, this development reflects a lack of critical analysis on the part of commentators and scholars who desire a categorization of contemporary conflicts. This is probably the result not of a real shift in the nature of warfare but of a dearth in conceptual categories (Kalyvas 2001). Cramer (2007) maintains that modern conflicts may not have the same political sheen as those of the Cold War but that there is little basis for claiming that these wars are apolitical. Furthermore, the seeming proliferation of warlords and rebellious greed are not new phenomena (Cramer 2007).

14. See Collier 2000a.

15. Kalyvas 2006.

16. Ibid.

17. Ibid.

18. Marks 2001.

19. Tarrow (2007) gives Ted Gurr's earlier works the credit for sparking initial interest in political violence. He writes that Gurr "founded an entire school of 'conflict studies' that took the study of contentious politics beyond the largely narrative traditions that were current in the 1960s" (Tarrow 2007). See Gurr 1968, 1970, 1986, 1994, and 2000.

20. See, for example, Keen 1998; Collier 2000a; Ross 2004; and Weinstein 2006.

21. Collier and Hoeffler 2001.

22. Humphreys and Weinstein 2006; Weinstein 2006.

23. Weinstein 2006.

24. Ibid.

25. Confidential source 2006.

26. NGO representatives 2006; priest 2006a; Restrepo et al. 2005.

27. In light of events of 2008, including the death of the FARC's leader and several high-ranking individuals, this statement may no longer be accurate. This does not, however, change the analysis of past FARC practices.

28. Weinstein 2006.

29. See, for example, Frum 2004; Hannity 2004; Ignatieff 2004; Ehrenfeld 2005.

30. I thank an anonymous reviewer for this insight.

31. Sovereignty is based on two principles: international legal sovereignty, which comprises mutual recognition of independent entities with certain rights of membership in international organizations, treaty making, and diplomatic immunity; and Westphalian sovereignty, which dictates the principles of nonintervention into the domestic affairs of other states (Krasner 2003). Sovereignty creates a challenging environment for insurgents. It acts as one of the main constraints of contemporary state building.

Not all insurgent rebellions take place in environments of scarcity. The Basque insurgency, for example, locates itself in northern Spain and southern France. Terrorist organizations often establish cells in developed countries as well. Several Al Qaeda cells have been discovered in Europe, for example.

32. Some studies point to a wider range of opportunities that play significant roles in causing conflicts, such as increasing access to small arms and the growth of opportunities to participate in lucrative global criminal networks. See Collier and Sambanis 2002. This approach to thinking about behavior is not far removed from Weinstein's (2006) explanation for insurgent abuse of civilians.

33. I have adapted this definition of competition from the one provided by Hunt and Morgan (1995), who develop their theory of competition as it applies to marketing.

34. A contractual relationship does not necessarily mean that the insurgent group will receive popular support. Rather, a contractual relationship implies obedience.

35. Zartman 1995; Herbst 1996–97, 2000; Beissinger and Young 2002; Rotberg 2003, 2004; and Fukuyama 2004.

36. Zartman 1995; Weber 1946.

37. Eriksen 2005.

38. See, for example, Jackson and Rosberg 1982; Tilly 1985, 1990; Jackson 1990; Mann 1993; Zartman 1995; Hansen and Stepputat 2001; Krasner 2001; Bates 2005.

39. Maslow 1943.

NOTES TO CHAPTER 3

1. *No Standing, Few Prospects* 2008.

2. Y. Kuol 2001.

3. The phrase "Afro-Arab State" is from Hale 1996, 180.

4. Hale (1996) claims that the African-Arab distinction in Sudan is largely a social construct rather than a map of biological or cultural traditions.

5. As Douglas Johnson points out, most people use *tribe* and *clan* interchangeably, associating both with units of kinship and blood line. Political affiliation is thus based on lines of descent. In reality, a *tribe* is the largest unit of combined political sections. The organizing principles of a tribe vary from people to people, and even within peoples; combinations vary over time; and the people within a tribe do not necessarily claim direct common descent or kinship links with each other (D. Johnson 2003).

6. Ibid.

7. Ibid.

8. For the text, translation, and commentary on Herodotus 3.97.2–3, see Eide, Hägg, Pierce, and Török 1994, 312–314.

9. D. Johnson 2003.

10. The Ummayid and Abbasid were two great dynasties of the Muslim Empire of the Caliphate. The Ummayid caliphate ruled until 750 A.D., when it was overthrown by the Abbasid. The Abbasid caliphate lasted until 1258, when the Mongols conquered it. For more, see Gibb 1982; Lapidus 2002.

11. D. Johnson 2003.

12. Ibid.

13. Ibid.

14. Ibid.

15. Deng 1995.

16. Ibid.

17. Ibid., 50.

18. Ibid.

19. Ibid.

20. D. Johnson 2003.

21. Ibid.

22. Ibid.

23. The ordinance was also instituted to facilitate the abolition of the internal slave trade in Sudan. It did not apply to the entire south, however, nor did it exclude all northern Sudanese or Muslims from the south. The Upper Nile Province in the south from Renk to the north was excluded, for example, because merchants from the north had established economic interests in that region. The ordinance did not stimulate any sort of commercial class in southern Sudan that would have balanced the influence of trading companies based in the north (D. Johnson 2003).

24. Ibid.

25. Ibid.

26. Warburg 1992.

27. D. Johnson 2003.

28. Ibid.

29. Ibid.

30. International Crisis Group 2002.

31. Deng 1995.

32. Lesch 1998.

33. International Crisis Group 2002.

34. There is a diverse literature on southern Sudan and the second civil war. Some scholars stress the distinctive cultures of the north and south, emphasizing the radical differences between the two regions as a major cause of the war (Deng 1995; Lesch 1998). Other scholars analyze the humanitarian conditions in areas of the south and focus on the efforts of the international aid community in an attempt to develop general approaches to studying the effects of NGOs in the international environment (Burr and Collins 1995; Tvedt 1994, 1998). Others look more specifically at refugee issues (James 2001). Some scholars write on the role of humanitarian aid and how it has been used in the Sudanese civil war as a tool to fuel the conflict. Duffield et al. (1995) claim that commanders on both sides of the fighting starved civilians to attract more food aid. Another robust area of academic research on Sudan is in anthropological studies (Evans-Pritchard 1969; Fukui and Markakis 1994; S. Hutchinson 1996). Academic attention to the SPLA in particular, however, has been absent from conflict studies literature, with a few notable exceptions (D. Johnson 2003; Rolandsen 2005).

35. Johnson and Prunier 1993.

36. International Crisis Group 2002.

37. SPLA/SPLM 1983, 16–17.

38. Tvedt 2000.

39. Deng 1995.

40. Lino 2001.

41. Nyaba 1997.

42. Ibid.; Metelits 2004.

43. Paul 2003.

44. David 2003.

45. Garang 1992.

46. That the two men were from different groups further reinforces the claim that the original tensions within the SPLA were neither tribally nor ethnically defined.

47. D. Johnson 2003.

48. Nyaba 1997.

49. D. Johnson 2003.

50. Confidential source 2003.

51. Deng 1995.

52. D. Johnson 2003.

53. Ibid.

54. Salih and Harir 1994.

55. Lino 2005.

56. D. Johnson 2003.

57. Ibid.

58. Ibid., 85.

59. Ibid.

60. Nyaba 1997.

61. D. Johnson 2003.

62. Confidential source 2001.

63. Prunier, forthcoming.

64. Although the SPLA itself never changed its name, the original group led by Garang was, during this period, often referred to as SPLA-Torit or SPLA-Mainstream (D. Johnson 2003).

65. Scott 1979.

66. UNHCR 2005.

67. UN News Centre 2006.

68. Human Rights Watch 1998, 1999a.

69. Human Rights Watch 1994.

70. Human Rights Watch 2001c.

71. Efuk 2000; de Waal 1993.

72. Marko 2001.

73. Gleditsch and Lacina 2005.

74. SPLA-United was retained by Lam Akol as the name of his Tonga-based group following the creation of the SSIM/A.

75. Monybut 2001.

76. For a detailed analysis of this system, see M. Kuol 1997.

77. Rolandsen 2005.

78. European-Sudanese Public Affairs Council 2001.

79. Migdal 1988.

80. Ferrero 1942.

81. Schutz 1995. There is an extensive literature on insurgent groups that have turned into political parties and governments. For information on Renamo in Mozambique, see Vines 1996; Manning 1998, 2002. For information on Hamas, see Ahmad 1994; Mishal and Avraham 2006; Gunning 2008.

82. The *payam* is the successor to the district or rural district council that existed during the Condominium era.

83. SPLA 1991.

84. Clark 2001; Connell 1999.

85. The local levels of governance in southern Sudan include the *boma* and the *payam,* the former being the smaller of the two.

86. M. Olson 1993.

87. In parts of Africa, rural social institutions such as courts and grassroots organizations play an important role and serve as arenas for discussion, influence, and the promotion of accountability within governmental structures (Newbury 1992).

88. Marko 2001.

89. Awat, Woll, and Deng 2001.

90. "Supremacy of Laws," in First Equatoria Regional Congress 2002; "Contribution of Women," in ibid.

91. Rolandsen 2005.

92. Sudan People's Liberation Movement 1996, 2.

93. Arol 2001.

94. Magnong 2001.

95. Sudanese indigenous NGOs (SINGOs) were allowed to operate in insurgent-held areas as early as 1989, but the SPLA prohibited many of these groups from taking part in political and military affairs.

96. Isaac 2001; Buoc 2001.

97. Riel 2001.

98. Arol 2001.

99. R. Kok 2001.

100. Deng and Nyahong 2001. Although I never saw documents that verified that local people were being elected to councils, this action was verified by everyone I spoke with, including those southerners in minority tribes (Oloya 2001).

101. Riel 2001.

102. Buoc 2001.

103. Maguat 2001.

104. Legally enacting the draft constitution would have meant that it had been voted on by representatives of southern Sudan. If it had been enacted, then this document, though not legally binding in the eyes of the international community, would have carried with it more legitimacy among southerners (and therefore perhaps among the international diplomatic and aid community).

105. Rolandsen 2005.

106. Garang 2000.

107. Rolandsen 2005.

108. Tilly 1990.

109. Rolandsen 2005.

110. Africa Watch 1993, 1995; Human Rights Watch 1999b.

111. Human Rights Watch 1994.

112. Protocol I of the Geneva Conventions relates to the protection of victims of international armed conflict. Protocol II of the Geneva Conventions relates to the protection of victims of noninternational armed conflict (civil wars). Part II, Article 4, of Protocol II states that "children who have not attained the age of

fifteen years shall neither be recruited in the armed forces or groups nor allowed to take part in hostilities," and it states that the "special protection provided by this Article to children who have not attained the age of fifteen years shall remain applicable to them if they take a direct part in hostilities . . . and are captured" (Protocol II 1977). For additional information on basic humanitarian law, see Gasser 1993.

113. Human Rights Watch Africa and Human Rights Watch Children's Rights Project 1994.

114. Human Rights Watch 1996.

115. Oloya 2001.

116. Ibid.

117. Quoted in Ashcraft 1991, 524.

118. Cobb 2002, 1.

119. Public Law 106-113, 106th Congress (1999), *U.S. Statutes at Large*, 1501A-122.

120. USAID 2002.

121. I argue elsewhere that the SPLA's cooperation with international humanitarian relief is merely a veneer for the purposes of acquiring significant resources and continued support from local populations (Metelits 2004). Such behaviors have been studied in other international entities. During the enlargement of the European Union (EU) and the North Atlantic Treaty Organization (NATO), the Central and Eastern European countries overcame member states' unfavorable views of their membership by employing rhetorical action. Candidates used arguments based on the norms and values of the Western community to induce acquiescence for enlargement. As demonstrated by various modern rebel organizations, rhetorical action can consist of—among other things—expressive actions such as dress, mimics, and gestures (Schimmelfennig 2003).

122. Moses 2001.

123. Lemin and Odera 2001.

124. Deng and Nyahong 2001.

125. Maguat 2001.

126. Ibid.

127. Despite the SPLA's signing this agreement, NGO reports indicated that the SPLA continued the practice of using child soldiers. See IRIN 2003 and United Nations Briefing Report 2003.

128. Uppsala notes that for 1997, the best estimate for 1997 was 146, while the high estimate was 746. It claims that the sources describing these attacks were often imprecise and thus it was difficult to obtain independent confirmation on what really happened. This is the reason for the big difference between the high and the best estimate for this year. I have reported the best estimates for all years represented.

129. Rolandsen 2005. Various estimates exist. One scholar cites 350,000 (S. Hutchinson 2001), another 200,000 (Karim 1996), while another puts the number around 130,000–150,000 (D. Johnson 1996).

130. New Sudan Council of Churches 1991, 2.

131. Rolandsen 2005, 78.

132. Ibid.

133. Ibid., 46, 52.

134. Kevane and Stiansen 1998; P. Kok 1996. The Umma party is a secular Islamic party with a centrist agenda that was established in 1945.

135. Rolandsen 2005.

136. Ibid.

137. Duffield et al. 1995; D. Johnson 1994.

138. Rolandsen 2005.

139. SPLA/SPLM 2000.

140. Duffield, Young, Ryle, and Henderson 1995, 98.

141. African Rights 1997, 88–89.

142. Human Rights Watch 2002.

143. DeMars 1993.

144. Rolandsen 2005.

145. Though the SPLA touted democratic structural reforms, much of it was merely window-dressing, for the SPLA and its institutions remained firmly under Garang's personal control. During my interviews in Sudan and Kenya, several individuals repeatedly and openly stated that the democratic institutions of the SPLA, much like the civil-society structures, appeared to be independent but in reality were not (Muriel and Dhel 2003). The newly created NEC, for example, possessed limited political power; commanders who may have proven to be rivals to Garang found themselves stripped of effective power upon appointment to the NEC. Garang furthered his monopoly of control within the leadership of the SPLA by habitually elevating subordinates to positions of authority and then discarding them before they could create their own power bases. "You need to make dummy appointments" to satiate the desires of some individuals, Garang was once quoted as saying (Garang 1996), and several individuals in different locations testified to his having said it. Moses, the chairman of the Nuer community living in Kakuma Refugee Camp in northern Kenya, claimed that "the man in the uniform still [received] the lion's share" of the benefits from the democratic structures (Moses 2001). Micah, a county judge in the town of Nimule, claimed that the SPLA was still very much a military movement, despite the formal separation of the military and the political wings in 1994 and the internationalization of the group's democratic intentions. The SPLA, he said, often interfered in Nimule's judicial system (Oloya 2001). These statements are but a few that were communicated to me regarding the SPLA's military grip on the south shortly after 2000, and they attest to the manipulation by the SPLA leader in regard to the local political environment. For more on this subject, see Metelits 2004.

146. Rolandsen 2005.

147. Statement from the Funj Civil Society 2003.
148. *Comprehensive Peace Agreement* 2005.
149. Ibid.
150. Ibid.
151. In October 2008, it was revealed that several Ukrainian tanks hijacked off the Somali coast were bound for southern Sudan. A source within the SPLA apparently said that it was not in the south's interest to start another war but that if one wanted peace, one had to prepare for war. See Henshaw 2008.
152. International Crisis Group 2007.
153. See, for example, Hacaoglu 2007.

NOTES TO CHAPTER 4

1. Pastora Maria 2006.
2. Weinstein 2006.
3. There is no shortage of literature analyzing the evolution of the FARC. Much of the scholarly analyses of this insurgent group can be found in historical accounts of Colombia. Safford and Palacios (2002) provide one of the broadest contemporary accounts of this country's economic, political, and social history. Bushnell (1993) looks specifically at the nineteenth and twentieth centuries in Colombia. A comprehensive history of the violence in Colombia is found in the volumes edited by Guzmán Campos, Fals Borda, and Umaña Luna. These works analyze *La Violencia* (1948–1958), during which an estimated two hundred thousand people were killed, as a social process (Guzmán Campos, Fals Borda, and Umaña Luna 1962, 1964). Sánchez Gómez and Aguilera, in *Memoria de un país en guerra* (Memory of a Country at War) (Sánchez Gómez and Aguilera 2001), also contribute analyses of this violent period. Works that provide a more specific analysis of the violence in Colombia include the edited volume by Bergquist, Peñaranda, and Sánchez (1992) called *Violence in Colombia*. Richani (2002) argues that the causes for the country's protracted civil war are found in the intersection of political, economic, and military factors. Colombian scholars and those who have lived and worked in the region for several years, including Juan Guillermo Ferro Medina and Graciela Uribe Ramón (2002), provide detailed and intimate accounts of the FARC's formation and ideologies. Román Ortiz (2002) details the development of the FARC through an examination of post–Cold War insurgent movements. Journalists also provide valuable accounts, as these are often the individuals with the best access to groups such as the FARC. One notable study is Steven Dudley's work, which provides one account of the FARC's political development and eventual decimation, as well as an intimate look at some of the group's members and ideologies (Dudley 2004). Guillermoprieto (2001) provides a more objective account in her focus on the problematic relationship between the Colombian government and the various armed actors in the country

and the U.S. role in this interplay. Many of the studies of the coca industry and the consequent economic and political dynamics created between the guerrillas, the *paras,* and the state focus on Colombian and U.S. government policies. Murillo (2004) provides one of the more objective policy analyses and examines the impact of U.S. policies on Colombia's internal affairs. A work that examines the nexus of history, the insurgents, and the cultivation of coca is Jaramillo, Mora, and Cubides 1986.

4. Murillo 2004.

5. Ibid.; Richani 2002.

6. Bushnell 1993.

7. Murillo 2004.

8. In Colombia (what was then called the New Kingdom of Granada), the Spaniards institutionalized several types of Indian labor exploitation. In one, the *encomiendo* (derived from the Spanish verb *encomendar,* "to entrust") was a legal system enforced by the Spanish crown throughout the Americas. In the New Kingdom of Granada, the *encomenderos* obtained tribute from Indian communities in exchange for protection and religious instruction. Under this system, the indigenous people owned the land (Richani 2002). Under a second labor system, a wage laborer called a *concierto* exchanged work for the right to use a parcel of land owned by a large landowner (Pallares 2002). The *mita* (mining) system was forced procurement of Indian slaves in mines. These systems of labor exploitation were abolished under the viceroyalty of Nuevo Grenada (New Grenada), 1718–1810, and a new system of exploitation called the *hacienda* (estate) system was introduced. This estate system depended on servile labor and limited access to land and included not only the Indians, or indigenous people, but also the *mestizos,* or mixed populations, as tenants and sharecroppers tied to the system through bondage debts (Richani 2002). These systems laid the foundation for future agrarian conflict and general ethnic/class tensions in the nineteenth and early twentieth centuries.

9. UNHCR 2006.

10. Human-rights lawyer 2006.

11. Safford and Palacios 2002.

12. Ibid.

13. Ibid.

14. During the late eighteenth century, Creole elites had become increasingly critical of the Spanish regime. The Spanish gave them much to be critical of. For example, the colonialists preferred their own in positions of government, despite the fact that many Creoles were trained in law. Many Creoles came to believe as well that the Spanish viceregal government purposely kept New Granada in an era of technical backwardness. The American and French revolutions of this period gave these individuals inspiration to throw off foreign rule. However, it was the disappearance of the Spanish monarchy in 1808—as a result of, among other

incidents, the occupation of Spain by French troops under Napoleon—that led to widespread Spanish insurgent resistance in the form of local juntas. These local juntas did not have the loyalty of the New Granadans, particularly the Creole elites. What ensued was a succession of wars of independence and the eventual declaration of freedom from Spanish rule in 1819 (Safford and Palacios 2002).

15. Ibid.

16. The Conservative and Liberal parties were well on their way to formation by the middle of the nineteenth century. Colombian scholars do not agree on when specifically these two political parties were created or on what sectors of the population they represented. To oversimplify the matter a bit, the Conservatives were backed by individuals loyal to the liberator, Simón Bolívar, and the Liberals were loyal to his vice president and rival, Francisco de Paula Santander (Bushnell 1992).

17. Safford and Palacios 2002. There are various interpretations of these divisions in society. Historians have traditionally presented the division between the Liberals and the Conservatives as a divide in the provinces due to different socioeconomic perspectives. However, contemporary scholars interpret the divisions in terms of a "master political narrative" (ibid., 135).

18. LeGrand 1992.

19. Safford and Palacios 2002.

20. LeGrand 1992.

21. Safford and Palacios 2002.

22. Bergquist 1992.

23. LeGrand 1992; Moore 1966.

24. LeGrand 1992.

25. Ibid., 35.

26. Archivo del Congreso Nacional 1992.

27. Academia Nacional de Ciencias de Bolivia 1907.

28. Safford and Palacios 2002.

29. LeGrand (1992) defines conflict as involving more than twenty-five settlers.

30. Smyth 1967; Fals Borda 1985.

31. LeGrand 1986.

32. Richani 2002.

33. Osterling 1989.

34. However, the force behind this proposal lost steam, and instead, in 1936 a law supporting large landowners was passed (Safford and Palacios 2002).

35. Manwaring 2002.

36. Safford and Palacios 2002.

37. Sánchez 1992, 77.

38. Ibid.

39. Fluherty 1956; Hanratty and Meditz 1990.

40. Sánchez 1992, 83.

41. Ibid.

42. Roldán 2002.

43. Bailey 1967.

44. Sánchez and Meertens 2001, xv.

45. Sánchez 1992.

46. Ibid., 88–89.

47. Safford and Palacios 2002.

48. Modesto Campos 1975, 3.

49. Sánchez 1992.

50. Ibid.

51. Ibid.

52. Ibid., 95.

53. Safford and Palacios 2002.

54. Although most accounts point to this agreement as the end of *La Violencia*, Sánchez and Meertens (2001) interpret this development as a new phase of the violence. They claim it was a multidimensional, ambiguous process resembling both a nineteenth-century-type civil war and a peasant revolution.

55. Hartlyn 1988. For more on this period of Colombian history, see Dix 1967.

56. Sánchez 1992.

57. Pizarro 1992.

58. Ibid.

59. Arenas 1985; FARC 1993.

60. Pizarro 1992.

61. Debray 1967.

62. For more on the ELN and smaller groups, see Safford and Palacios 2002.

63. Ibid.

64. The exception was Jacobo Arenas, a leader in the FARC, who came from a working-class background (Richani 2002).

65. Ibid.

66. Mario 2006.

67. Guevara maintained that revolution had to be led by an armed vanguard strictly of urban origins. However, for a revolution to be successful, he further claimed, vanguard leaders had to establish a revolutionary focus (*foco*) in the countryside among the peasantry, which would expand the revolution's base. Furthermore, the contact with the peasantry would transform the urban vanguard and make them more revolutionary (Safford and Palacios 2002).

68. Matta Aldana 1999.

69. Ortiz 2002.

70. Manwaring 2002.

71. Guerra 2006.

72. Pizarro 1992.

73. Richani 2002.

74. Mario 2006.

75. Dudley 2004, 62.

76. Richani 2002.

77. Dudley 2004, 52.

78. *Rent seeking* can be defined as efforts to gain wealth by obtaining favorable actions from the government rather than by producing goods or offering services. These actions can be anything from legitimate requests of elected officials to overt bribery. The term was coined by Anne Krueger in 1974. See Krueger 1974.

79. Ferro Medina and Uribe Ramón 2002.

80. Dudley 2004.

81. Just as the FARC has evolved over the forty-odd years of its existence, so has its structure of governance. Originally, the group adopted a traditional top-down hierarchical structure. However, according to one scholar, the "total war" launched against the FARC by the Gaviria administration during the 1990s forced the insurgent group to reassess the structure of its military command. The group, adapting to the Colombian military's renewed assault, transformed its hierarchical structure to one of (at the time of this writing) seven regional blocs, each with anywhere from five to fifteen fronts (Rabasa and Chalk 2001). Although this change has probably made the group much more efficient, it has also meant more autonomy and independence for the regional units (Murillo 2004). One could argue that this structural change contributed to the transformation in the FARC's treatment of peasant civilians. However, I argue that these regional blocs and fronts are not without their own hierarchies; they are not ragtag groups that lack discipline and command-and-control.

82. Dudley 2004.

83. Ferro Medina and Uribe Ramón 2002.

84. Dudley 2004.

85. Mario 2006.

86. Quoted in Dudley 2004, 94.

87. Ferro Medina and Uribe Ramón 2002.

88. Ibid.

89. Quoted in Dudley 2004, 128.

90. Restrepo 2001.

91. Dudley 2006.

92. Ferro Medina and Uribe Ramón 2002.

93. Some observers claim that FARC wanted the UP to fail. A defunct UP would show Colombians that only military insurrection would transform the country. A former UP member said, "We [the UP] were the sacrificial battalion so [the FARC] could justify their war. . . . We were the disposable ones" (quoted in Dudley 2004, 95).

94. Priest 2006a; Safford and Palacios 2002.
95. Betancourt and Garcia 1994.
96. Dudley 2004.
97. Safford and Palacios 2002.
98. *Jane's* 2001; Kovaleski 1999; Leech 2000; Molano 2000.
99. Rabasa and Chalk 2001.
100. Ibid.
101. Marks 2001.
102. Richani 2002. Richani reports that he interviewed Arteta, one of the highest ranking FARC commanders in captivity. See ibid., appendix, p. 174.
103. Gonzalez et al. 1998.
104. Human-rights lawyer 2006; Richani 2002.
105. Molano 1992, 214.
106. Richani 2002.
107. Dudley 2004.
108. FARC 1989; Vargas 1994
109. Dudley 2006.
110. Mario 2006.
111. Molano 1992.
112. Dudley 2004.
113. Guillermoprieto 2001.
114. Human-rights lawyer 2006.
115. Ibid.
116. Molano 1992.
117. The Colombian government officially began using civic-military brigades in its fight against the FARC in 1982. Civilian populations were mobilized in units of militias. Within the framework of trying to establish a peace deal with the insurgents, Betancur and the Colombian army—with the support of Texaco, several cattlemen, the Civil Defense, merchants, and local government officials—developed a strategy to retake the Middle Magdalena from the FARC. Complaints from the civilian populations in the region concerning the excesses of security forces soon arose and reached a high point in February 1983 with a report from the attorney general of the country on paramilitary activities. The report highlighted abuses by 163 individuals, of whom 59 were active members of the Colombian military (Safford and Palacios 2002).
118. Molano 1992.
119. Richani 2002. For an account of the development of paramilitaries in Cordoba and Uraba, see Garcia 1996 and Ramirez Tabon 1997.
120. Richani 2002.
121. Whereas there was a uniform political development of the various paramilitaries (they all began as reactive groups aimed at self-defense and over time developed a more preventive character meant to decrease popular support for

the insurgents in Colombia), their social features vary. Some members of these groups are purely local, clusters of young men who defend communities from the FARC and the ELN. These local groups maintain somewhat ambiguous relations with local officials and government security forces. Other members of the paramilitaries, however, do not belong to any local community and have joined merely to kill. This combatant type of paramilitary is often a part of a distant, hierarchically structured organization. They are often former members of the Communist Party or ex-insurgents compelled to fight with a passion similar to the newly converted (Safford and Palacios 2002).

122. Human Rights Watch 2001b. The AUC is made up of semiautonomous self-defense groups with regional alliances, although some observers argue that there is a central authority that plans national coordinated strategies against groups such as the FARC (Manwaring 2002). The link between the AUC and the paramilitaries is not always clear. Recently, in the paramilitary demobilization process, all the groups are referred to alternately as both AUC and *paras*. As it was explained to me, when the AUC ceases to protect a group of landowners or drug traffickers and joins the Colombian armed forces, it is then that it becomes the paramilitary (human-rights lawyer 2006).

123. UNHCR 2006.

124. Richani 2002.

125. Ibid., 103.

126. Garcia-Marquez 2006.

127. Safford and Palacios 2002.

128. Human Rights Watch 2001b.

129. Arizmendi 2000.

130. Safford 2006.

131. Rangel 2005.

132. Manwaring 2002.

133. Human Rights Watch 2001b, 15.

134. Rangel 2005.

135. Dudley 2004.

136. *Campesino* 2006.

137. Restrepo et al. 2005.

138. Wilson 2001, 14.

139. Spagat 2006.

140. McDermott 2002.

141. Center for International Policy 2006.

142. Mondragon 2007.

143. McDermott 2002.

144. Aviles 2006.

145. Mondragon 2007.

146. *AlJazeera.net* 2007.

147. Centro de Investigación y Educación Popular 2001.

148. Human Rights Watch 2000.

149. NGO representatives 2006; priest 2006a; Restrepo et al. 2005.

150. Although data for the FARC's earliest years of combat are not available, figure 4.1 shows that there has been an increase in violence against civilians during the period when the paramilitaries were most active. The last two years of data recorded show a significant decrease, however. This decrease is in line with my theory, as it was during this period that the AUC and many other paramilitary groups began to demobilize. See Arias and Escobar 2007.

151. The international laws breached include Article 3 to the Geneva Conventions of 1949 and the 1977 Protocol II Additional to the Geneva Conventions. Common Article 3 covers internal armed conflicts. Protocol II applies when forces in such an internal conflict are situated under a central command, exercise control over an area such that they can execute sustained and coordinated military operations, and have the ability to implement Protocol II (Human Rights Watch 2001b).

152. Amnesty International 2005.

153. Human Rights Watch 2000.

154. Amnesty International 2005.

155. Human-rights lawyer 2006.

156. *Campesino* 2006.

157. Murillo 2004.

158. Human-rights lawyer 2006.

159. Jorge 2006.

160. Ibid.

161. Policzer 2005.

162. Kirk 2001.

163. United Nations 1989.

164. Human Rights Watch 2000.

165. NGO representative 2006.

166. McDermott 2006.

167. Ibid.

168. Carmen 2006.

169. Ibid.

170. Human Rights Watch 2001b.

171. Centro de Investigación y Educación Popular 2000; Human Rights Watch 2001b. According to the U.S. State Department's Bureau for International Narcotics and Law Enforcement Affairs, Putumayo has Colombia's largest registered number of plots dedicated to the cultivation of coca (Human Rights Watch 2001b; Vicepresidencia de la República 2000).

172. Confidential source 2006.

173. Restrepo et al. 2005, 18.

174. Mario 2006.
175. Sagan 1988; O'Hanlon 1998; Cha 2002.
176. Kang 2003.
177. Dudley 2006.
178. *Campesino* 2006.
179. Ibid.
180. Pastora Maria 2006.
181. Priest 2006a.
182. Carmen 2006.
183. Confidential source 2006.
184. Pastora Maria 2006.
185. See *BBC News* 2006a.
186. El Tiempo 2007.
187. *GlobalSecurity.org* 2008.
188. For more on this story, see *International Herald Tribune* 2008; *BBC News* 2008.
198. For more on the desertions, see Forero 2008; Maloney 2008.
190. *BBC News* 2009.
191. *CNN.com* 2009.

NOTES TO CHAPTER 5

1. Dilan 2004.
2. The PKK is listed as an international terrorist organization by several states and international organizations including the United States, the European Union, and NATO. See U.S. Department of State 2005; *Christian Science Monitor* 2007.
3. Kreyenbroek 1992.
4. For more on this general topic, see Hutchinson and Smith 1996. For a discussion of how insecurity affected the Kurdish ethnic movement, and vice versa, see İçduygu, Romano, and Sirkeci 1999.
5. Kurdish insurgents have been a regular feature of the Turkish landscape since the 1920s, although other communal divisions have been important. Just a few of these groups include the Armenians and the Hatay, as well as those who speak Lazi and Arabic (Smith/Kocamahhul 2001).
6. This data is based on estimates by İçduygu, Romano, and Sirkeci (1999), obtained from the State Institute of Statistics.
7. İçduygu, Romano, and Sirkeci 1999.
8. A variety of statistics on the situation in southeastern Turkey come from a variety of different sources. See Criss 1995 and Beriker-Atiyas 1997.
9. Gunter 1990, 57.
10. Barkey and Fuller 1998.
11. Ibid.

12. Ibid.

13. Ibid. *Tarikats* are multiethnic religious orders. During the 1920s and 1930s, Kurdish revolts against the Turkish state were dominated by *tarikats* (Bozarslan 1996a).

14. Barkey and Fuller 1998.

15. Kansu 1997.

16. Barkey and Fuller 1998.

17. The official Turkish position on the Kurdish issue is that it is separatist terror that jeopardizes the integrity of the Turkish state (Criss 1995), though this view of the situation is considered by some scholars to be simplistic and narrow (İçduygu, Romano, and Sirkeci 1999).

18. Entessar 1989; van Bruinessen 1992; H. Barkey 1993; Robins 1993; McDowell 2004.

19. Kemalism is the ideology that constitutes the ground rules for state nationalism in Turkey.

20. Approximately 99 percent of Turkey's population professes to be followers of Islam. The government recognizes three minority religious communities— Greek Orthodox Christians, Armenian Orthodox Christians, and Jews—and counts the rest of the population as Muslim, although other non-Muslim communities exist (CIA 2007; Nezan 1997).

21. Gürbey 1996. The concept of nation developed by Atatürk cannot be separated from the principle of "the indivisible unity of a state's people and its territory," according to Turkey's constitution (See Turkish Constitution 1982, article 3).

22. Gellner 1983; Chatterjee 1993.

23. Zurcher 1993.

24. Watts 1999.

25. Socialist Party of Turkish Kurdistan 1984.

26. Socialist Party of Turkish Kurdistan 1985. The ban on Kurdish traditional costume, which dated back to 1924, was strictly enforced after the military coup of 1980.

27. During this period, the Kurds were not the only minority population causing consternation in Turkey's central government. Turkey's difficulty with the Armenian populace, and the Turkish response to Armenian political activities, is notorious.

28. Kinzer 2006a.

29. McDowell 1992.

30. Romano 2006.

31. Kutschera 1994.

32. Media 2004.

33. Kutschera 1994.

34. PKK 1995.

35. Diyarbakir is a southeastern city in Turkey that is often considered to be the capital of Turkey's Kurdish region.

36. PKK 1983.

37. Kutschera 1994.

38. H. Barkey 1993.

39. Gunter 1990.

40. Bulloch and Morris 1992, 168.

41. Henri Barkey, a scholar on the Kurds, maintains that the PKK is very much Öcalan's creation. See H. Barkey 1993.

42. Dilan 2004.

43. PKK soldiers claimed that they also received training in Greece.

44. Gunter 1990.

45. Ibid.

46. Van Bruinessen 1988.

47. Imset 1988–89.

48. Gunter 1990.

49. Quoted in Mardin 1989, 155.

50. Imset 1988–89.

51. Quoted in ibid., 20.

52. Kutschera 1995.

53. Barkey and Fuller 1998.

54. One could argue that, still, the United States (up until the first American invasion of Iraq) funded groups that gave money to the PKK. How much money was funneled to the PKK is a matter for further investigation.

55. Nezan 1997, 61.

56. *DozaMe.org* 2004.

57. McDowell 1992; Barkey and Fuller 1998.

58. Van Bruinessen 1988, 42.

59. Imset 1992.

60. Sirin 2004.

61. PKK 1985.

62. Ibid., 236.

63. Quoted in Imset 1988–89.

64. PKK 1985, 236.

65. Imset 1988–89, 10.

66. Tilly 1985.

67. Debray 1967; Guevara 1985.

68. Human Rights Watch 2005; *BBC News* 2006b.

69. Gunter 1990.

70. Barkey and Fuller 1998.

71. Bulloch and Morris 1992.

72. Imset 1988–89.

73. Ibid.

74. *Briefing* 1988c.

75. *Briefing* 1988b, 11.

76. Sirin 2004.

77. Dilan 2004.

78. Nezan 1997, 58.

79. Male PKK soldiers 2004.

80. Nezan 1997, 57.

81. Kutschera 1994, 13.

82. Zana was awarded the 1995 Sakharov Prize by the European Parliament, though she was unable to collect it until her release from prison in 2004.

83. Kutschera 1994; Watts 1999.

84. Kutschera 1994.

85. Watts 1999.

86. Kutschera 1994.

87. Watts 1999.

88. Kutschera 1994.

89. Watts (1999) argues that from this period on there existed a struggle among Turkish politicians over how to treat the issue of Kurdish identity politics. Mainstream politicians struggled between what appeared to be a genuine desire for a democratic solution to the Kurdish issue and party and popular pressure to carry out the traditional state platform of nationalism.

90. Gunter 1990.

91. Barkey and Fuller 1998.

92. Imset 1988–89.

93. Newroz 2004.

94. Quoted in *Briefing* 1988a.

95. Gunter 1990.

96. Dilan 2004.

97. Newroz 2004.

98. Media 2004.

99. Sirin 2004. Indeed, the PKK has an all-female battalion. For more information, see Damon 2008.

100. PKK 1995.

101. Media 2004.

102. Dilan 2004.

103. Newroz 2004.

104. Ibid.

105. Stein 1994.

106. Barkey and Fuller 1998; Stein 1994.

107. Turkish Ministry of Foreign Affairs 2005.

108. Adamson 2005.

109. Turkish Ministry of Foreign Affairs 2005.

110. Casteel 2003.

111. Cornell 2001; Rubin and Kirisci 2001; Nachmani 2003.

112. Schleifer 2006.

113. *GlobalMarch.org* 1999.

114. R. Olson 1996.

115. Collier (2000a) argues that diasporas play an important role because they produce a sixfold increase in the likelihood of rebellions.

116. Kaya 2000.

117. Van Bruinessen 1998; Adamson 2005; *BBC News* 2007.

118. A. Hutchinson 2002.

119. Assembly of Turkish American Associations 2007.

120. Federation of American Scientists 2007.

121. Assembly of Turkish American Associations 2007.

122. *BBC News* 2007.

123. Öcalan's death sentence was largely symbolic, as Turkey had maintained a moratorium on executions since 1984, and in 2002 the death penalty was abolished during peacetime. The European Court of Human Rights has claimed that there were several violations of Öcalan's right to a fair trial (Trilsch and Ruth 2006) and ruled in 2005 that his trial was unfair, as he did not have access to lawyers. However, the Council of Europe ruled in February 2007 that Öcalan was not entitled to a retrial, saying that one was "unnecessary."

124. Quoted in World Media Watch 1999, 1.

125. *CNN.com* 1999.

126. Ibid.

127. Trilsch and Ruth 2006.

128. Ibid.

129. Sirin 2004.

130. Anonymous source. I have chosen not to identify this individual for her own safety, despite the fact that she willingly gave me her name.

131. *KurdishMedia.com* 2004.

132. Bulloch and Morris 1992.

133. Zaman 2004a.

134. *KurdishMedia.com* 2004.

135. Kinzer 2006b.

136. Birch 2004.

137. The group is also referred to as the Patriotic Democratic Party (PWD).

138. Yilmaz 2004.

139. *KurdishMedia.com* 2004.

140. Partiya Welatpareza Demokratik 2004.

141. Bilgin 2004.

142. Ibid., 2.

143. Cited in Bilgin 2004, 2.

144. Zaman 2004a.

145. İçduygu, Romano, and Sirkeci 1999, 999.

146. Ibid.

147. Agence France-Presse 2005.

148. *BBC News* 2006b; *DozaMe.org* 2006.

149. Arsu 2005.

150. Agence France-Presse 2005.

151. *DozaMe.org* 2006.

152. As of this writing, Turkish prosecutors have moved to ban the DTP for colluding with the PKK.

153. Agence France-Presse 2004; Anadolu Agency 2004.

154. Zaman 2004b.

155. Bulloch and Morris 1992, 185–186.

156. Diker 2004; Nebahat 2004.

157. *Hürriyet* 2009.

158. Enginsoy 2009b.

159. As of this writing, PJAK maintains a functional website at http://www.pjak.org/english.php.

160. Enginsoy 2009a.

161. Assembly of Turkish American Associations 2007.

162. Adamson 2005.

163. Nezan 1997, 59.

164. Partiya Welatpareza Demokratik 2004.

NOTES TO CHAPTER 6

1. A network can be understood as a series of connected nodes. These nodes can be individuals or groups (even computers), but the key element is that there are linkages among them. They can be large or small, local or global, centrally directed or highly decentralized, narrowly focused or broadly oriented toward several goals (Williams 1998). Traditionally, criminal organizations have been characterized as strictly hierarchical organizations. For example, in a 1969 study of La Cosa Nostra in the United States, Cressey (1969) made the seminal observation that an organized criminal group was a bureaucracy. Its organizational structure, he argued, was directly related to the level of its presence in society; the greater the presence, the greater the complexity and hierarchy of the structure. His interpretation of organized crime as a highly centralized structure sparked numerous studies, many contesting his claim. Scholars such as Ianni (1974) and Albini (1979) questioned this rigid interpretation, arguing that criminal groups were akin to networks. Ianni wrote that a criminal group's structure can more accurately be described as a loose system of network relationships. A few years later,

Block (1979) reinforced this growing perception of criminal groups as horizontal structures when he described them as "webs of influence." Collectively, this body of scholarship established the fact that criminal organizations, though no less complex than their centralized counterparts, were more likely to be operating through fluid, horizontally organized structures.

2. Cenarrusa 2007.

3. Fanon 1982.

4. Kitson 1960; Kriger 1992.

5. Sarkesian 1975.

6. Ford 2005.

7. North 1981.

8. Williams and Godson 2002.

9. Ibid.

10. T. Johnson 2007a, 2007b; Jones 2008.

11. Karzai and Jones 2006.

12. Williams and Young 2007. I was conducting fieldwork in Kabul during the July 2008 bombing of the Indian embassy there.

13. Luqman 2008.

14. See, for example, Sikkink 1993; Chayes and Chayes 1995; Evans and Whitefield 1995; Legro 1995; Booth and Richard 1998; Keck and Sikkink 1998; McLaughlin Mitchell 2002; Schedler 2002; Flockhart 2005.

15. My definition of *norms* draws from Finnemore and Sikkink (1998), who claim that there is a concurrence on norms as "standard[s] of appropriate behavior for actors with a given identity" (251).

16. Adapted from IDEA website, www.idea.int/democracy/.

17. Gleditsch 2002, 13.

18. Osaghae 1999.

19. Sorenson 1998.

20. McColm 1993; Karatnycky 1994.

21. See Reagan 1982.

22. Apodaca and Stohl 1999.

23. O'Ballance 2000; Holt and Daly 2005.

24. Muriel and Dhel 2003.

25. Zaman 2004b.

26. Diker 2004; Nebahat 2004.

27. İçduygu, Romano, and Sirkeci 1999.

28. Metelits 2004.

29. Berry 2007.

Bibliography

Academia Nacional de Ciencias de Bolivia. 1907. v. 42, f. 177.

Archivo del Congreso Nacional. 1992. Leyes autografas de 1882 [Senado]. v. 2, fs. 250, 266.

Adamson, Fiona B. 2005. Globalisation, transnational political mobilisation, and networks of violence. *Cambridge Review of International Affairs* 18(1): 31–49.

African Rights. 1997. *Food and Power: A Critique of Humanitarianism*. London: African Rights.

Africa Watch. 1993. Sudan: Human rights developments. Human Rights Watch website, www.hrw.org/reports/1993/WR93/Afw-10.htm.

———. 1995. Sudan: Human rights developments. Human Rights Watch website, www.hrw.org/reports/1995/WR95/AFRICA-10.htm.

Agence France Presse. 2004. Kurdish activist to form new party. 24 October. (accessed 26 October 2004).

———. 2005. PKK denies responsibility for Turkish resort bombing. 17 July (accessed 18 July 2005).

Ahmad, Hisham H. 1994. *Hamas: From Religious Salvation to Political Transformation*. Jerusalem: Palestinian Academic Society for the Study of International Affairs.

Albini, Joseph. 1979. *The American Mafia: The Genesis of a Legend*. New York: Irvington.

AlJazeera.net. 2007. Banana grower's paramilitary links. http://english.aljazeera.net/News/aspx/print.htm (accessed 21 March 2007).

Amnesty International. 2005. Colombia. www.web.amnesty.org/report2005/col-summary-eng (accessed 19 October 2006).

Anadolu Agency. 2004. Former DEP deputy says they will launch democratic society movement. 22 October (accessed 24 October 2004).

Anderson, Perry. 1979. *Lineages of the Absolutist State*. London: Verso.

Apodaca, Claire, and Michael Stohl. 1999. United States human rights policy and foreign assistance. *International Studies Quarterly* 43(1): 185–98.

Arenas, Jacobo. 1985. *Cese el Fuego: Una Historia Politica de Las FARC*. Bogotá: Oveja Negra.

Arias, Desmond, and Gipsy Escobar. 2007. Defusing contention: The effectiveness of paramilitary demobilization programs in reducing violent crime and political violence in Colombia, 2000–2006. Paper presented at the annual meeting of the American Society of Criminology, Atlanta, 14 November. Available online at http://www.allacademic.com/meta/p201320_index.html.

Arizmendi, Dario. 2000. Interview with Carlos Castaño. *Cara a Cara.* Caracol Television, Colombia. 1 March.

Arol, Reuben Madol (judge). 2001. Interview with author. 29 October. Rumbek, Sudan.

Arsu, Sebnem. 2005. Official says Turkish blast was not by suicide bomber. *New York Times,* 18 July, A3.

Ashcraft, Richard, ed. 1991. *John Locke: Critical Assessments.* London: Routledge.

Assembly of Turkish American Associations. 2007. *PKK and Terrorism: A Report on the PKK and Terrorism.* http://www.ataa.org/ataa/ref/pkk/mfa/report-pkk-terrorism.html (accessed 10 March 2007).

Aviles, William. 2006. Paramilitarism and Colombia's low-intensity democracy. *Journal of Latin American Studies* 38: 379–408.

Awat, Daniel, Lwal Deng Woll, and David Deng (SPLA officials). 2001. Interview with author. 12 October. Nairobi, Kenya.

Azam, Jean-Paul. 2002. Looting and conflict between ethno-regional groups: Lessons for state formation in Africa. *Journal of Conflict Resolution* 46(1): 131–153.

Bailey, Norman A. 1967. La violencia in Colombia. *Journal of Inter-American Studies* 9(4).

Barkey, Henri J. 1993. Turkey's Kurdish dilemma. *Survival* 35(4): 51–70.

Barkey, Henri J., and Graham E. Fuller. 1998. *Turkey's Kurdish Question.* New York/Lanham, MD: Carnegie Commission on Preventing Deadly Conflict/ Rowman and Littlefield.

Barkey, Karen. 1994. *Bandits and Bureaucrats: The Ottoman Route to State Centralization.* Ithaca, NY: Cornell University Press.

Bates, Robert H. 2001. *Prosperity and Violence.* New York: Norton.

———. 2005. *Markets and States in Tropical Africa: The Political Basis of Agricultural Policies.* Berkeley: University of California Press.

BBC News. 2006a. Colombia's Uribe wins second term. 29 May. http://news.bbc.co.uk/go/pr/fr/-/2/hi/americas/5024428.stm (accessed 14 February 2009).

———. 2006b. Explosion rocks SE Turkish city. 13 September. http://news.bbc.co.uk/2/hi/europe/5340408.stm (accessed 6 January 2009).

———. 2007. PKK members held in Paris raids. 6 February. http://news.bbc.co.uk/go/pr/fr/-/2/hi/europe/6332215.stm.

———. 2008. Colombia calls for Chavez charges. 4 March. http://news.bbc.co.uk/2/hi/americas/7277313.stm (accessed 15 February 2009).

———. 2009. Colombia FARC attack "kills four." 14 January. http://news.bbc.co.uk/go/pr/fr/-/1/hi/world/7828037.stm (accessed 13 February 2009).

Beckett, Ian. 2005. The future of insurgency. *Small Wars and Insurgencies* 16(1): 22–36.

Bergquist, Charles. 1992. Introduction: Colombian violence in historical perspective. In *Violence in Colombia: The Contemporary Crisis in Historical Perspective,* edited by Charles Bergquist, Ricardo Peñaranda, and Gonzalo Sánchez G., 1–10. Wilmington, DE: Scholarly Resources.

Bergquist, Charles, Ricardo Peñaranda, and Gonzalo Sánchez G., eds. 1992. *Violence in Colombia: The Contemporary Crisis in Historical Perspective.* Wilmington, DE: Scholarly Resources.

Beriker-Atiyas, N. 1997. The Kurdish conflict in Turkey: Issues, parties and prospects. *Security Dialogue* 28(4).

Bermeo, Nancy. 1986. *The Revolution within the Revolution: Workers' Control in Rural Portugal.* Princeton, NJ: Princeton University Press.

Berry, Christina. 2007. Negotiating with FARC: Arms vs. words. *Diplomatic Courier,* 20 December. http://www.diplomaticourier.org/kmitan/articleback. php?ncwsid=29.

Beissinger, Mark, and M. Crawford Young. 2002. *Beyond State Crisis? Post-Colonial Africa and Post-Soviet Eurasia in Comparative Perspective.* Princeton, NJ: Woodrow Wilson Center Press.

Betancourt, Dario, and Martha Garcia. 1994. *Contrabadistas, Marimberos y Mafiosos.* Bogotá: Tercer Mundo.

Bilgin, M. Sirac. 2004. Letter to Kurdish people of Turkey. 31 July. Available online at www.bilgin.nu/articles/2004/2004-04-01.php.

Birch, Nicholas. 2004. Turkey's Kurdish rebels face uncertainty. *Christian Science Monitor,* 30 March.

Block, Alan. 1979. *East Side–West Side: Organizing Crime in New York, 1939–1959.* Swansea, UK: Christopher Davis.

Booth, John, and Patricia Richard. 1998. Civil society, political capital, and democratization in Central America. *Journal of Politics* 60(3): 780–800.

Bozarslan, Hamit. 1996a. Political crisis and the Kurdish issue in Turkey. In *The Kurdish Nationalist Movement in the 1990s,* edited by Robert Olson, 135–153. Lexington: University Press of Kentucky.

———. 1996b. Turkey's elections and the Kurds. *Middle East Report,* 16–19.

Briefing. 1988a. The case of the "Apo" interview.

———. 1988b. PKK: The European breakup.

———. 1988c. Will the PKK be a regional issue?

Bulloch, John, and Harvey Morris. 1992. *No Friends but the Mountains.* New York: Oxford University Press.

Buoc, Isaac Makur (commissioner). 2001. Interview with author. 29 October. Rumbek, Sudan.

Burr, J. M., and R. O. Collins. 1995. *Requiem for Sudan: War, Drought, and Disaster Relief on the Nile.* Boulder, CO: Westview.

Bushnell, David. 1992. Politics and violence in nineteenth-century Colombia. In *Violence in Colombia: The Contemporary Crisis in Historical Perspective*, edited by Charles Bergquist, Ricardo Peñaranda, and Gonzalo Sánchez G., 11–30. Wilmington, DE: Scholarly Resources.

———. 1993. *The Making of Modern Colombia: A Nation in Spite of Itself.* Berkeley: University of California Press.

Campesino. 2006. Interview with author. 25 October. Department of Sucre, Colombia.

Carmen (civilian). 2006. Interview with author. 27 October. Zambrano, Department of Bolivar, Colombia.

Casteel, Steven W. 2003. Statement of Assistant Administrator for Intelligence before the Senate Committee on the Judiciary. Available online at U.S. Drug Enforcement Administration website, http://www.usdoj.gov/dea/pubs/cngrtest/cto52003.html (accessed 15 March 2007).

Center for International Policy. 2006. "Mission accomplished," says State's Nicholas Burns. Washington, DC: CIP.

Centro de Investigación y Educación Popular (CINEP). 2001. *Situación de Derechos Humanos, Derecho Internacional Humanitario y Derechos Económicos, Sociales y Culturales en el Departamento del Putumayo: CINEP, MINGA, CODHES.* Available online at www.derechoshumanos.gov.co/observatorio_de_DDHH/documentos/indicadoresdico5.pdf.

Cha, V. 2002. Hawk engagement and preventive defense on the Korean peninsula. *International Security* 27: 40–79.

Chaliand, Gérard. 1969. *Armed Struggle in Africa: With the Guerrillas in Portuguese Guinea.* New York: Monthly Review Press.

Chaliand, Gérard, and Arnaud Blin. 2007. *The History of Terrorism: From Antiquity to Al Qaeda.* Berkeley: University of California Press.

Chatterjee, Partha. 1993. *The Nation and Its Fragments: Colonial and Postcolonial Histories.* Princeton, NJ: Princeton University Press.

Chayes, Abram, and Antonia Chayes. 1995. *The New Sovereignty: Compliance with International Regulatory Agreements.* Cambridge, MA: Harvard University Press.

Christian Science Monitor. 2007. Turkish Kurds: Some back the state. 6 July. http://www.csmonitor.com/2007/0706/p06s02-wosc.html (accessed on 6 January 2009).

CIA. 2007. Turkey. 15 March. https://www.cia.gov/cia/publications/factbook/geos/tu.html (accessed 17 April 2007).

Clark, John F. 2001. Explaining Ugandan intervention in Congo: Evidence and Interpretations. *Journal of Modern African Studies* 39(2): 261–287.

CNN.com. 1999. Kurds seize embassies, wage violent protests across Europe. 16 February (accessed 15 March 2007).

———. 2009. Colombian guerrillas kill 17 Indians, human rights groups say. 11 February. http://www.cnn.com/2009/WORLD/americas/02/11/colombia.indians/index.html (accessed 13 February 2009).

Cobb, Charles. 2002. Sudan: Government, rebels sign promise not to target civilians. *AllAfrica.com*, 26 March. http://allafrica.com/stories/200203260777.html.

Collier, Paul. 2000a. *Economic Causes of Civil Conflict and Their Implications for Policy.* Washington, DC: World Bank Development Research Group.

———. 2000b. Rebellion as a quasi-criminal activity. *Journal of Conflict Resolution* 44(6): 839–853.

Collier, Paul, and Anke Hoeffler. 2001. Greed and grievance in civil war. World Bank research paper. Washington, DC: World Bank.

Collier, Paul, and Nicholas Sambanis. 2002. Understanding civil wars. Special issue, *Conflict Resolution* 46(1).

Comprehensive Peace Agreement between the Government of the Republic of the Sudan and the Sudan People's Liberation Movement/Sudan People's Liberation Army. 2005. January. United Nations Mission in Sudan website, www.unmis.org/english/documents/cpa-en.pdf (accessed 14 February 2009).

Confidential source (SPLA member). 2006. Interview with author. 29 October. Cartagena, Colombia.

——— (SPLA member). 2003. Interview with author. 17 June. Rumbek, Sudan.

———. 2001. Interview with author. 26 October. Nairobi, Kenya.

Connell, Dan. 1999. Field report: What's new in the new Sudan? *Middle East Report* 212: 2–3, 7.

Cornell, Svante E. 2001. The Kurdish question in Turkish politics. *Orbis* 45(1): 31–46.

Cramer, Christopher. 2007. *Violence in Developing Countries.* Bloomington: Indiana University Press.

Cressey, Donald. 1969. *The Theft of the Nation.* New York: Harper and Row.

Criss, Nur Bilge. 1995. The nature of PKK terrorism in Turkey. *Studies in Conflict and Terrorism* 18(1): 17–37.

Damon, Arwa. 2008. Female fighters: We won't stand for male dominance. *CNN.com.* http://www.cnn.com/2008/WORLD/meast/10/06/iraq.pkk/index.html (accessed 6 January 2009).

Daniel (SPLA commander). 2001. Interview with author. 15 November. Yei, Sudan.

David (former Rumbek County commissioner). 2003. Interview with author. 12 June. Nairobi, Kenya.

de Waal, Alex. 1993. Some comments on militias in the contemporary Sudan. In *Civil War in the Sudan,* edited by M. W. Daly and A. Alawad. London: British Academic Press.

Debray, Régis. 1967. *Revolution in the Revolution?* New York: Grove.

DeMars, William Emile. 1993. Helping people in a people's war: Humanitarian organizations and the Ethiopian conflict, 1980–1988. Ph.D. diss., University of Notre Dame.

Deng, Francis M. 1995. *War of Visions: Conflict of Identities in the Sudan.* Washington, DC: Brookings Institution Press.

Deng, Mary Achol, and Priscilla Nyahong. 2001. Interview with author. 18 November. Nimule, Sudan.

Diker, Seyhmus (assistant to mayor). 2004. Interview with author. 24 December. Diyarbakir, Turkey.

Dilan (PKK soldier). 2004. Interview with author. 2 July. PKK camp, northern Iraq.

Dix, Robert H. 1967. *Colombia: The Political Dimensions of Change.* New Haven, CT: Yale University Press.

DozaMe.org. 2004. Clashes in Bingol between village guards and the Kurdish HPG. 5 May (accessed 5 May 2004).

———. 2006. Cunning attack by TAK leaves 18 wounded in Adana. 7 August (accessed 7 August 2006).

Dudley, Steven. 2004. *Walking Ghosts: Murder and Guerrilla Politics in Colombia.* New York and London: Routledge.

——— (journalist). 2006. Interview with author. 24 January. Bogotá, Colombia.

Duffield, Mark, Helen Young, John Ryle, and Ian Henderson. 1995. *Sudan Emergency Operations Consortium (SEOC): A Review.* Birmingham: University of Birmingham.

Efuk, Soforonio. 2000. Humanitarianism that harms: A critique of NGO charity in southern Sudan. *Civil Wars* 3(3): 45–73.

Ehrenfeld, Rachel. 2005. *Funding Evil, Updated: How Terrorism Is Financed and How to Stop It.* Santa Monica, CA: Bonus Books.

Eide, Tormund, Tomas Hägg, Richard Holton Pierce, and László Török, eds. 1994. *Fontes Historiae Nubiorum: Textual Sources for the History of the Middle Nile Region between the Eighth Century BC and the Sixth Century AD,* vol. 1 Bergen: University of Bergen.

El capo de las drogas de las FARC. 2007. *Eltiempo.com,* http://www.eltiempo.com/conflicto/noticias/ARTICULO-WEB-NOTA_INTERIOR-3705978.html (accessed 3 September 2007).

Enginsoy, Ümit. 2009a. Iraqi Kurds reveal anti-PKK measure. *Hürriyet,* 11 February. http://arama.hurriyet.com/tr/arsivnews.aspx?id=10973358 (accessed 13 February 2009).

———. 2009b. U.S. says Iranian arm of PKK terror group. *Hürriyet,* 6 February. http://arama.hurriyet.com/tr/arsivnews.aspx?id=10938380 (accessed 13 February 2009).

Entessar, Nader. 1989. The Kurdish mosaic of discord. *Third World Quarterly* 11(4): 83–100.

Enzensberger, Hans Magnus. 1994. *Civil Wars: From L.A. to Bosnia*. New York: New Press.

Eriksen, Stein S. 2005. The politics of state formation: Contradictions and conditions of possibility. *Journal of European Development Research* 17(3): 396–410.

European-Sudanese Public Affairs Council. 2001. The war on terrorism: The United States and the SPLA in Sudan. *Sudan.net*, http://www.sudan.net/news/press/postedr/43.shtml (accessed 29 March 2007).

Evans, Geoffrey, and Stephen Whitefield. 1995. The politics and economics of democratic commitment: Support for democracy in transition societies. *British Journal of Political Science* 25(4): 485–514.

Evans-Pritchard, Edward E. 1969. *The Nuer: A Description of the Modes of Livelihood and Political Institutions of a Nilotic People*. New York: Oxford University Press.

Fals Borda, Orlando. 1985. *Historia de la Cuestion Agraria en Colombia*. Bogotá: Carlos Valencia Editores.

Fanon, Frantz. 1982. *Wretched of the Earth*. New York: Grove.

FARC. 1989. Pleno 1989: Conclusiónes sobre Plan Militar Estratégico de 8 años, Organización, Escuela Nacional y Finanzas.

———. 1993. Declaración Politica de la Octava Conferencia Nacional FARC-EP.

Federation of American Scientists. 2007. The PKK's role in international drug trafficking. *FAS.org*. http://www.fas.org/irp/world/para/docs/studies5.htm (accessed January 2007).

Ferrero, Gugliermo. 1942. *The Principles of Power: The Great Political Crises of History*. Salem, NH: Ayer.

Ferro Medina, Juan Guillermo, and Graciela Uribe Ramón. 2002. *El Orden de la Guerra: Las FARC-EP Entre la Organización y la Politica*. Bogotá: Centro Editorial Javeriano.

Finnemore, Martha, and Kathryn Sikkink. 1998. International norm dynamics and political change. *International Organization* 52(4): 887–917.

First Equatoria Regional Congress. 2002. Yei, New Sudan.

Flockhart, Trine. 2005. *Socializing Democratic Norms: The Role of International Organizations for the Construction of Europe*. Basingstoke, UK: Palgrave.

Fluherty, Vernon Lee. 1956. *Dance of the Millions: Military Rule and the Social Revolution in Colombia, 1930–1956*. Pittsburgh: University of Pittsburgh Press.

Ford, Christopher. 2005. Speak no evil: Targeting a population's neutrality to defeat an insurgency. *Parameters* (Summer): 51–66.

Forero, Juan. 2008. FARC desertions hit record high. Radio broadcast. *NPR News*, 28 March. http://www.npr.org/templates/story/story.php?storyId=89186915 (accessed 15 February 2009).

Frankel, Glenn. 2005. Police pin bank heist on IRA. *Washington Post*, 8 January.

Frum, David. 2004. *An End to Evil: How to Win the War on Terror*. New York: Ballantine Books.

Fukui, K., and J. Markakis, ed. 1994. *Ethnicity and Conflict in the Horn of Africa.* London: James Currey.

Fukuyama, Francis. 2004. *State-Building: Governance and World Order in the 21st Century.* Ithaca, NY: Cornell University Press.

Garang, John. 1992. *The Call for Democracy in Sudan,* 2nd ed. London: Kegan Paul.

———. 1996. Speech to the National Executive Council following the conference on Civil Authority, Himan–New Cush, May.

———. 2000. Message to all units. January. Nairobi, Kenya.

Garcia, Clara Ines. 1996. *Uraba: Region, Actores y Conflicto, 1960–1990.* Bogotá: CERAC.

Garcia-Marquez, Captain (head of navy). 2006. Interview with author. 30 October. Cartagena, Colombia.

Gasser, Hans-Peter. 1993. *International Humanitarian Law, an Introduction.* Geneva: Henry Dunant Institute.

Gellner, Ernest. 1983. *Nations and Nationalism.* Ithaca, NY: Cornell University Press.

Gibb, Hamilton. 1982. *Studies on the Civilization of Islam.* Princeton, NJ: Princeton University Press.

Gleditsch, Kristian S. 2002. *All International Politics Is Local.* Ann Arbor: University of Michigan Press.

Gleditsch, Nils Petter, and Bethany Lacina. 2005. Monitoring trends in global combat: A new dataset of battle deaths. *European Journal of Population* 21(2–3): 145–166.

GlobalMarch.org. 1999. Belgium. http://www.globalmarch.org/resourcecentre/world/belgium.pdf (accessed 15 March 2007).

GlobalSecurity.org. 2008. Military: Revolutionary Armed Forces of Colombia. www.globalsecurity.org/military/world/para/farc.htm (accessed 13 February 2009).

Gonzalez, Jose Jairo, Roberto Ramirez, Alberto Valencia, and Reinaldo Barbosa. 1998. *Conflictos Regionales: Amazonia y Orinoquia.* Bogotá: Fundación Friedrich Ebert de Colombia and IEPRI.

Goodwin, Jeff. 1995. The vogue of revolution in poor countries. *Political Science Quarterly* 110(3): 490–492.

Grossman, Herschel I. 1999. Kleptocracy and revolution. *Oxford Economic Papers* 51(2): 267–283.

Guerra, Wilder (anthropologist). 2006. Interview with author. 30 October. Cartagena, Colombia.

Guevara, Ernesto "Che." 1985. Introduction and case studies. In *Guerrilla Warfare,* edited by J. Brian Loveman and Thomas M. Davies. Lincoln: University of Nebraska Press.

Guillermoprieto, Alma. 2001. *Looking for History: Dispatches from Latin America*. New York: Vintage Books.

Gunning, Jeroen. 2008. *Hamas in Politics: Democracy, Religion, Violence*. New York: Columbia University Press.

Gunter, Michael M. 1990. *The Kurds in Turkey: A Political Dilemma*. Boulder, CO: Westview.

Gürbey, Gülistan. 1996. The Kurdish nationalist movement in Turkey since the 1980s. *The Kurdish Nationalist Movement in the 1990s*, edited by Robert Olson, 9–37. Lexington: University Press of Kentucky.

Gurr, Ted Robert. 1968. A causal model of civil strife: A comparative analysis using new indices. *American Political Science Review* 62: 1104–1124.

———. 1970. *Why Men Rebel*. Princeton, NJ: Princeton University Press.

———. 1986. Persisting patterns of repression and rebellion: Foundations for a general theory of political coercion. In *Persistent Patterns and Emerging Structures in a Waning Century*, edited by M. Karns. New York: Praeger.

———. 1994. Peoples against states: Ethnopolitical conflict and the changing world system: 1994 presidential address. *International Studies Quarterly* 38(3): 347–377.

———. 2000. *Peoples versus States: Minorities at Risk in the New Century*. Washington, DC: USIP.

Guzmán Campos, German, Orlando Fals Borda, and Eduardo Umaña Luna, eds. 1962. *La Violencia en Colombia*. Vol. 1. Bogotá: Ediciónes Tercer Mundo.

———, eds. 1964. *La Violencia en Colombia*. Vol. 2. Bogotá: Ediciónes Tercer Mundo.

Hacaoglu, Selcan. 2007. Kurds return to Turkey's parliament. *USA Today*, 3 August. http://www.usatoday.com/news/topstories/2007-08-03-3796946200_x.htm.

Hale, Sondra. 1996. The new Muslim woman: Sudan's national Islamic front and the invention of identity. *Muslim World* 86(2): 176–199.

Hannity, Sean. 2004. *Deliver Us from Evil: Defeating Terrorism, Despotism, and Liberalism*. New York: Harper.

Hanratty, Dennis M., and Sandra W. Meditz, eds. 1990. *Colombia: A Country Study*. Washington, DC: Federal Research Division, Library of Congress.

Hansen, Thomas Blom, and Finn Stepputat. 2001. *States of Imagination: Ethnographic Explorations of the Post-Colonial State*. Durham, NC: Duke University Press.

Hartlyn, Jonathan. 1988. *The Politics of Coalition Rule in Colombia*. Cambridge: Cambridge University Press.

Hechter, Michael. 2000. *Containing Nationalism*. Oxford: Oxford University Press.

Henshaw, Amber. 2008. Pirates reveal Sudan's precarious peace. *BBC News*, 7 October. http://news.bbc.co.uk/2/hi/africa/7657359.stm (accessed 14 February 2009).

Herbst, Jeffrey. 1996–97. Responding to state failure in Africa. *International Security* 1(3): 120–144.

———. 2000. *States and Power in Africa: Comparative Lessons in Authority and Control*. Princeton, NJ: Princeton University Press.

Hoffman, Bruce. 2006. *Inside Terrorism*. New York: Columbia University Press.

Holsti, Kalevi J. 1996. *The State, War, and the State of War*. Cambridge: Cambridge University Press.

Holt, P. M., and M. W. Daly. 2005. *A History of the Sudan: From the Coming of Islam to the Present Day*. 5th ed. Harlow, UK: Pearson Education.

Human-rights lawyer. 2006. Interview with author. 24 October. Cartagena, Colombia.

Human Rights Watch. 1994. Civilian devastation: Abuses by all parties in the war in southern Sudan. New York: Human Rights Watch/Africa.

———. 1996. Children in combat. *Human Rights Watch Children's Rights Project* 8, no. 1 (G) (January). www.hrw.org/sites/default/files/reports/general961.pdf.

———. 1998. Sudan: How human rights abuses caused the disaster. *hrw.org*. http://www.hrw.org/campaigns/sudan98/sudfam.htm (accessed February 2006).

———. 1999a. Bahr El Ghazal and the famine of 1998. In *Famine in Sudan, 1998*. *hrw.org*. http://www.hrw.org/reports/1999/sudan/SUDAWEB2-01.htm.

———. 1999b. Sudan: Human rights developments. *hrw.org*. http://www.hrw.org/wr2k/Africa-11.htm (accessed February 2006).

———. 2000. Colombia: Human rights developments. *hrw.org*. http://www.hrw.org/wr2k1/americas/colombia.html (accessed 19 October 2006).

———. 2001a. Colombia: Rebel abuses worsening. *hrw.org*. July. www.hrw.org/en/news/2001/07/08/colombia-rebel-abuses-worsening.

———. 2001b. *The "Sixth Division": Military-Paramilitary Ties and U.S. Policy in Colombia*. New York: Human Rights Watch.

———. 2001c. Sudan: Analysis of the current fighting and its relation to famine. *hrw.org*, February. http://www.hrw.org/en/news/2001/02/28/sudan-analysis-current-fighting-and-its-relation-famine (accessed 7 September 2006).

———. 2002. Slavery and slave redemption in the Sudan. *Human Rights Watch Backgrounder*. www.hrw.org/backgrounder/africa/sudanupdate-print.htm.

———. 2005. A face and a name: Civilian victims of insurgent groups in Iraq. *hrw.org*. http://www.hrw.org/en/reports/2005/10/02/face-and-name (accessed 6 January 2009).

Human Rights Watch/Africa and Human Rights Watch Children's Rights Project. 1994. Sudan: The lost boys; Child soldiers and unaccompanied boys in southern Sudan. *Children's Rights Project and HRW/Africa* 6(10) (November).

Humphreys, Macartan, and Jeremy M. Weinstein. 2006. Handling and manhandling civilians in civil war. *American Political Science Review* 100(3): 429–447.

Hunt, Shelby D., and Robert M. Morgan. 1995. The comparative advantage theory of competition. *Journal of Marketing* 59 (April): 1–15.

Hürriyet. 2009. Turkish army bombs PKK lairs. 7 February. http://arama.hurriyet. com/tr/arsivnews.aspx?id=10946395 (accessed 13 February 2009).

Hutchinson, Asa. 2002. *International Drug Trafficking and Terrorism: Testimony before the Senate Judiciary Committee Subcommittee on Technology, Terrorism, and Government Information.* U.S. Department of State, http://www.state. gov/p/inl/rls/rm/2002/9239.htm (accessed 15 March 2007).

Hutchinson, J., and A. D. Smith, eds. 1996. *Ethnicity.* Oxford: Oxford University Press.

Hutchinson, Martha Crenshaw. 1978. *Revolutionary Terrorism: The FLN in Algeria, 1954–1962.* Stanford, CA: Hoover Institution Press.

Hutchinson, Sharon E. 1996. *Nuer Dilemmas: Coping with Money, War and the State.* Berkeley: University of California Press.

———. 2001. A curse from God? Religious and political dimensions of the post-1991 rise of ethnic violence in south Sudan. *Journal of Modern African Studies* 39(2).

Ianni, Francis J. 1974. *Black Mafia: Ethnic Succession in Organized Crime.* New York: Simon and Schuster.

İçduygu, Ahmet, David Romano, and Ibrahim Sirkeci. 1999. The ethnic question in an environment of insecurity: The Kurds in Turkey. *Ethnic and Racial Studies* 22(6): 991–1010.

Ignatieff, Michael. 2004. *The Lesser Evil: Political Ethics in an Age of Terror.* Princeton, NJ: Princeton University Press.

Imset, Ismet G. 1988–89. Briefing study. *Briefing.* An analysis of the PKK published by the independent Turkish weekly *Briefing* and written by its news editor over the period of several weeks.

———. 1992. *PKK: Ayrilikci Siddetin 20 Yili (The PKK: 20 Years of Separatist Violence in Turkey).* Ankara: Turkish Daily News Yayinlari, 1992.

International Crisis Group. 2002. God, oil and country: Changing the logic of war in Sudan. ICG Africa Report No. 39. Brussels: International Crisis Group.

———. 2007. A strategy for comprehensive peace in Sudan. ICG Africa Report No. 130. Brussels: International Crisis Group.

International Herald Tribune. 2008. Dead rebel's laptop shows Chavez is funding rebels, Colombian police say. 3 March. http://www.iht.com/articles/ ap/2008/03/03/america/LA-GEN-Colombia-Chavez-FARC.php (accessed 15 February 2009).

IRIN. 2003. Sudan: Monitoring body documents more violations. 24 June.

Isaac (Archdeacon of Episcopal Church of Sudan). 2001. Interview with author. 30 October. Rumbek, Sudan.

Jackson, Robert. 1990. *Quasi-States: Sovereignty, International Relations, and the Third World.* Cambridge: Cambridge University Press.

Jackson, Robert H., and Carl G. Rosberg. 1982. Why Africa's weak states persist: The empirical and the juridical in statehood. *World Politics* 35(1): 1–24.

James, Wendy. 2001. "People-friendly" projects and practical realities: Some contradictions on the Sudan-Ethiopian border. Paper presented at Sudan Workshop, Copenhagen, 9 February.

Jane's. 2001. FARC: Finance comes full circle for bartering revolutionaries. 19 January.

Jaramillo, Jaime, Leonidas Mora, and Fernando Cubides. 1986. Colonización, coca y guerrilla. Universidad Nacional de Colombia.

Johnson, Douglas H. 1994. Destruction and reconstruction in the economy of the southern Sudan. In *Short-Cut to Decay: The Case of the Sudan*, edited by S. Harir and T. Tvedt. Uppsala: Nordiska Afrikainstitutet.

———. 1996. Increasing the trauma of return: An assessment. In *In Search of Cool Ground: War, Flight and Homecoming in Northeast Africa*, edited by T. Allen. London: James Currey.

———. 2003. *The Root Causes of Sudan's Civil Wars.* Oxford: James Currey, in association with Indiana University Press and Fountain Publishers.

Johnson, Douglas H., and Gerard Prunier. 1993. The foundation and expansion of the Sudan People's Liberation Army. In *Civil War in the Sudan*, edited by M. W. Daly and A. A. Sikainga. London: British Academic Press.

Johnson, Thomas H. 2007a. On the edge of the big muddy: The Taliban resurgence in Afghanistan. *China and Eurasia Forum Quarterly* 5(2): 93–129.

———. 2007b. The Taliban insurgency and an analysis of *Shabnamah* (night letters). *Small Wars and Insurgencies* 18(3) (September): 317–344.

Jones, Seth G. 2008. The rise of Afghanistan's insurgency: State failure and jihad. *International Security* 32(4) (Spring): 7–40.

Jorge (farmer). 2006. Interview with author. 25 October. Chinulito, Chengue, Colombia.

Kaldor, Mary. 1999. *New and Old Wars: Organized Violence in a Global Era.* Stanford, CA: Stanford University Press.

Kalyvas, Stathis N. 2001. "New" and "old" civil wars: A valid distinction? *World Politics* 54(1): 99–118.

———. 2006. *The Logic of Violence in Civil War.* Cambridge: Cambridge University Press.

Kandeh, Jimmy D. 1999. Ransoming the state: Elite origins of subaltern terror in Sierra Leone. *Review of African Political Economy* 81: 349–366.

Kang, David C. 2003. International relations theory and the second Korean war. *International Studies Quarterly* 47: 301–324.

Kansu, Aykut. 1997. *The Revolution of 1908 in Turkey.* Leiden: Brill.

Karatnycky, Adrian. 1994. Freedom in retreat. *Freedom Review* 25.

Karim, Ataul, et al. 1996. *Operation Lifeline Sudan: A Review.* Geneva: Operation Lifeline Sudan.

Karzai, Hekmat, and Seth G. Jones. 2006. How to curb rising suicide terrorism in Afghanistan. *Christian Science Monitor*, July 18.

Kaya, Yasar. 2000. *Ozgur Politika. KurdishMedia.com,* 11 July. http://www.elif-savas.com/articles%20about%20elif/KurdishMedia%20News%20Issue%20390%20-%20July%2011,%202000.htm (accessed 2007).

Keck, Margaret, and Kathryn Sikkink. 1998. *Activists beyond Borders: Advocacy Networks in International Politics.* Ithaca, NY: Cornell University Press.

Keen, David. 1998. *The Economic Functions of Violence in Civil Wars.* Oxford: Oxford University Press.

Kevane, M., and E. Stiansen. 1998. Introduction. In *Kordofan Invaded: Peripheral Incorporation and Social Transformation in Islamic Africa,* edited by M. Kevane and E. Stiansen. Leiden: Brill.

Kinzer, Stephen. 2006a. The big change. *New York Review of Books,* 12 January.

———— (journalist). 2006b. Interview with author. Evanston, Illinois.

Kirk, Robin. 2001. Interview with Pablo Policzer. 3 July.

Kitson, Frank. 1960. *Gangs and Counter-Gangs.* London: Barrie and Rockliff.

Kok, Peter. 1996. *Governance and Conflict in the Sudan, 1985–1995: Analysis, Evaluation and Documentation.* Hamburg: Deutches Orient Institut.

Kok, Rebecca Yar Joseph. 2001. Interview with author. 31 October. Rumbek, Sudan.

Kovaleski, Serge F. 1999. Rebel movement on the rise: Colombian guerrillas use military force, not ideology to hold power. *Washington Post,* 5 February.

Krasner, Stephan D. 2001. *Problematic Sovereignty: Contested Rules and Political Possibilities.* New York: Columbia University Press.

————. 2003. The exhaustion of sovereignty: International shaping of domestic authority structures. Institut du Developpement et des Relations Durable Internationales, Paris.

Kreyenbroek, Philip G. 1992. On the Kurdish language. In *The Kurds: A Contemporary Overview,* edited by P. Kreyenbroek and S. Sperl. London and New York: Routledge.

Kriger, Norma J. 1992. *Zimbabwe's Guerilla War.* New York: Cambridge University Press.

Krueger, Anne. 1974. The political economy of the rent-seeking society. *American Economic Review* 64(3): 291–303.

Kuol, M. L. 1997. *Administration of Justice in (SPLA/M) Liberated Areas: Court Cases in War-Torn Southern Sudan.* Oxford: Oxford Refugee Studies Programme.

Kuol, Yar (data officer, SPLA). 2001. Interview with author. 15 November. Yei, Sudan.

KurdishMedia.com. 2004. The long and winding road of the major split from the PKK to PWD. 24 October (accessed 2005).

Kutschera, Chris. 1994. Mad dreams of independence: The Kurds in Turkey and the PKK. *Middle East Report,* 12–15.

———. 1995. Kurdistan Turkey: Parliament in exile, a propaganda ploy? *Middle East Magazine.* 1 June.

Lapidus, Ira. 2002. *A History of Islamic Societies.* Cambridge: Cambridge University Press.

Leech, Gary M. 2000. An interview with FARC commander Simon Trinidad. *NACLA Report on the Americas,* September–October.

LeGrand, Catherine. 1986. *Frontier Expansion and Peasant Protest in Colombia, 1850–1936.* Albuquerque: University of New Mexico Press.

———. 1992. Agrarian antecedents to the violence. In *Violence in Colombia: The Contemporary Crisis in Historical Perspective,* edited by Charles Bergquist, Ricardo Peñaranda, and Gonzalo Sánchez G., 31–50. Wilmington, DE: Scholarly Resources.

Legro, Jeffrey. 1995. Which norms matter? Revisiting the "failure" of internationalism in World War II. Paper presented at the annual conference of the American Political Science Association, Chicago.

Lemin, Joseph, and George Odera (chairman and secretary of County Development Committee). 2001. Interview with author. 18 November. Nimule, Sudan.

Lesch, Ann Mosely. 1998. *The Sudan: Contested National Identities.* Bloomington: Indiana University Press.

Lino, Edward (commander, SPLA). 2005. Interview with author. 30 December. Nairobi.

———. 2001. Interview with author. 12 October. Nairobi.

Luqman (Deputy Director of Institute of Diplomacy, Ministry of Foreign Affairs). 2008. Interview with author. 30 June. Kabul, Afghanistan.

Magnong, Mangar Chol (Payam administrator). 2001. Interview with author. 30 October. Rumbek, Sudan.

Maguat, Monica Ayen (coordinator, New Sudan Women's Federation for Rumbek). 2001. Interview with author. 31 October. Rumbek, Sudan.

Male PKK soldiers. 2004. Interview with author. 3 July. PKK camp, northern Iraq.

Maloney, Anastasia. 2008. After desertions, demise of leaders, Colombia's FARC appears in decline. *World Politics Review,* 13 June. http://www.worldpoliticsreview.com/Article.aspx?id=2285 (accessed 15 February 2009).

Mann, Michael. 1993. *The Sources of Social Power.* Cambridge: Cambridge University Press.

Manning, Carrie L. 1998. Constructing opposition in Mozambique: Renamo as political party. *Journal of Southern African Studies* 24(1): 161–89.

———. 2002. *The Politics of Peace in Mozambique.* Westport, CT: Praeger/Greenwood.

Manwaring, Max G. 2002. *Nonstate Actors in Colombia: Threat and Response.* Carlisle Barracks, PA: Strategic Studies Institute, U.S. Army War College.

Mardin, Serif. 1989. *Religion and Social Change in Modern Turkey.* Albany: State University of New York Press.

Mario (former Colombian journalist, asylum seeker). 2006. Interview with author. February. Chicago.

Marko (southern Sudanese refugee). 2001. Interview with author. 22 October. Kakuma Refugee Camp, Kenya.

Marks, Thomas A. 2001. Colombian crossroads: COLAR adapts to FARC insurgency. *Soldier of Fortune* (September): 56–61, 72.

Maslow, Abraham. 1943. A theory of human motivation. *Psychological Review* 50: 370–396.

Matta Aldana, Luis Alberto. 1999. *Colombia y las FARC-EP: Origen de la Lucha Guerrillera/Testimonio del Comandante Jaime Guaraca*. Tafalla, Nafarroa (Spain): Txalaparta.

McLaughlin Mitchell, Sara. 2002. A Kantian system? Democracy and third-party conflict resolution. *American Journal of Political Science* 46(4): 749–759.

McColm, Bruce R. 1993. The comparative survey of freedom. *Freedom Review* 3.

McDermott, Jeremy. 2002. Colombia's growing paramilitary force. *BBC News*, 7 January. http://news.bbc.co.uk/2/hi/americas/1746943.stm (accessed 30 January 2007).

———. 2006. Colombia conflict draws in minors. *BBC News*, 12 December. http://news.bbc.co.uk/1/hi/world/americas/6171709.stm (accessed 22 January 2007).

McDowell, David. 1992. The Kurdish question: A historical review. In *The Kurds: A Contemporary Overview*, edited by P. G. Kreyenbroek and S. Sperl. London and New York: Routledge.

———, 2004. *A Modern History of the Kurds*. London: I. B. Tauris.

Media (PKK soldier). 2004. Interview with author. 1 July. PKK camp, northern Iraq.

Metelits, Claire. 2004. Reformed rebels? Democratization, global norms, and the Sudan People's Liberation Army. *Africa Today* 51(1): 65–84.

Migdal, Joel S. 1988. *Strong Societies and Weak States*. Princeton, NJ: Princeton University Press.

Mishal, Shaul, and Selva Avraham. 2006. *The Palestinian Hamas: Vision, Violence, and Coexistence*. New York: Columbia University Press.

Modesto Campos, Jose. 1975. Las formas superiores de lucha en Colombia: Experiencia creadora de las masas. *Estudios Marxistas* 10.

Molano, Alfredo. 1992. Violence and land colonization. In *Violence in Colombia: The Contemporary Crisis in Historical Perspective*, edited by Charles Bergquist, Ricardo Peñaranda, and Gonzalo Sánchez G. Wilmington, DE: Scholarly Resources.

———. 2000. The evolution of the FARC: A guerrilla group's long history. *NACLA Report on the Americas*.

Mondragon, Hector. 2007. Democracy and plan Colombia. *NACLA Report on the Americas* (January–February): 42–44.

Monybut, Santino (former SPLA soldier). 2001. Interview with author. 19 October. Kakuma Refugee Camp, Kenya.

Moore, Barrington. 1966. *Social Origins of Dictatorship and Democracy*. Boston: Beacon.

Moses, Gideon Mathai (Nuer chairman). 2001. Interview with author. 22 October. Kakuma Refugee Camp, Kenya.

Muriel and Dhel (deputy brigade commanders, SPLA). 2003. Interview with author. 17 June. Rumbek, Sudan.

Murillo, Mario A. 2004. *Colombia and the United States: War, Unrest, and Destabilization*. New York: Seven Stories.

Nachmani, Amikam. 2003. *Turkey: Facing a New Millennium*. Manchester: Manchester University Press.

Nebahat (leader of local women's rights group). 2004. Interview with author. 23 December. Diyarbakir, Turkey.

Newbury, Catherine. 1992. The resurgence of civil society in Rwanda. Paper presented at Conference on Civil Society in Africa, Hebrew University, Jerusalem.

Newroz (congresswoman from Kongra-Gel). 2004. Interview with author. 3 July. PKK camp, northern Iraq.

New Sudan Council of Churches. 1991. Press release. Nairobi, Kenya.

Nezan, Kendal. 1997. Postscript. In *Prison No. 5: Eleven Years in Turkish Hails by Mehdi Zana*. Cambridge, MA: Blue Crane Books.

NGO representative. 2006. Interview with author. 24 October. Cartagena, Colombia.

NGO representatives. 2006. Interview with author. 26 October. Sincelejo, Colombia.

North, Douglass C. 1981. *Structure and Change in Economic History*. New York: Norton.

No Standing, Few Prospects. 2008. Sudan Issue Brief No. 13. September. Geneva: Small Arms Survey.

Nyaba, Peter A. 1997. *The Politics of Liberation in South Sudan: An Insider's View*. Kampala, Uganda: Fountain.

O'Ballance, Edgar. 2000. *Sudan, Civil War and Terrorism, 1956–1999*. Basingstoke, UK: Macmillan.

O'Hanlon, M. 1998. Stopping a North Korean invasion: Why defending South Korea is easier than the Pentagon thinks it is. *International Security* 22: 135–170.

Oloya, Micah (county judge). 2001. Interview with author. 18 November. Nimule, Sudan.

Olson, Mancur. 1993. Dictatorship, democracy and development. *American Political Science Review* 87(3): 567–576.

———. 2000. *Power and Prosperity: Outgrowing Communist and Capitalist Dicta-torships.* New York: Basic Books.

Olson, Robert, ed. 1996. *The Kurdish Nationalist Movement in the 1990s: Its Impact on Turkey and the Middle East.* Lexington: University Press of Kentucky.

O'Neill, Bard E. 1990. *Insurgency and Terrorism: Inside Modern Revolutionary Warfare.* Dulles, VA: Brassey's.

Ortiz, Román D. 2002. Insurgent strategies in the post–cold war: The case of the Revolutionary Armed Forces of Colombia. *Studies in Conflict and Terrorism* 25: 127–143.

Osaghae, E. 1999. Democratization in sub-Saharan Africa: Faltering prospects, new hopes. *Journal of Contemporary African Studies* 17(1): 5–28.

Osterling, Jorge P. 1989. *Democracy in Colombia: Clientelist Politics and Guerrilla Warfare.* Piscataway, NJ: Transaction.

Pallares, Amalia. 2002. *From Peasant Struggles to Indian Resistance: The Ecuadorian Andes in the Late Twentieth Century.* Norman: University of Oklahoma Press.

Partiya Welatpareza Demokratik. 2004. Press release on Kongra-Gel split: Osman Öcalan leads new group. 17 August.

Pastora Maria. 2006. Interview with author. 26 October. Sincelejo, Colombia.

Paul (former Lakes County governor). 2003. Interview with author. 17 June. Rumbek, Sudan.

Pizarro, Eduardo. 1992. Revolutionary guerrilla groups in Colombia. In *Violence in Colombia: The Contemporary Crisis in Historical Perspective,* edited by Charles Bergquist, Ricardo Peñaranda, and Gonzalo Sánchez G. Wilmington, DE: Scholarly Resources.

PKK. 1983. Serxwebun [PKK], Programme. English translation. Cologne, West Germany.

———. 1985. *Gallows in Kurdistan, Barracks Culture, and Our Duty of Revolutionary Revenge.* July. In Turkish.

———. 1995. 5. Kongresine Sunulan Eyalet Çalışma Raporları. *Provincial Working Reports Submitted to PKK's 5th Congress.* Vol. 1. Damascus.

Policzer, Pablo. 2005. *Human Rights Violations and Non-State Armed Groups: A New Framework.* Available online at www.iir.ubc.ca/Papers/Policzer-WP40.pdf (accessed 19 October 2006).

Priest. 2006a. Interview with author. 26 October. Sincelejo, Colombia.

———. 2006b. Interview with author. 28 October. Cartagena, Colombia.

Protocol II: Protocol Additional to the Geneva Conventions of 12 August 1949, and relating to the protection of victims of non-international armed conflicts. 1977. Available online at http://fletcher.tufts.edu/multi/texts/BH708.txt.

Prunier, Gerard. Forthcoming. The SPLA crisis. In *Contemporary Sudan,* edited by F. Ireton, E. Denis, and G. Prunier.

Pye, Lucien. 1971. *Warlord Politics: Conflict and Coalition in the Modernization of Republican China.* New York: Praeger.

Rabasa, Angela, and Peter Chalk. 2001. *Colombian Labyrinth.* Santa Monica, CA: RAND.

Ramirez Tabon, William. 1997. *Los Inciertos Confines de una Crisis.* Bogotá: Planeta.

Rangel, Alfredo. 2005. Prologo. In *El Poder Paramilitar,* edited by A. Rangel. Bogotá: Editorial Planeta Colombiana.

Reagan, Ronald. 1982. Speech to the House of Commons. 8 June. Available online at http://www.fordham.edu/halsall/mod/1982reagan1.html.

Reno, William. 1998. *Warlord Politics and African States.* Boulder, CO: Lynne Rienner.

Restrepo, Jorge, Michael Spagat, Patrick Reanier, and Nicolás F. Suárez. 2005. Civilian casualties in the Colombian conflict: Georeferencing human security. Paper presented at the twenty-fifth annual ESRI International User Conference, San Diego, CA.

Restrepo, Luis Alberto. 2001. The equivocal dimensions of human rights in Colombia. In *Violence in Colombia, 1990–2000: Waging War and Negotiating Peace,* edited by Charles Bergquist, Ricardo Peñaranda, and Gonzalo Sánchez G. Wilmington, DE: Scholarly Resources.

Rice, Edward. 1988. *Wars of the Third Kind: Conflict in Underdeveloped Countries.* Berkeley: University of California Press.

Richani, Nazih. 2002. *Systems of Violence: The Political Economy of War and Peace in Colombia.* Albany: State University of New York Press.

Riel, Rafael (vicar-general). 2001. Interview with author. 30 October. Rumbek, Sudan.

Robins, Philip. 1993. The overlord state: Turkish policy and the Kurdish issue. *International Affairs* 69(4): 657–676.

Rolandsen, Oystein H. 2005. *Guerrilla Government: Political Changes in the Southern Sudan during the 1990s.* Uppsala: Nordiska Afrikainstitutet.

Roldán, Mary. 2002. *Blood and Fire: La Violencia in Antioquia, Colombia, 1946–1953.* Durham, NC: Duke University Press.

Romano, David. 2006. *The Kurdish Nationalist Movement: Opportunity, Mobilization and Identity.* Cambridge: Cambridge University Press.

Ross, Michael L. 2004. How do natural resources influence civil war? Evidence from thirteen cases. *International Organization* 58 (Winter): 35–67.

Rotberg, Robert I. 2003. *State Failure and State Weakness in a Time of Terror.* Washington, DC: Brookings Institution Press.

———, ed. 2004. *When States Fail: Causes and Consequences.* Princeton, NJ: Princeton University Press.

Rubin, Barry M., and Kemal Kirisci, eds. 2001. *Turkey in World Politics: An Emerging Multiregional Power.* Boulder, CO: Lynne Rienner.

Safford, Frank. 2006. Changing phases and modalities of violence. Presentation at the Center for International and Comparative Studies, Northwestern University, Evanston, Illinois.

Safford, Frank, and Marco Palacios. 2002. *Colombia: Fragmented Land, Divided Society*. New York: Oxford University Press.

Sagan, S. 1988. The origins of the Pacific war. *Journal of Interdisciplinary History* 18: 893–922.

Salih, M. A. Mohamed, and Sharif Harir. 1994. Tribal militias: The genesis of national disintegration. In *Short-Cut to Decay: The Case of Sudan*, edited by S. Harir and T. Tvedt. Uppsala: Nordiska Afrikainstitutet.

Sánchez Gómez, Gonzalo, and Mario Aguilera, eds. 2001. *Memoria de un País en Guerra: Los Mil Días 1899–1902*. Bogotá: Planeta.

Sánchez, Gonzalo. 1992. The violence: An interpretive synthesis. In *Violence in Colombia: The Contemporary Crisis in Historical Perspective*, edited by Charles Bergquist, Ricardo Peñaranda, and Gonzalo Sánchez G., 75–124. Wilmington, DE: Scholarly Resources.

Sánchez, Gonzalo, and Donny Meertens. 2001. *Bandits, Peasants, and Politics*. Translated by A. Hynds. Austin: University of Texas Press.

Sarkesian, Sam C., ed. 1975. *Revolutionary Guerilla Warfare*. Chicago: Precedent.

Schedler, Andreas. 2002. Menu of manipulation. *Journal of Democracy* 13(2): 36–50.

Schimmelfennig, Frank. 2003. *The EU, NATO and the Integration of Europe*. Cambridge: Cambridge University Press.

Schleifer, Yigal. 2006. Denmark, again? Now it's under fire for hosting Kurdish TV station. *Christian Science Monitor*, 21 April.

Schmid, Alex P., and Albert J. Jongman. 2005. *Political Terrorism: A New Guide to Actors, Authors, Concepts, Data Bases, Theories, and Literature*. New Brunswick, NJ: Transaction.

Schutz, Barry. 1995. The heritage of revolution and the struggle for governmental legitimacy in Mozambique. In *Collapsed States: The Disintegration and Restoration of Legitimate Authority*, edited by I. W. Zartman. Boulder, CO: Lynne Rienner.

Scott, James C. 1979. Revolution in the revolution: Peasants and commissars. In State and revolution, special double issue, *Theory and Society* 7(1–2): 97–134.

Shelley, Louise, John T. Picarelli, Allison Irby, et al. 2005. *Methods and Motives: Exploring Links between Transnational Organized Crime and International Terrorism*. Project report, Department of Justice. 23 June.

Sikkink, Kathryn. 1993. Human rights, principled issue-networks, and sovereignty in Latin American. *International Organization* 47(3): 11–41.

Sirin (PKK soldier). 2004. Interview with author. 1 July. PKK camp, northern Iraq.

Skocpol, Theda. 1979. *States and Social Revolutions: A Comparative Analysis of France, Russia and China*. Cambridge: Cambridge University Press.

———. 1985. Bringing the state back in: Strategies of analysis in current research. In *Bringing the State Back In*, edited by P. B. Evans, T. S. D. Reuschemeyer, and Theda Skocpol. Cambridge: Cambridge University Press.

Smith/Kocamahhul, Joan. 2001. In the shadow of Kurdish: The silence of other ethnolinguistic minorities in Turkey. *Middle East Report* 219: 45–47.

Smyth, T. Lynn. 1967. *Colombia: Social Structure and the Process of Development*. Gainesville: University Press of Florida.

Snow, David. 1996. *Uncivil Wars: International Security and the New Internal Conflicts*. Boulder, CO: Lynne Rienner.

Snyder, Jack, and Robert Jervis. 1999. Civil war and the security dilemma. In *Civil Wars, Insecurity and Intervention*, edited by Barbara F. Walter and Jack Snyder. New York: Columbia University Press.

Socialist Party of Turkish Kurdistan. 1984. A report of the address by Kemal Burkay, General Secretary of the SPTK, to the Labour Movement Conference on Turkey. Headquarters of the NUR.

———. 1985. Appeal to the delegates of the 23rd General Conference of the UNESCO. Sofia, Bulgaria.

Sorenson, Georg. 1998. *Democracy and Democratization*. Boulder, CO: Westview.

Spagat, Michael. 2006. Colombia's paramilitary DDR: Quiet and tentative success. August. Available online at Conflict Analysis Resource Center website, http://www.cerac.org.co/pdf/UNDP_DDR_V2.pdf (accessed 18 January 2007).

Spears, Ian S. 2004. States-within-states: An introduction to their empirical attributes. In *States within States: Incipient Political Entities in the Post–Cold War Era*, edited by Paul Kingston and Ian S. Spears. New York: Palgrave Macmillan.

SPLA. 1991. Resolution 7. *The SPLM/SPLA Torit Resolutions*.

SPLA/SPLM. 1983. Manifesto, chapter 7, article 21. N.p.

———. 2000. Memorandum of understanding. 12 January.

Spruyt, Hendrik. 1994. *The Sovereign State and Its Competitors: An Analysis of Systems Change*. Princeton, NJ: Princeton University Press.

Statement from the Funj Civil Society. 2003. *Let Us Not Be Denied the Right to Decide on Our Future*. South Blue Nile, Southern Sudan.

Stein, Gottfried. 1994. *Endkampf um Kurdistan? Die PKK, die Turkei und Deutschland* (*The Ultimate Battle for Kurdistan? The PKK, Turkey and Germany*). Munich: Aktuell.

Sudan People's Liberation Movement. 1996. Programme. Paper presented at Conference on Civil Society and the Organization of Civil Authority of the New Sudan, 30 April–4 May, Himan-New Cush.

Tarrow, Sydney. 2007. Inside insurgencies: Politics and violence in an age of civil war. *Perspectives on Politics* 5(3): 587–600.

Tellez, Dora Maria. 2008. Interview with author. 25 July. Managua, Nicaragua.

Thornton, Thomas P. 1964. Terror as a weapon of political agitation. In *Internal War: Problems and Approaches,* edited by Harry Eckstein. New York: Free Press.

Tilly, Charles. 1985. War making and state making as organized crime. In *Bringing the State Back In,* edited by P. B. Evans, T. S. D. Reuschemeyer, and Theda Skocpol. Cambridge: Cambridge University Press.

———. 1990. *Coercion, Capital, and European States.* Cambridge, MA: Blackwell.

Trilsch, Mirja, and Alexandra Ruth. 2006. Ocalan v. Turkey. App. no. 46221/99. *American Journal of International Law* 100(1): 180–186.

Turkish Constitution. [1924–28] 1982. In *Suna Kili, Turk Anayasalari.* Ankara: Tekin Yayinevi.

Turkish Ministry of Foreign Affairs. 2005. Terrorism. http://www.mfa.gov.tr/MFA/ForeignPolicy/MainIssues/Terrorism/ (accessed 1 December 2005).

Tvedt, Terje. 1994. The collapse of the state in southern Sudan after the Addis Ababa agreement: A study of internal causes and the role of NGOs. In *Short-Cut to Decay: The Case of the Sudan,* edited by S. Harir and T. Tvedt. Uppsala: Nordic Afrikainstitutet.

———. 1998. *Angels of Mercy or Development Diplomats? NGOs and Foreign Aid.* Oxford, UK: Africa World Press.

———. 2000. *An Annotated Bibliography on the Southern Sudan, 1850–2000.* Vol. 2. Bergen, Norway: University of Bergen.

UNHCR. 2005. *2003 UNHCR Statistical Yearbook Country Data Sheet—Sudan.* http://www.unhcr.org/cgi-bin/texis/vtx/country?iso=sdn&expand=statistics (accessed 7 September 2006).

———. 2006. Chapter 7: Internally displaced persons. In *The State of World's Refugees.* Available online at http://www.unhcr.org/publ/PUBL/4444d3cc11.html.

United Nations. 1989. *Convention on the Rights of the Child.* Available online at http://www.cirp.org/library/ethics/UN-convention/.

United Nations Briefing Report. 2003. *Child Soldier Use 2003: A Briefing for the 4th UN Security Council Open Debate on Children and Armed Conflict.* 16 January.

UN News Centre. 2006. First Sudanese refugees from Ethiopia arrive home under UN programme. http://www.un.org/apps/news/story.asp?NewsID=18055&Cr=Sudan&Cr1=unhcr (accessed 7 September 2006).

Uppsala Conflict Data Program. 2008. *UCDP One-Sided Violence Dataset, v. 1.3, 1989–2006.* Uppsala University, www.ucdp.uu.se/database (accessed 5 August 2008).

USAID. 2002. Sudan: Southern sector OFDA program summary for FY 2002. http://www.usaid.gov/about/sudan/ofda_southern.html (accessed July 2002).

U.S. Department of State. 2005. Chapter 6: Terrorist groups. In *Country Reports on Terrorism.* 27 March. http://www.state.gov/s/ct/rls/crt/2006/82738.htm (accessed on 6 January 2009).

van Bruinessen, Martin. 1988. Between guerrilla war and political murder: The workers' party of Kurdistan. *Middle East Report* 153: 40–42, 44–46, 50.

———. 1992. *Agha, Shaikh and State: The Social and Political Structures of Kurdistan.* London: Zed Books.

———. 1998. Shifting national and ethnic identities: The Kurds in Turkey and the European Diaspora. *Journal of Muslim Minority Affairs* 18(1): 39–52.

Vargas, Ricardo, ed. 1994. *Drogas, Poder y Región en Colombia.* Vols. 1 and 2. Bogotá: CINEP.

Vicepresidencia de la República (Colombia). 2000. Panorama Actual del Putumayo: Análisis Regional: Observatorio de Derechos Humanos.

Vines, Alex. 1996. *Renamo: From Terrorism to Democracy in Mozambique?* Oxford, UK: James Currey, 1996.

Walter, E. Victor. 1969. *Terror and Resistance: A Study of Political Violence.* New York: Oxford University Press.

Warburg, Gabriel R. 1992. *Historical Discord in the Nile Valley.* Evanston, IL: Northwestern University Press.

Watts, Nicole F. 1999. Allies and enemies: Pro-Kurdish parties in Turkish politics, 1990–94. *International Journal of Middle East Studies* 31(4): 631–656.

Weber, Max. 1946. *From Max Weber: Essays in Sociology.* Edited and translated by H. H. Gerth and C. Wright Mills. New York: Oxford University Press.

Weinstein, Jeremy. 2006. *Inside Rebellion: The Politics of Insurgent Violence.* Cambridge: Cambridge University Press.

Williams, Brian, and Cathy Young. 2007. Cheney attack reveals Taliban suicide bombing patterns. *Terrorism Focus* 5(4).

Williams, Phil. 1998. The nature of drug-trafficking networks. *Current History* 97(618): 154.

———. 2008. Violent non-state actors and national and international security. International Relations and Security Network. Zurich: Eidgenössische Technische Hochschule.

Williams, Phil, and Roy Godson. 2002. Anticipating organized and transnational crime. *Crime, Law and Social Change* 37: 311–355.

Wilson, Scott. 2001. Massacre in a Colombian village. *Washington Post,* 5 February, 11, 14–15.

World Media Watch. 1999. Kurdish reaction to Öcalan's arrest. 18 February (accessed 15 March 2007).

Yilmaz, Kani (former Kongra-Gel parliament member). 2004. Interview with *KurdishMedia.com,* 30 July.

Zaman, Amberin. 2004a. Kurds say changes merely gesture by Turkey for EU. *Los Angeles Times,* 24 October.

———. 2004b. *New Formation of Zana Combines Outlawed Leaders?* 4 November (accessed 12 November 2004).

Zartman, I. William. 1995. *Collapsed States: The Disintegration and Restoration of Legitimate Authority.* Boulder, CO: Lynne Rienner.

Zurcher, Erik J. 1993. *Turkey: A Modern History.* London: I. B. Tauris.

Index

Abbasid dynasty, 34, 186
active rivalry theory, 11–12, 14, 26, 47, 49, 66, 76–77, 80, 114, 117, 119, 161, 164–166, 172, 175; policy implications of 166–176
Adamson, Fiona B., 203n108, 204n117, 205n162
Addis Ababa Agreement, 40–41, 45
Afghanistan, 146, 168–169, 176; suicide bombings in, 168
African Rights, 69, 191n141
Afro-Arab State, 32. *See also* Sudan
agrarian reform: in Colombia, 88, 93; in Sudan, 35, 83, 85, 87
Ahmad, Hisham H., 188n81
Akol, Lam, 48–49, 188n74
Al Qaeda, 17, 21, 137, 177n6; in the Philippines, 177n6; Abu Sayyaf and, 177n6
Albini, Joseph, 205n1
al-Bashir, Omar Hassan Ahmad, 42, 64, 71
al-Mahdi, Muhammad Ahmed, 36–39, 42. *See also* Mahdiyya
Anderson, Perry, 179n7
Anglo-Egyptian Condominium, 37–39, 188n82
Angola, 21
Ankara Democratic Patriotic Association of Higher Education, 131. *See also* Kurdistan Workers' Party
Ankara, Turkey, 9, 28, 127, 129, 130–132, 145, 147–148, 154–155

Anya-Nya, 40–41, 45–46
Anya-Nya II, 46
Apo, 132, 138. *See also* Öcalan, Abdullah
Apodaca, Claire and Michael Stohl, 206n22
Archivo del Congreso Nacional: Colombia, 194n26
Arenas, Jacobo, 97, 195n59, 195n64
Argentina, insurgencies in, 93–94
Arias, Desmond and Gipsy Escobar, 199n150
Arizmendi, Dario, 198n129
Armenians, in Turkey, 126, 200n5
Arsu, Sebnem, 205n149
Ashcraft, Richard, 190n117
Atatürk, Mustafa Kemal, 127. *See also* Turkey
Aviles, William, 198n144
Azam, Jean-Paul, 184n13

Baader Meinhoff Gang, 173
Bailey, Norman, 195n43
bandits, 94, 96, 178, 180–181; roving, 178; stationary, 13, 178–179. *See also* Olson, Mancur
Barkey, Henri J., 201n18, 202n38, 202n41
Barkey, Henri J., and Graham E. Fuller, 200n10, 201n14, 201n16, 202n53, 202n57, 202n70, 203n91, 203n106
Barkey, Karen, 190n7
Barzani, Massoud, 134

Cuban Revolution: influence on Colombian insurgents, 93–94

dan Fodio, Usman, 182n8
Darfur, 21, 34, 36, 64, 74–75
de Paula Santander, Francisco, 194n16
de Waal, Alex, 188n71
Debray, Regis, 137, 195n61, 202n67
DeMars, Williams Emile, 191n143
Demirel, Süleyman, 135
Democratic People's Party (DEHAP),
141, 155
democratization as a policy: by the
PKK, 148, 172; by the SPLA, 57, 72,
172; general, 75, 169–176; Inter-
national Monetary Fund and, 172;
World Bank and, 172
Deng, Francis, 186n15, 187n31,
187n34, 187n39, 187n51
Dinka, 32, 35, 39, 47, 50, 70,
Dix, 195n55
Diyarbakir, 9, 121, 129–131, 139, 154,
156, 173, 202n35
Donmez, Sahin, 136
DozaMe.org, 202n56, 205n148, 205n151
Dudley, Stephen, 96, 102, 192n3,
196n75, 196n77, 196n80, 196n82,
196n84, 196n86, 196n89, 196n91,
196n93, 197n96, 197n107, 197n109,
197n112, 198n135, 200n177
Duffield, Mark, Helen Young, John
Ryle, and Ian Henderson, 69,
187n34, 191n137, 191n140

East Kurdistan Defense Forces, 157
Efuk, Soforonio, 188n71
Egypt, 34, 36–37, 39
Ehrenfeld, Rachel, 185n29
Eide, Torumund, Tomas Hägg, Richard
Holton Pierce, and László Török,
186n8
Enginsoy, Ümit, 205n158, 205n160

Entessar, Nader, 201n18
Enzensberger, Hans Magnus, 16,
183n14, 184n3
Eriksen, Stein, 185n37
Eritrean People's Liberation Front
(EPLF), 70
Ethiopia, role in Sudanese civil war, 3,
31, 35, 41–45, 48–49, 60, 65, 68, 70,
76, 162
European Union (EU), 147, 149–150,
154, 156, 159–160, 173, 175,
190n121, 200n2
European-Sudanese Public Affairs
Council, 188n78
Euskadi Ta Askatasuna (ETA), 165,
173. *See also* Basque insurgency
Evans, Geoffrey, and Stephen White-
field, 206n14
Evans-Pritchard, Edward E., 187n34
extortion by the FARC, 3, 15, 80, 91

failed state, 28
Fals Borda, Orlando, 194n30
Fanon, Frantz, 166, 206n3
FARC. *See* Revolutionary Armed
Forces of Colombia (FARC)
Fenian Movement, 17
Ferrero, Gugliermo, 188n80
Ferro Medina, Juan Guillermo, and
Graciela Uribe Ramón, 192n3,
196n79, 196n83, 196n87, 196n92
Finnemore, Martha, and Kathryn Sik-
kink, 206n15
First Equatoria Regional Congress, 55,
189n90
Flockhart, Trine, 206n14
Fluherty, Vernon Lee, 194n39
foco theory, 93, 195n61, 195n67
France, ETA in, 185n31
Frankel, Glenn, 177n6
Frum, David, 185n29
Fukui, K., and J. Markakis, 187n34

About the Author

CLAIRE METELITS is Assistant Professor of Political Science at Washington State University.